5-11-23

To Marita Golden,

My friend, My Mentor.
Thanks for being such
a role model for me.

Louis F. Kerry

Only on Sundays

Mahalia Jackson's Long Journey

JANIS F. KEARNEY

A Creative Nonfiction Book

Edited by Mellonee Carrigan
Cover Design by Andre Hawkins

Only on Sundays: Mahalia Jackson's Long Journey / Janis F. Kearney
www.wowpublishing.org
First Writing Our World Publishing Edition, Volume 1

ISBN: 978-0-98896-446-4
Library of Congress Control Number: 2020918393

Printed in the United States of America

"You'd have a person like Mahalia who is a kind of priestess. She was a priestess in the Negro church just as Bessie Smith was a priestess when she sang the blues among those people who really knew them and felt them. She stood there and evoked these emotions, evoked these images, evoked this sense of life. This is a very important thing. Of course, this woman just knocks me out. There's something that sounds through the voice, there's something which goes beyond the mere technique and eloquence of phrasing, although she has all of these things.

"It is an art which was acquired during those years when she sang in the comparative obscurity of the Negro community."

—Ralph Ellison, Saturday Review (1958)

TABLE OF CONTENTS

Part 4 — Halie's Hard Childhood

Part 5 — Goodbye Nigger Town, Hello Promised Land (1927)

Part 6 — Love and Horses and Fish and Bread

Part 11 — A New Beginning

Part 12 — The Return of the Gospel Queen

Part 13 — Mahalia's Encore in Europe (1967)

Part 14 — The Death of a Dreamer

A NOTE
from the Author

Most African Americans born in the early 1950s knew Mahalia Jackson's music. Part of our rite of passage growing up was watching the 1959 movie *Imitation of Life* each year with our families. Mahalia Jackson appeared in the movie as a soloist in a church choir singing at a funeral. During a 40-year career, Mahalia Jackson was the best-known gospel singer in the world, touring in Europe and around the globe. Still, which of us could claim that we knew Mahalia Jackson, until now.

In recent years, I made it my intention to learn as much as I could about this giant of a woman through research, books, and talking with those who knew Mahalia Jackson. What I learned, deducted, intimated about Mahalia Jackson, I will share here. I am calling my book historical nonfiction. It is the product of more than 15 years of a *re-investigation* of Mahalia Jackson's complex life based on written and spoken stories, and from her own words as shared in interviews, books, and songs.

I am not a historian by academic measurements. I am a lover and curator of stories and their historical background. I chose to write Mahalia's story as a creative nonfiction book rather than as a biography. I am a firm believer that every story about a subject that is not his or her own—actually, even our own stories—is a re-interpretation of the subject's life and stories. Because Mahalia Jackson is no longer here for me to speak with and because I did not gain an entrée into her family's stories, I relied on stories shared with me by others and the research collected by others.

Many of whom had sparse substantive connection to Ms. Jackson's culture and experiences.

This book is one author's interpretation of a great American's life story. In the literary vernacular, this book falls within the recent genre of creative nonfiction—whereas the author offers a unique interpretation of the subject's story based on research and written and oral history through the lens of the writer's own experiences as a woman of African descent who also grew up in the American South.

In creative nonfiction, writers take the liberty of imagining some of their subjects' thoughts and actions based on their patterns, their experiences, how they describe themselves and their lives. Then, of course, the writers lean heavily on the most objective of archival material. Even so, creative nonfiction must be based on truth. One of America's most treasured poets, Emily Dickinson, wrote that, while it is important that we write with truth, the best telling of stories is when truth is told "with a slant."

Spring 2020, more than any other time since the Great Depression, was a cross-point in Black Americans' evolution as Americans. A time of immense introspection and reassessments of this thing we call American democracy. Spring 2020 was an era of immense pain for America, but far more painful for Black America. A central part of that pain was the revelation that so much of the important racial and social justice work done over the last century has nearly all been undone within the last decade.

For writers of color, it was a collective realization that our stories, our histories, when told, were most often not told from our own perspectives. The stories about us lacked the slant from people of color. When we hold our own archives up to the light of day, we find the annals of American literature and history sorely lacking in the rich stories of African Americans who lived, survived, and even thrived during these last four centuries.

First came the universal sigh in Black America, knowing how difficult and complicated an assignment this would be—a disruption of African American history and literature. How to address this historical problem. The mission in time became clear: to tell and write new stories about who we are, about our unique experiences as multilayered Americans, and by "retelling" the stories that have been told by others.

This story of the great Mahalia Jackson, America's Queen of Gospel, is in her honor and a step toward this new beginning to tell our stories and to tell them from our slant. Finally.

Part 1

HANNAH'S DREAM

AUDUBON PARK, NEW ORLEANS
(NEW ORLEANS HISTORICAL ARCHIVES).

Halie Leaves Nigger Town

In 1963, well into the heyday of her stardom, Mahalia Jackson visited the James Weldon Johnson Elementary School in her hometown of New Orleans. After a warm welcome by the school principal, Mahalia looked out into the beaming faces of the children and offered them her most precious gift, a song. They were delighted.

After she finished the song, the children smiled and clapped and begged Mahalia to sing more. She was on a schedule and needed to leave, but she was deeply moved by the children's reaction. At their age, they reminded her of herself—young Halie (Mahalia's childhood nickname), full of life and questions and dreams in that long ago place called Pinchers Town.

At the end of Mahalia's visit, the school administrators presented her with a plaque. As she accepted it, she couldn't steel herself to hold back her tears until she left. She wept as she accepted the plaque because it was the first time this place of her birth and childhood had recognized her. She would treasure the lovely gift and the recognition by the school forever. The children's adoring faces were etched with love into her memory.

Throughout her illustrious career, Mahalia seldom spoke openly of her early childhood in New Orleans, of how she'd never owned a doll as a child, and how her short-lived education and childhood ended when her aunt Mahala "Duke" Paul, her adopted mother, decided the family needed extra income to pay the bills and 9-year-old Halie had to go to work. Halie was introduced to jobs usually held by grown colored women—hotel maid, laundress, domestic, cook, and housemaid in white families.

Halie didn't share the nickname "Fishhooks" that her older brother Peter gave her because of her deformed legs that scissored across each other as she walked, and she rarely complained about her lot in life. Her smile, even then, was something to behold. Halie had somehow learned that her big smile made others forget she wasn't pretty like her mother—Halie's skin was chocolate, not paper sack brown like her mother's, and her legs were crooked. *"And, those legs! Poor child!"* the grown-ups would whisper. Halie learned early on that her smile endeared her to her family and friends and the white people for whom she worked.

Perhaps Halie, even then, was wise enough to understand that complaining rarely led to real change in her lot. Instead, she learned to put her family and friends, and the white people she worked for, at ease with her joy and dancing and singing.

A life full of hardships was made easier by the songs in her heart, a heart swelled to overflowing with dreams of what could be. Work, it seemed, erased any sadness for young Halie. Besides, it was a way for her to save for the life she dreamed about. Something better. It wasn't something she talked about with even those in her closest circle, but it was an important part of her dreams.

By the time she was in her teens, Halie was tall and straight; her ebony skin so perfectly smooth and clear. There was a pure and natural beauty in the 16-year-old girl, though no one knew enough about Black beauty in Uptown New Orleans to call her that. She would never in all her years see that beauty when she looked in a mirror. What she did know, without a doubt, was that God had endowed her with a wonderful gift—a voice that no one would ever be able to take away.

Halie was a smart girl from the very beginning, always thinking, always questioning. She was thrifty, too. It wasn't from the bare-bones ways of Aunt Duke that Halie picked up her thriftiness. Duke would, if she just could, but she never seemed to be able to hold onto an extra dollar to save. *"Every penny come into this house, going toward living,"* she'd say.

Halie would look back later and decide that it was God's way of saving her by giving her this knack for pinching pennies, saving every extra nickel or dime she could, whatever was left after Aunt Duke's portion to help with food and lodging.

What Halie Left Behind

Halie left New Orleans for Chicago in November 1927, smack in the middle of the Jim Crow era in Louisiana. The same Jim Crow that haunted Mississippi, Arkansas, Alabama, Tennessee, and the rest of America's South.

Halie, as she was known in her community, dreamed of something more than New Orleans and something different from what Aunt Duke could offer her. She'd convinced herself and her other aunts that she wanted to be a nurse. She'd failed, however, to convince her adopted guardian, Aunt Duke. Duke was an older sister of Halie's mother Charity and the one who took Halie in after the child's mother died—after all, Halie was Duke's namesake. Duke had quietly taken on the role of the Clark family matriarch, though she was not the oldest of the seven sisters.

Duke, whose word was almost always the last, had never believed Halie's story. With her piercing gray eyes that saw straight through into the girl's heart, Duke reminded her sisters how even before the child could walk on those little crooked legs, she'd loved to dance to New Orleans's devil music, and how, at 5 years old, Halie had latched onto the church music. Duke had decided then that it was the music, not God, that had the girl hurrying to the church door on Sunday mornings. Mostly, Duke whispered to her sisters, it was the performing in front of crowds and the loud applause that most attracted Halie; the smiling faces that made her feel special.

Truth is, it scared the hard and strict Duke that the girl was bent on moving up North, following what would become known as the Great Migration. During the Great Migration, millions of Blacks moved from rural communities in the South to cities in the North between 1916 and 1970. What did Halie know about the kind of fast living she heard about? Duke worried. The kind that killed her own boy who had followed his dream of being a musician.

The mostly silent tug-of-war between Halie and Aunt Duke took them both by surprise. Even from a small child, Halie had been stubborn, set in her ways, but always in the end, a compliant child. Now, it seemed she'd

4

made her mind up about something that Duke couldn't change, no matter how hard she tried. From all outward appearances, Halie had won this tug-of-war. She left New Orleans for Chicago a few days past Thanksgiving in 1927, as most of the world's minds were focused on Christmas.

Aunt Duke's sadness was masked by a hard obstinance as Mahalia tearfully hugged her goodbye; this woman who was the closest thing to a mother young Halie had known. How the girl had exasperated her aunt with her early love for the "devil's music," her growing up being a tomboy sneaking to play baseball, climbing trees, and giving as good as she got when she fought with the neighborhood boys.

The 16-year-old had already lived a lifetime by the time she left New Orleans. She'd been a maid, a washerwoman and laundress, had minded the white families' children, and cooked their meals. Except for her mother's funeral, held down in Legonier County where her mother was born, Halie hadn't set foot outside the community where she was born. It was the place where people loved her and accepted her imperfections.

In spite of those comforts that hold most people in one place all their lives, Halie had made up her mind to leave. As she and her Aunt Hannah left for the train station, Halie clasped a crumpled newspaper clipping announcing admissions for Chicago's nursing school. She tried her hardest to ignore Aunt Duke's steely gray eyes boring into her back.

Halie boarded the train with Aunt Hannah, who had been visiting from Chicago. Looking forward not backward as she clutched the newspaper posting, Halie was also remembering what Aunt Hannah, the family's seer, had foretold—that Halie wouldn't always be a crippled child and that she'd one day walk with queens and kings. The miraculous straightening of her crooked legs had happened just a few years ago. Halie believed it was God's way of preparing her for the realization of the rest of Hannah's dream.

Mahalia's dreams were part of something so much larger than her and Hannah's trip up North. They were part and parcel of the hundreds of thousands of other Black Southerners' hopes and dreams as they fled all they'd known for Northern and Midwestern states. It was a leap of faith—fear of the unknown mixed with faith that what lay ahead would be better than what they left behind.

Amid this fear and faith was also guilt. Halie was going against Aunt Duke in a big way. Was she disrespecting the fact that Duke had volunteered to adopt Halie and her brother Peter when Charity, their mother, died? Only 6 years old at the time, Halie barely remembered her real mother now, and Duke didn't understand the need to keep their mother alive in the children's hearts.

So, there was that…the missing piece, the still gaping hole inside Halie that she had to believe could be filled by something in her future. Something to remove the aloneness that never left her and seemed to come alive at night during those quietest hours.

As the train moved down the tracks toward Chicago, Halie left the hard questions behind. She was on her way to something, and not just better work or education. The 16-year-old girl was in search of Hannah's dream—something far beyond what others expected of her. Chicago was the highway to that dream. If she started nursing school, so be it. That wouldn't be the end. She never fooled herself that it would fulfill her. It was a means to an end, something that would afford her work and pay while she pursued what she truly loved—singing.

New Orleans would never leave Mahalia. It would forever be a part of the breath she took, the blood in her veins. As Halie left her home, Duke had stared her straight into her eyes and shook her head. *"I want to be a nurse and help people,"* Halie had whined to Aunt Duke, who knew that music was the most important thing to the girl. Nothing came close. Duke's fear was that Halie would fall into singing any kind of music to get herself an audience and applause. Bound for the promised land. Surely God was preparing her. Hadn't God miraculously straightened her legs?

All during the train ride, Halie was remembering Aunt Duke's hard face. Didn't her aunt know how scared she was? How hard it was to leave everything she knew? All that she had loved, and yes, the parts she hadn't loved. Oh, how she'd miss her Sundays at Mt. Moriah Baptist Church. She didn't imagine there would ever be such wonderful Sundays as those again. The church had been her safe haven where she was loved and protected by the women and men who were moved by her weekly deliverance. As brave as she tried to be, Halie's exhilaration in leaving was dampened by her fear of the unknown.

Those Sundays would just have to be another part of her past now that she was on her way to something, to that dream Aunt Hannah had shared with her. Yes, nursing was a faint passion. It tapped her love to heal and help others, but it wasn't her deepest passion. Halie could learn to do good by others as she waited for her own destiny.

Chicago was full of possibilities, with not one guarantee. Poor, undereducated, and, to a great extent, hungry for the affection that Aunt Duke couldn't supply, Halie was on her way to something to fill that hole inside her.

Since childhood, Halie was a princess at Mt. Moriah Church where she and Aunt Duke attended each Sunday and most Wednesdays. She'd be the farthest thing from royalty as she arrived in Chicago. The only thing she had to offer was a reminder of the South that most Negroes had purposely left behind. That rousing young voice that excited and calmed the good church people of New Orleans was for the longest a discomfort for the "up North" Southerners. Whatever it took, Halie decided, she was prepared to do. She'd never lose sight of Hannah's dream.

Part 2

MAHALIA'S ROOTS

Mahalia Jackson had deep roots in south Louisiana where both her maternal and paternal grandparents lived and toiled. Both sets of grandparents were enslaved during their childhoods. While her maternal grandparents would remain in rural Louisiana and take on the harsh existence of sharecropping, her paternal grandparents left the farms and moved to New Orleans where they became domestics or river workers. The one threat throughout Louisiana and the rest of the South during the Jim Crow era was the lynching of Blacks. No matter which part of Louisiana one lived or worked, lynching was a very real and active part of Blacks' existence.

LEFT: POINTE COUPÉE PARISH SIGN (POINTE COUPÉE PARISH HISTORICAL ONLINE IMAGES). **RIGHT:** PAUL CLARK, MAHALIA'S GRANDFATHER, POINTE COUPÉE PARISH, CIRCA 1935 (TULANE CREDIT).

Mahalia's Slave History—Pointe Coupée Parish

Mahalia Jackson's ancestors, the Clarks and Fiendleys were not long removed from enslavement when the horrors of Jim Crow and lynching became stark realities in the American South.

The abolition of slavery came with its own chains—second-class citizenship and a lifetime of fearing for your life. The Clark family of Pointe Coupée Parish had for years served the white masters in their homes; in their fields; late at night suckling the white babies who would later become somebody's master; combing their hair and dressing the white mothers; bathing the white children; and cooking the meals that fed the white families and their friends, and relations of their masters.

After Abraham Lincoln called an end to the subjugation of one man over another, the enslaved were called sharecroppers. It was a new kind of slavery, without the visible chains, but chains no less. Laboring from can, to can't. Working the fields, doing the handy work, the hard work, the dirty work for their share of the profits that they rarely saw because they had to live, and the landowner held the key to their living. Whites, their former masters and mistresses, owned the land and the shacks the Blacks called home and the food the Blacks must buy to feed their children who helped work the fields that allowed them to live not unlike the slaves they were before.

It was no different on the Merrick Plantation in Pointe Coupée, the place in south Louisiana that impacted Halie's bloodline, her lifeline, in ways she might never see but that would flow through her veins until the day she died. Mahalia Jackson's story is intricately woven into this complex story of the American South—and certainly within the unlikely relationships between slaveowners and their wards, their unpaid and involuntary laborers, including Mahalia Jackson's maternal grandparents Paul and Ophelia Clark.

Pointe Coupée Parish, like most of Louisiana, claimed a rich and dark history of slavery. The area was settled by French colonists and French Creoles as well as Africans from the French West Indies. It was later settled by African Americans, Anglo-Saxons, and Italians.

The parish was created on March 31, 1807. It is one of the 19 parishes which were created by dividing the Territory of New Orleans. Pointe Coupée Parish was named in honor of the French phrase *la pointe coupée* or in English, "the place of the cut-off."

Maybe the darkest moment in the parish's history was the infamous Pointe Coupée Conspiracy. On May 4, 1795, 57 slaves and three white men were put on trial in Point Coupée after a slave insurrection at one of the plantations. During the insurrection, several planters' homes were burned down. Planters discovered the book *Theorie de l'impot,* which included the document the "Declaration of the Rights of Man and of the Citizen" from the 1789 French Revolution, in one of the slave cabins. After a speedy trial, 23 slaves were hung. Their decapitated heads were posted along the road beside the Mississippi River. Another 31 slaves were sentenced to flogging and hard labor. The three white men were deported, with two sentenced to six years forced labor in Havana, Cuba.

In Louisiana, the number of lynchings spiked following Reconstruction (1865-1877)—the era following the Civil War (1861-1865) when efforts were made to reunify the divided nation and integrate Blacks into society— though signs of the problem emerged far earlier. As Louisiana struggled with the new political order imposed during Reconstruction, many disenfranchised whites struck out at the Republican Party's faithful, regardless of their race. Terrorist or white supremacist groups such as the White League spread fear throughout the state, mixing threats with violence.

In an 1884 incident known as the Coushatta Massacre, members of the league lynched four Blacks and six white Republicans in Coushatta, the parish seat in Red River Parish, Louisiana. The violence that engulfed the state and the South played a pivotal role in turning Northern opinion against Reconstruction.

When Reconstruction finally ended in 1877, Louisianans faced a different sequence of challenges and a more aggressive and racially motivated spate of lynchings. As the 1880s dawned, a new era of violence ensued as Bourbon Democrats strengthened their hold on power in Louisiana. Bourbon Democrats were a conservative faction in the Democratic Party. White supremacy represented a central tenant of their platform and led to even greater levels of violence as they tried to reverse the advances made by Negroes during Reconstruction.

Although most lynching victims were African Americans, other "outsiders" sometimes ran afoul of Louisiana's white ruling class. In 1891, at the height of the lynching epidemic in Louisiana, the lynching of 11 Italians in New Orleans for allegedly killing Police Chief David Hennessey garnered the most attention. It marked the first of several attacks on the rapidly expanding Italian community in southeastern Louisiana.

Further north, in the Madison Parish village of Tallulah, five Sicilians were killed because of little more than rumors that the men possessed fiery and violent tempers. Scant evidence existed that the men, all of whom sold fruits and vegetables, were anything but law-abiding citizens. At a time when outsiders were viewed with suspicion, however, the economic success of the Sicilians—when many in the surrounding community suffered—heightened hostility toward them.

Twentieth Century Lynching in Louisiana

In the early 20th century, the number of lynchings generally decreased as state and local authorities began cracking down on the crime, partly because of outside pressure. The establishment of a legally sanctioned system of racial segregation, known as Jim Crow, decreased contact between the races and contributed to this reduction, albeit unintentionally. Once this system was firmly ensconced, the need for frequent demonstrations of terror gradually dissipated.

There was one New Orleans lynching in the early 20th century used as a warning to young people in the community about the dangers of moving outside one's appointed space—geographically, culturally, or socially.

The summer of 1900 sparked a week of murder, mayhem, mutilation, and a manhunt. Slavery had only been abolished for 35 years in 1900, and New Orleans' blueprint had expanded far beyond the French Quarter. Jim Crow segregation was at its peak, and lynchings were a regular occurrence in the South.

The 1900 New Orleans lynching had its roots in a brutal Georgia lynching in 1899 where Sam Hose was murdered by a lynch mob after killing his white employer in self-defense. The white mob tortured his body, burned him alive, and sold his remains as "souvenirs."

Blacks around the country were outraged by this blatant inhumanity. It struck an especially sensitive nerve in New Orleans resident Robert Charles, a Mississippi-born child of former slaves who moved to New Orleans at the age of 28 in search of better paying jobs.

Well-educated, well-dressed, Charles resided in Uptown New Orleans and was a paid member of a society promoting the migration of Black people "back to the homeland," the country of Liberia. He was an outspoken advocate for civil rights and who spoke out against the race problems unique to the American South, including the especially cruel killing and lynching of Sam Hose in Georgia.

On July 23, 1900, Charles and a friend sat on a white family's porch on Dryades Street. This was not unusual. They were waiting for Charles's girlfriend to end her work day. Around 11p.m., a police report was made insinuating that the "two suspicious-looking Negroes" were up to no good.

The policemen, upon arrival at the home, demanded to know what the two men were doing on the white family's porch. The interaction quickly escalated, and one of the officers later reported that Charles pulled away when the officer tried to grab him. The two men struggled, and the officer drew his gun. Charles also drew his weapon. Both men were shot. Charles, bleeding, left the scene.

An all-out search began for Charles, including an unruly lynch mob. After days of searching, Charles was caught and hung without a trial. His body parts were parceled out to the crowd.

The Ties That Bind—The Merrick Plantation

> **CAPT. D. T. MERRICK.**
>
> Capt. David T. Merrick, a distinguished son of Louisiana both in war and peace, and prominent in the public life of Point Coupee Parish, died at Merrick on March 14. He was a son of the late Chief Justice Merrick, of one of the noted families of the South; and whether in war or peace, he was always a leader. Born in Clinton, La., in 1841, he was sent to Centenary College at Jackson; and when the war broke out, though but nineteen years of age, he left school and entered the Confederate army. He raised a company of infantry, and commanded it under General Jackson, participating in more than a dozen hard-fought battles. At Gettysburg he had but one man of his company left. He afterwards commanded a company of sharpshooters, and was subsequently placed on the staff of Gen. Leroy Stafford as inspector general of the 2d Louisiana Brigade. He was badly wounded at Payne's Farm, in Virginia, a Minie ball passing through the side of his head over the cavity of the mouth and cutting off the lobe of his left ear. Recovery from such a wound was wonderful in the annals of surgery. Returning to his Point Coupee plantation after the war, he spent the remainder of his life in upbuilding the South for which he had fought. He was a Mason of high rank and prominent in Confederate circles for many years. His wife, a son, and a daughter are left to mourn their loss.

Mahalia's uncle and grandfather shared stories about the young Captain David Merrick, who went off at 17 to fight in the Civil War to protect slavery. Merrick would become a young slave master for a brief period before President Lincoln's abolition of slavery. Merrick and the slave's relationship changed almost overnight to tenant farmer.

Merrick wasn't much more than 20 years old when he returned home tragically wounded by a Minié ball during a battle at Payne's Farm, Virginia. The Minié ball, with its conelike front end, was designed to inflict devastating injuries, much more so than the round musket balls. After his tragic wound in 1864, Captain Merrick returned to Louisiana. Though he miraculously recovered, he lived the rest of his life with complete loss of hearing and the loss of sight in one eye. In spite of his incapacities, Merrick took on the role of plantation owner and overseer of a sharecropper operation and remained in that role on his farm until his death in Merrick, Louisiana.

Paul Clark—Mahalia's grandfather, whose parents were brought to Big Cane, Louisiana, by a white farmer in the early 1850s—was Captain Merrick's plantation foreman. Paul Clark managed the ginning and baling of cotton before it was loaded onto steamboats to travel down the Atchafalaya River, eventually connecting with the Mississippi River and on to its destination in New Orleans.

Captain Merrick's parents, Caroline Thomas Merrick and her husband Louisiana Chief Justice Edwin T. Merrick, resided in New Orleans before, during, and after the Civil War. Born into white gentility and privilege, Caroline Elizabeth Thomas was the quintessential Southern belle. In middle age, she transformed herself into the new, free white woman who challenged the American power system to include white women.

Born in 1825 on the Cottage Hall Plantation in East Feliciana Parish, Louisiana, Caroline, at 15, married the 37-year-old district judge Edwin Thomas Merrick from the Florida Parishes. During the early part of their marriage, they resided in Clinton, Louisiana, then moved with their children to New Orleans. Caroline had three children by the time she was 20, and her last child at 32. Her husband would eventually rise to chief justice of the Louisiana Supreme Court.

David Merrick was the couple's firstborn child, arriving shortly after they moved to New Orleans in 1841. David, "D.T.," was sent to Centenary

College at a young age but left school at 17 to join the Confederate Army, where he became a captain and served under General Andrew Jackson.

Judge and Caroline Merrick, like hundreds of other prosperous Southern landowners, lost much of their property and slaves during the War Between the States. Upon the Union's takeover of New Orleans, Judge Merrick took his slaves to Confederate territory to wait out the war. Caroline moved with her children to Myrtle Grove Plantation, her brother's home on Louisiana's Atchafalaya River, for the duration of the war.

Captain David Merrick was a hero of the Confederate army during the Civil War. He returned home to Pointe Coupée Parish a tragically wounded veteran, half-blind and deaf thanks to his meritorious Civil War efforts to save the South and its livelihood. He would spend the balance of his life on the Merrick farm in Point Coupée and manage the once prominent plantation with his wife Talulah Dowdell from the great Southern state of Alabama.

For the hundreds of thousands of slaves set free in the South, the chances of their finding work outside the places they had been enslaved were dismal at best. Paul Clark chose to remain on the Merrick farm after slavery ended.

The Clarks of Pointe Coupée Parish would now be designated as sharecroppers, only a slightly less penurious role than the one they were born into. They would marry and have their children on the very farmland many had worked as slaves.

Their former masters were not left unscathed by the war. Endless acres of fertile land and mansions once viewed as great and mighty were much less ostentatious farms. It was no longer a given that the fertile land would produce riches. For many formerly large plantations, the key goal was to keep their land, feed their families, and hold on to the Black men and women who still worked the land. Except for a lucky few, many Black families would live, work, and die on the Merrick farm.

While there is no proof that Mahalia's family ever intersected with the Merrick family in New Orleans, it is certainly a possibility. After Judge

Merrick's death, Caroline would continue to reside in the city and reinvent herself into a prominent women's rights activist in New Orleans and around the country. Caroline Merrick died four years before Mahalia came into the world.

Mahalia was well aware and spoke often of the relationship between her ancestors and the Merrick family, prominent Southern slave owners, and the young Civil War hero who would spend the rest of his life keeping the Confederacy alive in Louisiana and around the South. This, as Mahalia's beloved ancestors continued their subservient roles with the Merrick family as freed laborers.

The Merrick Plantation set facing the Atchafalaya River whose basin was the nation's largest river swamp and contained almost one million acres of America's most significant bottomland hardwoods, swamps, bayous, and backwater lakes. Two adjacent plantations were run by Captain David Merrick's son, E.T.

Sharecropping was the new term for the still unjust and unequal labor partnership between Blacks and their landowners. Southern plantations survived thanks to this new form of human labor. In the half-century after slavery, the relationship between Black workers and the landowners changed only slightly.

Legonier, Louisiana, was settled by Black former slaves who lived and worked in dire poverty on the Merrick Plantation. It was home to the Clark family who would later recall that the only times they had to look forward to were Sundays, Christmas, and the Fourth of July—the first day of the year that Black families could buy ice.

Sunday was the only day the laborers and their families lived and interacted in their own worlds. They were able to worship God and share their sorrows and gratitude freely. Worshipping was a treasured freedom that they looked forward to all week. It was a day to interact as free and equal humans to share their lives and dreams and fears with those who understood.

And then there was Christmas, the sharecroppers' favorite time of the year. Their happiness had less to do with what they had than the opportunity to spend uninfringed time with family. It was the joy of families gathering together, worshipping together, cooking for weeks, then enjoying Christmas meals together and the small gifts they exchanged. Other than Sundays, it was the only other time of the year that they didn't have to rise before sunup to work the fields or take care of the landowners' family and meals.

For most, holiday decorations were intricately cut patterns from newspapers plastered to the walls and adorned with colored pages from magazines or journals the landowners gave to the Black sharecroppers. The one complaint about Christmas was that it lasted just one day. If the landowner was in a good mood, he might let them take an extra day.

The rest of the year, Black men and women were forced to take care of the land, the homes, and the children of the landowners. Men and young boys plowed the fields for 75 cents per day and hoed the fields for 50 cents a day. Cotton picking was 75 cents per 100 pounds.

Paul Clark's oldest daughter, Isabell, was known as the cotton-picking queen. When she was old enough to keep part of the 75 cents per 100 pounds she earned, she picked twice as much.

The Merrick farmworkers received meager field wages and a parceling out of garden land for shares—share cropping—where the Black workers took care of the land, grew the crops, then shared any profits from their farm with the landowner.

The Family of Paul and Ophelia "Celie" Clark

Paul Clark was born into slavery around Big Cane, Louisiana, in St. Landry Parish. His parents are believed to have been enslaved in Virginia but transported in bondage to Louisiana in the mid-1800s. Paul was 9 or 10 years old when he and his family were given their freedom. Paul's family moved to the Merrick Plantation in the late 1880s and would remain on the land eking out their living as sharecroppers and laborers.

Paul's father was a coachman and his mother was a cook when emancipation set young Paul free. In spite of their new freedom, the family remained in Pointe Coupée Parish on the Merrick farm.

Paul met and married Ophelia "Celie" Fiendley in 1871. Celie was the eldest child of Bosmer and Charity Fiendley. As was common during the time, Ophelia's name was erroneously documented in the 1900 Census, as "Celie," the name her closest family members called her.

The Fiendley family migrated from Big Cane, Louisiana, to the old Merrick farm during and after the days of slavery, sometime around the same time as the Clarks arrived. The Clark and Fiendley families are thought to have been purchased by the same Louisiana landowner. Ophelia's siblings included George, the eldest Fiendley child; Rhoda, the middle child; and Prudy, the baby.

Paul and Ophelia Clark had 11 children. Three died on the Merrick farm. Boston Clark was the eldest boy; Isabell was the oldest; Mahala "Duke" was the next oldest girl; followed by Harrison, Charity, Cleveland, Hannah, Porterfield, Rhoda, Alice, and Bessie. Cleveland and Harrison died young. There were grandchildren, too, in the Clark household—Lisa Joseph, Fred Duskin, Porterfield, Roosevelt, and Olivia Joseph.

Both the Fiendley and Clark families continued to work on the Merrick farm up until 1910. Some family members left that year; others remained until the infamous flood of 1912. Paul Clark would remain in Legonier, long after all his children had left and begged him to join them in New Orleans. He finally did leave in the late 1920s, when he moved in with his daughter Mahala "Duke," her husband Emanuel "Manuel" Paul, his granddaughter Mahalia "Halie" Jackson, and grandson Peter. Halie would leave New Orleans shortly after her grandfather arrived.

Paul Clark was tall, distinguished, and charismatic. Some described him as an imposing figure. His slate gray eyes illuminated his smooth, dark skin. He had a natural flair for speaking, which came in handy as a part-time pastor of his church.

Unlike most in the community, Paul had received a limited amount of schooling during his childhood. More than anything, he used his literacy to read and learn the stories from the Bible. He was unique also in the fact that he became a licensed minister, Bible scholar, which made him a respected figure on the Merrick Plantation. Especially on Sundays.

Paul Clark, his wife Celie, and his houseful of children made up a large component of St. John the Baptist Church in Gumpstump Station on the edge of Legonier. Paul would often be asked to serve as guest pastor on Sundays. On weekdays, the church doubled as the Negro schoolroom—one room, one teacher teaching students from first through fifth grades.

Paul Clark was born with a slight advantage over most Blacks during the early post-slavery days. Somehow his parents had been given land and property, loosening the constraint of the sharecropping relationship that most Black families were remanded to. He was listed in one of the local Pointe Coupée newspapers, along with a long list of "Agents of EPA," whose membership required an annual fee and merited a card that proved they were free Black men.

Paul Clark ran Merrick's gin on the adjacent Belaire farm which baled for all three plantations. During the off-season, he took over the corn-grinding operation. On Saturdays, he stayed busy at his weekend job, barbering from dawn to dusk—most of his customers were white men. This made him a substantial man in the Black community. Blacks wouldn't call at his house without a coat and tie. When men visited, they removed their hats at the door.

As a father and husband, Paul Clark was remembered as a strict disciplinarian who never spared the rod and demanded that his children follow the teachings of the Bible. The Clarks were a close-knit family of four boys and seven girls. Boston and Porterfield were the only sons to survive beyond childhood. There were usually 10 to 11 children in the small frame house in the workers' quarters.

Like most plantations, the Merrick Plantation was situated near the river, making it easier to move the invaluable cotton; sugarcane or rice; livestock; and, years before, human chattel on the river and steamboats. Sitting west of New Orleans, Gumpstump—the name referencing the area surrounding the Merrick farm—relied heavily on river transportation which took their cotton, rice, and sugar up the river to ports in New Orleans to sell.

Ophelia Fiendley Clark died in 1910 at the age of 46, after a life of hardscrabble work and bringing babies into the world. Some said she just plain gave out after working herself to death. Widowed at 51 years old, Paul remained in Pointe Coupée Parish for the next decade or so, residing at Red Cross on River Road on the east bank of the Atchafalaya River. He lived in a rented home and opened his own barbershop where he was able to serve Blacks as well as whites. He also preached at St. John the Baptist Church located near the Merrick farm.

After Ophelia's death, the Clark children began leaving Legonier, striking out for the big city of New Orleans. Though Paul Clark wouldn't move for another decade, he often visited his children and grandchildren in New Orleans and joined his daughters at Mt. Moriah Baptist Church where his granddaughter Halie made her musical mark. He became such a regular there, he was eventually invited to preach at the church from time to time.

Porterfield Clark—Agent of Change

Porterfield Clark, born in 1883, Paul and Ophelia's youngest son, was as much mythology as real. Each of the Clark siblings remembered him differently for the disparate ways he impacted their lives. Though he loved his parents, he was nothing like them in their willingness to remain on a farm that didn't always treat them fairly. Porterfield knew early on that he was meant to make his life somewhere besides Legonier.

Early on, young Porterfield became fascinated with the steamboats that chugged up and down the Red River landing. At 10 years old, Porterfield Clark was said to have ask Captain Merrick for a pair of shoes, and the white man's answer was: *"Boy, you don't need any shoes. Go grease your legs! That will keep them warm in the winter and shiny in the summer!"*

Porterfield—nicknamed Porter—would later say that that one interaction fed his determination to leave the plantation as soon as he was old enough. More than that, the desire to travel the world and learn as much as he could about the world was in young Porter's blood.

As a young boy, he played along the levee watching the U.S. Army Corps of Engineers' riverboats charting the river bottom. Excited by the adventure of their work, he vowed he would find a way to leave plantation life and follow the steamboats. Whenever one of the engineers heaved a line to tie up to the riverbanks, Porter was right there to catch it and help the men tie up the boat. Within a few years, the engineers gave him a job on the boat.

After leaving Legonier, Porter shared stories about his childhood with anyone who would listen—about how the white landowners robbed the coloreds of their cotton during the new scheme called sharecropping, almost a mirror image to slavery.

He recalled how white men rode their fine-blooded saddle horses into the fields where colored men, women, and children were bent chopping or picking the cotton plants for 50 cents a day. He remembered the loud plantation bell that rang at 4 a.m. each morning, except on Sundays—a warning for the colored men and boys to hurry and get dressed, eat their sparse breakfasts, and begin their day of field work, which was always before the rising of the sun.

It would be another day of plowing behind the mules from sunup until sundown to earn 75 cents a day. The money, he recalled, was always kept on the books at the Merrick Plantation's store, the same place the owner sold laborers pickled pork and corn meal and molasses. Somehow, Porter recalled, it almost always turned out that the sharecropper could never get caught up on what he owed the white landowner. If a Negro bought a mule on time to plow a little for himself on his own patch of land, he kept on paying for that mule. It might be 10 years later and the worker would be told, "Nope, you don't own that mule, just yet."

The Black children on the plantation weren't expected to attend school unless it rained. On good days, they worked in the fields along with the adults. The only school for Black children was at St. John the Baptist Church, which served as a one-room school for students from first through fifth grades. School was not encouraged by landowners, and there were never enough Black teachers available. Porter and his siblings learned more about the Bible from Paul Clark's fire-and-brimstone teachings than about reading and writing.

When the destruction of the boll weevil arrived in Louisiana, Porter was convinced an angry God had cursed the proud and selfish white farmers in the South. The Black sharecroppers learned from white people's whispers that the destructive insect had destroyed thousands of acres of white farmers' cotton, sending many farmers straight into bankruptcy. Many Louisiana farmers lost everything and had to start all over. Others were never able to reclaim their cotton, rice, or sugar farms.

St. John the Baptist Church represented a sweet freedom for Blacks in Legonier. Sunday was more than a day for learning right from wrong, it represented Black families' opportunities to freely interact with each other. They weren't able to do so in the cotton field, as overseers watched to ensure they worked nonstop throughout the day and houseworkers went about their jobs nonstop inside the white landowners' homes. Blacks were not allowed to fraternize with each other or with whites for whom they worked.

The Negro community was proud of the legacy of St. John the Baptist Church. Slaves built the church in the Atchafalaya River swampland during the early 1800s with hand-cut cypress trees—some of which were 100 years old with dark red bark. The large trees were cut, then sawed into planks before the church structure was created.

Paul Clark and the other preachers baptized newly converted members in the Atchafalaya River where the currents ran so swiftly, they could turn a steamboat around. Young girls and boys sat on the mourners' bench where, within a week or two, they would acknowledge their dedication to God and Christianity. They would then be baptized and officially named new members of St. John the Baptist Church. Years later, most would be funeralized on the very same church grounds.

Porter and all of the Clark children were baptized in the Atchafalaya River and became members of St. John the Baptist Church before leaving home. Porter often said the experience of being baptized in the river never left him. As long as the church remained, Blacks born in Legonier were funeralized and buried on the church site.

Curious and ambitious from childhood, Porterfield, who everyone called Porter, would change the direction of the Clarks' lives after their mother died in 1910. Once he settled in New Orleans, he returned to his home and encouraged first his siblings, then other young people, to leave the Merrick farm. He began escorting young men from Legonier to New Orleans, mesmerizing them with stories of the New Orleans waterfront, of tall-stacked steamboats nine miles long.

Like his father, Porter was industrious and charismatic. He was considered one of the most intelligent young colored men on the river. The men on the boats liked him, including Captain Buddy Rucker, who took him under his wing. He called Porter "my colored son," and practically raised him right along with his own children. Throughout his life, the Rucker children referred to Porter as their colored brother.

The Mississippi River pilot who eventually became the captain of the excursion boat *The President* became a true friend and ally to Porter. When the boat sailed out of New Orleans, Porter was very often onboard as a crewman. He later said Captain Rucker was the first white man he knew to treat a colored man as an equal.

The prestigious boat captain gave Porter a ticket to the world. Porter learned to cook over coal and wood stoves in the galleys of the little steamboats that ran up the small rivers and creeks to the country cotton plantations. He learned to use a cup of cornmeal to settle the muddy river water to the bottom of the water barrel so he could get a dipper of clear water for his bread dough.

Later Porter would sail on the bigger riverboats. He cooked on the *Bessie Anne,* a fast mail boat that ran the Mississippi River between Natchez, Mississippi, and New Orleans; and he worked on stern-wheelers on the Red River and the Atchafalaya River from New Orleans to Vicksburg, Mississippi, as a chef cook. At the time, steamboats were the queens of the river. They had beautiful dining rooms and the best service. They prided themselves on serving the best food in the land.

Porter became a first-class cook, but he also realized that boat life attracted all kinds of people and often was filled with opportunities for trouble. Porter worked hard to stay away from the dangerous side of boat life. He found early on that most workers on boats carried pistols and dirks (daggers), and one little word could lead you into a terrible struggle.

One of the stories that came from the boats was that Boston Clark, Porter's oldest brother whom he had helped get a job on the boats, got into trouble with a white mate on a steamboat and was thrown overboard one dark night, never to be seen or heard from again. Porter often said it was that long ago baptism in the Atchafalaya River that saved him from a horrible fate.

Porter was convinced that God had commissioned him to lead the young people from the plantation to a better life. Once he was familiar with how to navigate the Mississippi and what to look out for in New Orleans, he made regular trips back to Gumpstump and coaxed young people off the plantation.

Duke, Alice, Bell, and Charity joined him on the steamboat *Julia Anne Partridge*, which had been built for the transport of cotton and slave passengers. In New Orleans, Porter got Charity a job with a white family who were friends of Captain Rucker.

Porter told young colored boys they could better themselves; find out there's more to life than chopping cotton. Many of them would train as cooks and waiters on the riverboats and later get jobs on the railroad or in the hotels in the big cities. None returned to the plantation once they left. Only the older residents remained on the Merrick farm. It was the place where they were born and had known all their lives, they said.

Porter settled in New Orleans, renting a room near the Uptown wharf. He soon married an 18-year-old named Bertha, someone he'd known for years in Big Cane, Louisiana. He continued to work the river clear up to Vicksburg and beyond. New Orleans was his love, and with his mother gone, he wanted to make sure his sisters were together and nearby. He convinced all except one, Isabell, to leave the farm.

Even when the Atchafalaya flushed her out, Bell only reluctantly moved to New Orleans near her family. She would always miss home, finding city life too fast. She swore she would go back to the security of Legonier.

Part 3

NIGGER TOWN, THE OTHER NEW ORLEANS
(1910)

MT. MORIAH BAPTIST CHURCH IN NEW ORLEANS
(AUTHOR'S PERSONAL ARCHIVES).

The Clarks of Nigger Town

Not even a year had passed after Ophelia "Celie" Clark's death back in Pointe Coupée Parish, before her children began their trek to New Orleans, as if her presence had been the only glue that held them in the oppressive parish all those years.

Porter believed Celie would want him to gather up his family, escort them out of their past, and help them settle into the only corner of New Orleans that accepted Louisiana's former slaves and children of slaves. She would want her children to leave the parish that bore such a painful history for Blacks.

This new home, called "Nigger Town" at the time, was home to families that the leadership of New Orleans designated the least desirable, the underclass that few members of the proper citizenry saw as equals. The community by the Mississippi River—also known as "Pinchers Town" in reference to residents' reliance on welfare assistance—was populated by Blacks from Louisiana and other Southern plantations as well as poor white immigrants, mostly Italians, from European countries. In a move toward political correctness, Nigger Town, aka Pinchers Town, would finally be renamed Black Pearl in the early part of the 21st century, long after Mahalia Jackson had left.

Although most of New Orleans residents never set foot in the community and may not have even known of its existence, Nigger Town was a living, breathing neighborhood with large and small families and working parents. When children weren't working to help the household, they attended one of the segregated schools in the Black communities.

Mahalia Jackson could never forget the place she called home for 16 of her 60 years on Earth. The houses, referred to as shanties by most, were bunched together in a narrow area in the 14th Ward, between Magazine and Walnut streets. It was as close as any New Orleans community to the Mississippi River, separated only by the fragile levee. Residents found some strange pride in saying they lived very near the beautiful, sprawling

Audubon Park that was separated from the community by thick groves of tall, mossy live oaks and cypress trees.

The community was also home to small shops and storefronts owned by Italians and some Creoles. None that Mahalia could recall were owned by Blacks. Bisso's was a grocery store and bar where children weren't allowed, though some parents sent their children there to pick up packages. Jungs', a busy grocery store, was close by, too. People would go there at least once every day for ice and food.

There was also Mr. Casserta's drugstore, which sold voodoo potions along with his regular pharmaceuticals. It was rumored that local voodoo priestesses taught Mr. Casserta how to create the potions.

Small shops and stands lined up all up and down Magazine Street—rolling carts selling sundries and trinkets and treats like the colorful shaved ice made into snowballs for 2 cents each.

Mahalia remembered Magazine Street humming each and every day with the sounds of people interacting, the swoosh of cars passing, or even the clip clop of horse-drawn carriages. On Fridays, the sounds changed. The sidewalks came alive with adult activities.

Magazine Street had the only paved sidewalk in Uptown New Orleans, and it was packed with gamblers with their own unique songs and sounds. Men on their knees shaking dice or throwing cards: Pitty Pat; Cotch; Georgia Skin, like Blackjack; and Coon Can, the only two-person game. The men would jump up and stroll off if a preacher came along. Mahalia's religion, however, prevented her from gambling of any type. She admitted that the main reason she didn't gamble was because she couldn't sit still that long, "just studying numbers on a piece of card paper."

The Clark sisters were as close as any family could be, with their sister Duke always at the lead. Though they would eventually begin to disperse and find their own places to live, they never completely left Duke's orbit. Bessie went to live with Uncle Porter's wife Bertha. Bell moved in with her daughter Celie. Porter lived just a couple of blocks away on Walnut Street. At the time, Porter was the only Black living on the 300 block of Walnut Street.

There were a handful of second-generation Clark children in New Orleans as well. Hannah had a son they called "Baby." Duke had a son, Fred "Chafalaye," who moved out at 15 and went to live with Charity, Mahalia, and Peter. Young Halie and Peter adored their older cousin, but the teenager was too busy to be followed around by younger cousins.

The seven Clark Sisters were all striking in appearance, statuesque, with soft brown eyes and warm smiles. They carried themselves with a natural grace and dignity. Mahala "Duke" had dark brown skin and gray eyes. Her nickname, Duke, came from her royal deportment. No matter what time of the day it was, she marched through life as erect as a drum major. Even as a child, she was a natural leader and always serious; never one with a quick smile.

Of all of Paul and Ophelia Clark's girls, Charity was considered the pretty one. She had an engaging laugh and an even more engaging personality. She loved life and was fun around family and close friends, though quite shy around strangers. She had a warm demeanor that easily drew suitors to her. Young men were drawn to her big smile and easy personality.

Charity was, however, "delicate," known to have female problems throughout her teen years. She had Peter at 18, when she was still working on the Merrick Plantation. Records show she married Roosevelt "Peter" Hunter the year her child was born. Hunter lived in Red Cross, just a few miles from Legonier. Charity's problems persisted after she arrived in New Orleans. Her sister Bell took her to Charity Hospital in New Orleans, but no reason for her ailment was ever documented.

Charity, the third eldest of the Clark sisters, was one of the earliest to leave Legonier with her young son Peter and settle in the poor shanty enclave called "Nigger Town." Enthralled by Porter's descriptions of life in New Orleans, it seems she may have left without legally divorcing her son's father.

Porter, however, was quite convincing in his description of life in New Orleans, where the opportunities were strikingly different from work on the plantation. None of the six Clark sisters who came to New Orleans was older than 20 at the time. Bessie was just 11.

It wasn't long after Charity arrived in New Orleans with her sisters and her young son that she caught the eye of another handsome young man by the name of Johnny Jackson, a barber and stevedore working on ships during the day and barbering in the evenings and on Saturdays. He was also a part-time minister at his parents' holiness church on weekends.

In a short time, Charity's new relationship resulted in a second pregnancy. Her daughter was born October 26, 1911. Charity's marital status during her short life is confused by census records that show she was married at least twice—neither time to her daughter's father, Johnny Jackson.

Mahalia wrote in her memoir *Moving on Up* that her mother and father settled on Water Street in the 16th Ward in an area called Front of Town. While it is true that Charity and her sisters lived on Water Street, Johnny Jackson lived around the corner on Walnut Street. No records were found to confirm the couple ever lived together or were ever married. Unexplainably, however, Charity was known to sign her name Charity Jackson, Charity Hunter, and even Charity Smith, the man she was in love with before her death.

Charity used the surname of Hunter, her son's father's name, at her workplace. Though she never claimed marriage to Roosevelt Hunter, records show they were married. There are also records confirming her marriage to a Clement Smith, a young man she courted around 1915 and 1916.

Halie's Coming

Wealthy white families in New Orleans lived on Fontainebleau Drive in grand homes with tall white pillars. Adorning the beautiful homes was Audubon Park, once a massive plantation. Another neighborhood in the area was the Garden District, another well-to-do enclave.

The Clark families lived on the opposite side of Audubon Park, along the levee that separated them from the Mississippi River. It's likely that very few residents of either Fontainebleau or the Garden District ever set foot in the area called Nigger Town. Downtown New Orleans was four miles down the river, and neither Mahalia Jackson nor other colored children had any reason to venture into the downtown area, except during holiday parades when even coloreds were welcome to partake of the festivities.

Young Roosevelt "Peter" Hunter was almost 5 when Mahala "Halie" was born. Charity had brought the boy with her to New Orleans after their mother died. The Clark siblings all moved into a small house at 268 Audubon Street. The shack was full of leaks and openings that allowed wind and rain inside during the worst of the seasons. The shack, which rented for $8 or $9 per month, came with no indoor plumbing or electricity. An outhouse sat behind the house. Back then, immigrants from the plantations could move into a shack and maybe live there for a few weeks before the landlord came around and asked for pay.

Duke and her son, 13-year-old Fred "Chafalaye" Duskin, lived on Water Street. She had moved to New Orleans soon after Hannah and Porterfield. Neither Hannah or Rhoda, nor Alice had children at that time, which was a blessing given that work was hard to come by. Wages for Black workers then were 35 cents to 50 cents per day.

Duke convinced her sisters to move in with her and her son Fred on Water Street just shortly before "the high water of 1912." The infamous flood ruined the Merrick Plantation and finally convinced Bell to move to New Orleans with her two children—Celie, named after their mother; and her newborn son little Porterfield, named after her brother.

Now there were 13 Clarks crammed into three rooms and a kitchen at Duke's home on Water Street. Really, not all that different from the way it had been in Legonier on the Merrick Plantation, which was nicknamed Gump-stump, in reference to the stumped over country and endless gum trees.

The Clark house wasn't the only one overrun with people. Both whites and Blacks were crammed into the houses in the thrown-together community of the poorest New Orleans residents. The lucky men got jobs on the wharf and its ferries. Women were employed in the white folks' imposing homes close by.

The week of October 26, 1911, was the same week that Orville Wright set a flying record; Saunders Terrell, the blind American blues harmonica player, was born; and the Philadelphia Athletics defeated the New York Giants and won the World Series in six games—making baseball history.

On that same date, the overrun household on Water Street was filled with Clark women. And the Clark sisters were excited about the coming of Charity Clark's second child—never mind the fact that they were poor as church mice, earning just enough to eat and sleep, and the baby's father was someone else's husband.

Baby Halie, as the family called her, wasn't unique in being born out of wedlock. Children, even those born with no father in sight, were considered gifts from God. Halie was sweet Charity's girl, and she would certainly be a gift.

Mahalia was born into a house ruled and run by women—aunts, mostly. Porter was in and out. He had his own family to see after and was often traveling on the boats. When he did return home, he made it his business to visit his sisters to make sure they were faring well.

Mahalia, named after Charity's sister Mahala "Duke," arrived on a Thursday, an October day like most in New Orleans—unusually warm, humid, and threatening rain. While Mahalia's arrival was exciting for the Clark family, the world outside paid little if any attention.

The neighborhood didn't miss a beat on October 26, 1911. It was one more Black child brought into the world in the poorest section of town. The vegetable and fruit markets kept right on humming; the river docks were as busy as ever with big, strong men, mostly Black or Italian, singing their work songs and hollering commands across the docks. The trains kept right on running, as long and hard as they always did, shaking the floor beneath the bed that held Charity Clark and her newborn baby as they rumbled by.

Mahalia slipped into the world rosy and pink, not the signature ebony color the world would know in later life. The crowd of aunts and the midwife Granny Lee immediately noticed the baby's crooked legs and the mucus that covered her red, inflamed eyes. The aunts looked at each other, understanding the nasty connotation of the infection before turning the lamp off to protect the infant's eyes. Granny Lee cautioned them to keep the child in darkness lest she go blind. She offered them unceasing prayer as the only fix for the child's legs.

The new addition to the Clark family was originally named Mahala after her Aunt Mahala "Duke" Paul. Later, the name would be softened, with an I added to the last syllable. How much did Charity and Duke know about the genesis of the name Mahala—that it was derived from the Bible, or from the Native American word for Mahala, meaning *woman*? Or that in the Hebrew culture, the name meant *tenderness* or *barren?* Mahala was a name given to creative and expressive women who were often speakers, writers, or singers. Women who yearned to have beauty around them; women who were passionate, compassionate, intuitive, romantic, had magnetic personalities; women who easily fell in love, thus were easily hurt.

Mahalia's father, Johnny Jackson, lived around the corner from the Clark sisters' home, on the corner of Walnut between Water and Magazine—180

Walnut Street. He had other children, including a son born just one month after Mahalia's birth, and another daughter who came not much later.

Mahala "Halie" Jackson was recorded in the New Orleans City Hall by Granny Lee who had done this very thing enough times to know that no law would demand a marriage license from a Negro woman to confirm the father of the child. It hadn't been that long ago that there was no such thing as a civil marriage between Blacks.

While she was still nursing her child, Charity was already figuring she'd have to return to work for the Rightor family in a hurry. No colored woman had the luxury of laying up with their baby, listening to their coos and smiles for very long. She knew she'd have to work to eat and keep a roof over hers and her children's heads.

Charity returned to her job once she gained enough strength to get up and move around. Without missing a beat, Charity asked her sister Bell, who had a baby son, to nurse Baby Halie while she went out and looked for work. Though some might deem it unnatural for one sister to breastfeed another sister's child, the Clark women had their own code of survival.

Bell marveled at how fast Halie took to her breast milk. It didn't seem to matter at all to the child whose breasts she was feeding from. Later, Porter's baby would feed from his aunt's breasts, as well. When the two cousins grew close in adulthood, they often joked that it had to do with the breastfeeding.

With patient tending, Halie's eyes cleared up, but the child wouldn't be weaned as easily as her cousin, little Porter, Bell's son. Bell sought every kind of remedy to wean Halie. She used hot pepper, vinegar, and bitter alum on her breast to deter the child. Nothing worked. Finally, Bell came up with the bright idea to use a chicken feather to tickle the child's nose each time she prepared to feed at Bell's breast. In time, this would do the job.

There was still the problem of Halie's crooked legs. Charity took her to the hospital near their neighborhood, ironically named Charity Hospital. The doctor who looked at Halie told Charity they'd have to operate and break the child's bones. Bell, outraged, refused the remedy. Worried that her daughter's legs would never straighten, Charity and her sisters gave in to the old wives' tale of rubbing a child's legs down every morning and night with greasy dishwater.

Growing up Halie

Halie spent the first 16 years of her life just miles from New Orleans' infamous Congo Park, with its haunting history of Black men, women, and children being delivered, examined, and sold into bondage to the highest bidder. She would grow up just a stone's throw from the Mississippi River, the transportation pathway for hundreds of thousands of slaves brought to Louisiana from the foreign Northern states. She learned that her maternal grandparents, the Clarks of Pointe Coupée Parish, remained on the Merrick Plantation after they were set free.

Both sets of Halie's grandparents were enslaved before being freed by President Lincoln's Emancipation Proclamation. During her childhood, Mahalia's paternal grandparents lived right around the corner from her. Her Grandpa Andrew Jackson served as part-time pastor of a neighborhood church. They were some of the first to witness the deep, resonant voice that came from the 4-year-old Halie.

Both Grandpa Jackson and his wife were born into slavery on a rice plantation about a hundred miles from New Orleans. After the Civil War was over, they continued working on the plantation farm as sharecroppers. When Andrew Jackson finally decided to leave, he picked up and walked into New Orleans on his own two feet. That was how most coloreds got around in those days. Mahalia wrote in her memoir: *"The Merricks raised cotton with Negroes and mules. The Negroes did the planting and hoeing and the cotton picking, and the mules did the plowing."*

As a child, Halie was surrounded by Clark women. Isabell "Bell" was the oldest of the seven Clark sisters, who were all quite young when Mahalia was born. Bessie, the youngest, was just 12. The second oldest was Mahala "Duke." Then came Charity, Hannah, Rhoda, and Alice "Big Alice." Charity, Duke, Alice, Hannah, and Bell, and their children, along with young Bessie, all moved on Water Street into a four-plex house in Uptown New Orleans. The small house was just blocks from Audubon Park and just a stone's throw from the Mississippi River, protected only by a levee.

If you had to say, Charity was the Clark girl with the inviting personality, beloved, and fun to be around. Paper sack brown would have been how men described her. But Charity with the sunshine personality was sickly. She'd brought "female ailments" with her from the plantation fields of Pointe Coupée Parish to their new home.

Though Duke was not the oldest of the sisters, she was a natural leader, the substitute mother the girls lost in 1910. Duke was born the boss, always directing, always making the final decision. She had, in reality, become the family's matriarch.

Who was brave enough to question Duke? She was the one who found a place for the sisters to live when the Great Flood of 1912 destroyed their home along with all the other homes on the levee. Duke was the one who sent for Granny Lee, the midwife, when Charity gave birth to Halie. Duke helped the midwife bring the baby into the world. Duke was the one who named the girl Mahala, after herself. Who would go up against Duke? Not even the baby's mother, Charity.

The Mississippi River had done it again, in 1912, shortly after Halie's birth. It wouldn't be the worst beating the city would endure. Another flood in 1927 would take that title. Yet again, the South's poor and struggling found themselves uprooted and displaced through no fault of their own.

The small shack in which the girls resided had floated away along with the thousands of other houses in Uptown New Orleans.

Thankfully, the Clark family survived the disaster. Duke's new abode sat on a plot of land that was just another Cypress swamp a few years before. Before that, it was a sugar plantation owned by early French immigrants, but had been wiped away in the tragic 1912 flood.

By May 1912, the Mississippi reached a height never before equaled. The giant river went tearing through levee after levee, rushing toward the sea at a maximum speed of 60 miles per hour, killing 1,000 people, and leaving 30,000 homeless. The damage from the flood would cost more than $50 million.

The endless rainstorms bloated the streams, unhinged the dikes, and broke new crevasses all the way from Vicksburg to New Orleans. Hundreds of farmers and their families, a majority of them Negroes, were cut off and overwhelmed by the flood. For several weeks New Orleans lived in fear that a large part of the city might be submerged.

Nearby, the sprawling sugar plantations in the prosperous town of Moreauville sat under water. The Red Cross and the Army set up refugee camps and deployed relief workers throughout the area. There were many sad stories of famished and suffering victims of the flood. Miles and miles of desolated country struck horror.

The Army Corps of Engineers was tasked with the job of relocating families—mostly colored families living near the levee—who'd lost their homes. The Corps chose the corner of New Orleans, a community tucked safely away from the city's proper communities, to house families like the Clarks, the second-class citizens, the laborers, and the house servants.

The Clark sisters were relocated to a place on Water Street, a short distance from the levee that let them down before. It overlooked the Mississippi

River on one side and the City Belt railroad tracks on the other. The community folk half-joked that the white people knew good and well the levee wouldn't protect them from the all-mighty Mississippi. When it was time for the great river to stretch itself, the people of New Orleans would suffer once again.

The stories of the floods were like the horrifying childhood nightmares that parents called "witches riding your dreams." Halie would later swear she lived so close to the river she could feel the pull of the water, hear the lapping when the wind rose high enough, feel the swaying of the boats, and hear the warnings from the river rats who worked the docks.

To think that the Army Corps of Engineers had built the small, drafty shacks for families was one of those things you laughed about to keep from crying. Surely, they kept in mind that the housing was mostly for Blacks and poor immigrants not used to much more.

The homes were little more than plantation shacks set inside a bustling city. Residents were so close to the train they could set their clocks by its horn and the loud rattling that shook their homes and woke babies from their sleep—until they grew so used to it, they could easily fall asleep as the train passed by.

Even so, the Mississippi would remain a source of innate fear for most Black New Orleanians—a constant threat of taking over their lives, leaving them helpless, uprooted all over again. There is the knowledge, always, that the levees won't help when the Mississippi decides to stretch.

Duke's three-room shotgun home was double-sided, with just room enough for the 11 people who lived there. There was one common pump at the end of the street, but it was, more often than not, filled with mud. Mothers would use cornmeal to sift out the mud.

The Clarks, like most families with no electricity, used kerosene lamps to light their homes and wood stoves to cook their food. Charity cooked the family's food on the stove using driftwood washed up by the Mississippi River and coal from the railroad tracks for fuel.

Halie was more a younger sister to the Clark girls than a niece, given their own young ages. Except for Duke, who never treated the girl as an equal. Watchful, strict Duke who would often call Halie "an odd little thing." She wondered where the child's constant questioning and that searing stare came from. Certainly, she had reason to be different, those legs crisscrossing like scissors when she walked; and that dark, smooth ebony skin you could almost see your own reflection in.

From the very beginning little Halie was entranced by sounds. It was New Orleans, and sounds were the backdrop of this exotic Southern city. The echoes of Uptown New Orleans entered Halie's being. She would later describe the sounds she grew up with as something spiritual. The noises of the river and passenger trains were a constant in her young years.

Halie loved the sounds that greeted her each morning and when she fell off to sleep at night. She loved the diverse red, green, blue, and black birds, including the woodpeckers of New Orleans. More than those sounds of nature, she loved the music that was so much a part of her childhood.

Music wafted through the streets from the cafes, the parks, the restaurants. The loud, melodic calls from peddlers and street sellers who marketed their wares—deviled crabs, blackberries, boiled shrimp—each had their own song of invitation to buy. Halie heard the sailors' work songs, too. She fell asleep to the tunes made by riverboats tooting and trains whistling, and sometimes men and women laughing together, outside her window.

And then there were the voices and the stories shared by those songs—blues, jazz, ragtime, and church music. When she heard Bessie Smith, the girl thought she'd died and gone to heaven. She learned every blues song of Bessie's she heard. She begged her cousin Fred to teach her to dance to Bessie's music.

But she also loved the Mardi Gras songs performed mostly by Black musicians who were members of the Mardi Gras Marching Club. She looked forward to this great spectacle that came every February. She was very young when she learned the Zulu Club's song:

If ever I cease to love
If ever I cease to love
May the fish get legs
And the cows lay eggs
If I ever cease to love

The high and grassy river levee was a dangerous place for children to play—likely the very thing that drew them to it. Halie remembered how they sat on the levee and sang songs with ukuleles, baked sweet potatoes in fires made from driftwood, and caught all the fish and shrimp and crabs they could eat.

And, then one day she learned that she had a daddy and that he lived right around the corner. Wild horses couldn't have kept her from him. She could only catch a glimpse of him on Saturdays when he worked at the barbershop. Those piercing eyes were set on Johnny Jackson a long time before she got up the nerve to walk into his barbershop and introduce herself.

This was "Nigger Town," in the early 20th century.

Mt. Moriah Church—Halie's Lifeline

If there was anything that represents Halie's childhood more than Aunt Duke, her adopted mother, it was Mt. Moriah Missionary Baptist Church. Halie loved the church at least as much as she loved most of her friends and many of her relatives. It was her rock, the one thing other than Duke she knew would always be there for her. Since the age of 4 when the choir accepted her as a certified member, Halie began getting excited on Saturdays in anticipation for walking into church on Sundays.

41

JANIS F. KEARNEY

The Clark family attended Mt. Moriah Church each Sunday, as they lived just three blocks from the church. When Halie turned 4 years old, she began singing in the church—music that was different, but not so different, from Bessie Smith's and the Mardi Gras jazz songs she loved so much.

Watchful Duke and Charity made sure Halie knew she couldn't straddle the fence. She would either sing church songs, or street songs. God or the Devil is how they put it. Mahalia liked them both and couldn't understand why she had to give up one, if she sang the other.

It was the singing, of course, the opportunity to open her mouth and share her innermost emotions with the congregation that excited Halie. It was seeing the grown people in awe of her, Halie, like she'd never experienced before. Of course, little Halie couldn't know that she was using the church to bare her soul, shed the confusion she couldn't articulate about her poverty; being the butt of jokes because of her crooked legs; and about the invisible father she only saw if she snuck a peek at him while he cut hair in his barbershop. God knew and understood. And, as long as she sang, the people of Mt. Moriah smiled and rocked and clapped right in time with the little girl's singing as if she was a pretty little princess.

Halie's father, Johnny Jackson, attended his parents' holiness church that was so different from the Clarks' Baptist church. There, members used musical instruments and tambourines. They shouted and danced. All of this was forbidden in the Baptist church where they sang Godly spirituals and congregational hymns. As much as she loved singing in her mama's church, Halie seemed naturally drawn to her father's church. It was the music, the feelings, the beat.

Charity tried again to patiently explain to her daughter that their singing was the music worthy of God's ears. No tambourines or guitars. Not even a piano, for the longest time. The difference between the two churches' music was the same as the difference between church songs and Mardi Gras music. The unsaved enjoyed the loud, dancing music, while good Christian folk liked something more spiritual that pleased God.

Halie's decision to sing in the Baptist church came with her commitment to Charity, and more importantly, to Duke, that she was turning away from the Mardi Gras, blues, and street songs. When she learned she had to be saved to sing in the choir, Halie asked to sit on the mourners' bench while members prayed that God would save her soul, protect her, and welcome her into the church. Duke warned Halie that she would have to confess her sins to the church.

Only then was Halie able to "try out" for the choir. There were no printed books in the church, and few members could read. The spirituals were passed on from the slave era to the era of freedom, and now to this new generation. At 5 years old, Halie learned the old songs that were so expressive of Black people's history of suffering and resiliency. Charity told the church, "I think little Halie's ready." At her very first tryout at Mt. Moriah, Halie sang, *"I'm so glad, I'm so glad, I'm so glad I've been in the grave an' rose again…."*

Aunt Duke was the last holdout for the girl's induction into the choir…and church. She had doubts that the child was ready to claim the Lord as her savior, but even she relented when she heard the girl open her mouth to sing in church that morning.

A stoic and proper church mother, Duke found herself moved and getting "happy" in spite of herself. People outside the church stopped to listen to this amazing young voice. When Halie finished her song, there was silence, swollen with awe, and then followed by thunderous applause. Little Halie's usually small eyes were big on that day as she watched the grown folks' reaction to her singing.

Ten years later, Halie was baptized during a Sunday baptism day where girls and boys and men and women were immersed in the muddy Mississippi River with their sparkling white baptism gowns. It was 1926, and Halie was now a certified member of Mt. Moriah Baptist Church. With a healthy glow to her dark skin and a smile that illuminated her narrow eyes, Mahalia was reborn and committed to the congregation that she would sing praises to God for the rest of her life.

Losing Charity

Wednesday, June 26, 1918, was the 177th day of the year. It was one year after America's entry into World War I and four months after the onset of the 1918-19 flu pandemic.

It was the day that something inside little Halie changed. Charity Clark, the brightest light in the Clark family, died, leaving her siblings locked inside a fog of quiet and grief. Leaving her young daughter Halie inconsolable and her young son Peter lost and angry.

Losing Charity left a hollow place inside Halie that would never fully fill over the years. For some time, 6-year-old Halie couldn't understand that Charity wouldn't wake from her deep sleep and call to her little girl to crawl into bed with her. Peter tried to tell his little sister that their mama was gone for good. Surely, the most painful part of Charity's short illness must have been the moment she realized she might die and her children would become orphans—a mother no longer with them and a father in name only.

Except for family, close friends, and neighbors, this dampening of the Clarks' bright light did not impact life outside their doors, on the streets of Uptown New Orleans. The sights and sounds of the streets—the street rhythm that made Charity smile so often as she walked to and from work, met her young man, raced her son and daughter to Audubon Park—continued without a hitch, with its own syncopation that had been a part of the city centuries before Charity set foot in the town.

The day Charity died the New Orleans streets forgave her leaving. Her death was part of the city's regeneration, part of the churning of life. The sun would keep rising, the trains would keep chugging, the street vendors would continue to sing about their wares, the New Orleans music would still waft into windows, and the great Mississippi River would keep right on rolling.

Yet, for Paul Clark and Duke and Porter, and the other Clark girls and Halie and Peter, losing Charity changed their world. It was a painful loss, for each of them loved her in their own secret way, and they all loved her best. Even more painful was how Charity's death reminded them all of losing that other sweet soul, Ophelia, just eight years earlier.

Why Charity? Why so quickly? Her oldest sister Bell had dark suspicions and whispered with her sisters about the boy named Clement Smith. The small, high-yellow boy who had come into Charity's life so suddenly would never have fit in with the close-knit Clark family. None of Charity's sisters took to him.

Charity knew she was dying a month earlier. Her 18-year-old nephew Allen, called "Son Baby," visited her on May 12th and shared that he was enlisting in the Navy. She startled him when she burst into tears, saying, "I won't see you again, Son Baby. When you come looking, I'll be gone." Because the dark premonition was so unlike Charity, he didn't tell her he was shipping out that day.

Not only Charity's immediate family, but also her white employers, the Rightor family, took her loss hard. She was truly a light for all who knew her. The Rightors had vocally disapproved of Clement Smith's coming around to take Charity out after work. They claimed a special place in their heart for Charity and the other Clark girls. They lauded the girls' industrious and efficient work habits and their affection for the Rightors' children.

After Charity's death, her siblings learned that Charity and Clement Smith had married in 1917, the year before her death. At 25, the pretty, life-loving Charity had wedded twice, the first time to her son's father. Both marriages would result in short lived unions.

The rumors ran rampant after Charity's passing; hints about poisoning, voodoo, a spell—all common suspicions in those days in the exotic New Orleans. According to rumor, it was not unusual for a woman or man to be targeted and given over to a voodoo practitioner who might place a spell on an enemy or an unfaithful lover.

The year that Charity fell ill was the same year Halie joined Mt. Moriah's choir. No one, not even the doctor, knew what the trouble was with Charity. If God saw fit to take her, Charity worried, what would become of her children? She hoped her sisters would not let Johnny Jackson's family take Mahalia. In spite of what Charity's wishes may have been when it came to Johnny Jackson, he was a married man when they met and remained a married man after his daughter was born.

What Charity did know about the Jackson family was that they didn't have the same religious restrictions the Clark family had. Johnny Jackson and his relatives not only attended the Holy Rollers' church, the Church of God in Christ, but Johnny was a part-time preacher there as well.

Charity's fears, however, concerned the family members who were honky-tonk entertainers. Some even performed with Ma Rainey, the blues singer from Columbus, Georgia. They called her, even then, the Mother of the Blues. It scared Charity that Halie might get wrapped up in a family that sang the very songs Halie loved, no matter how good she sang for Jesus.

Johnny Jackson's family performed and toured around the South with Ma Rainey's Rabbit Foot Minstrels. Charity was thinking forward. Halie's passion for singing scared her. The child loved singing more than anything else, more than she liked playing. And, on top of that, she loved to make grown folks smile and like her. Charity imagined Johnny taking her girl and having her traipsing behind that bunch of people in the minstrel show. She worried at night when she wasn't too sick. She needed to keep the girl safe from her demons.

The darkest day in young Halie's life was a Wednesday, the day she came in from playing to find that her mother had died. Not fully understanding, she watched as neighbors brought covered pots and dishes of food that they piled on Duke's table, the boiled pig feet, baked alligator tail, black-eyed beans and rice, corn bread, chitterlings, soups, and cakes and pies.

Halie's paternal grandparents and her father offered the use of their church to hold Charity's funeral. The church women there would take care of everything. Duke was shaking her head from left to right before she said a word. She wouldn't hear of it, and told them so.

Duke had quickly quashed the matter. She and Charity had had their talk before Charity slipped away. Who would dare go up against the formidable Duke? She knew she could rely on her position at Mt. Moriah Baptist Church and her leadership role in the neighborhood. Even those in the community who feared her also respected her. With Duke's nod, Mt. Moriah's burial society took charge of Charity's funeral. The burial society was already pooling together enough money to pay the undertaker and enough funds to ensure a decent burial and a little extra help for the family.

Duke had known Charity's final wishes for a while. One quiet night after everyone had gone off to bed, she and Charity had talked for a long time. That was the night Charity begged her sister to please take her home, back to Legonier and bury her at St. John Baptist Church cemetery at Gumpstump plantation beside their mother. When Porter, the unofficial leader of the family, arrived, he was so overwhelmed with grief he left everything, every decision to Duke. The family knew and accepted that Charity was the favorite of all the sisters, but for Porter she hung the sun. The family would hold the funeral at Mt. Moriah, then take Charity home to Legonier.

The wake was held in Aunt Duke's home. The undertaker had prepared the body for display throughout the all-night vigil attended by members of Charity's church, the burial society, her neighbors, and next of kin. Family and visitors filled the small house. There was no need to fear that evil spirits might harm Charity or steal her soul. The sisters took turns "sitting up" with Charity throughout the night. She couldn't be left alone until she was safely delivered into the hands of the Lord at the burial site.

That night, there was no laughter or common talk. Just sitting and singing and praying softly and eating and drinking, mostly coffee or tea. The next morning, neighbors came in and prepared a large breakfast for the family and friends still there, before everyone left on their journey, taking Charity home.

When Mahalia woke on the day of her mother's funeral, familiar sounds seemed changed...her little eyes were swollen from crying throughout the night. Her tears had disappeared when she entered Mt. Moriah Baptist Church later in the day. However, as someone began moaning the refrain of *"Mother's Gone on to Prepare a Place for Us,"* Halie wept anew.

After the singing ended and the preacher finished his sermon, the family went up for a last look at Charity. Aunt Duke held Mahalia and hugged Peter close so the children could see their mother one last time. Then the funeral directors put the lid on Charity's casket and took her to the train for the burial at Gumpstump.

Halie's first journey outside New Orleans, the first of thousands to come in her lifetime, was to Legonier, Louisiana, in Pointe Coupée Parish, her mother's home. It was where everyone who was part of her life had grown up. The place they still called home. It was also the place where her brother Peter was born, he reminded her. As a child, he boasted that Papa Paul and Grandma Ophelia used to feed him and play with him. That was before Charity followed Porter to New Orleans.

Six-year-old Halie would likely not remember most of what she saw or heard during her short visit to her mother's home at Gumpstump plantation. Her memory was through her Uncle Porter's eyes. He told her how she was walking on the same dirt roads Charity had walked during their trips to Sunday services where her grandfather preached, and about their weekly walks to school when they didn't have to work the fields. Halie loved Papa Paul and wondered why he didn't live with them in New Orleans.

Of all the stories Aunt Duke and Aunt Bell shared on the train ride down to Gumpstump, something stuck with Halie throughout her life. She would never forget the smell and feel of the place that was home to Charity. When she shared those memories with others, she would gain a richer sense of herself and who her mother was before New Orleans.

Halie missed Charity terribly that first year after her mother's death. Yet, she never asked to return to Gumpstump plantation. What she would remember, and never forget, was the sight of her mother's pine coffin following behind them as they traveled to the church at Gumpstump. She would remember the long ride with the clicking of the train wheels and the rushing steam she could see outside the window.

They had boarded "The Plug" in New Orleans, then switched to the Louisville and Nashville Railroad (L&N) train called "The Windy," which took them to a town called Torras. There she'd climbed down into Uncle Porter's arms, and he'd set her into a mule-drawn wagon that would take them to Red River Landing.

Torras was located in the extreme northeastern corner of Pointe Coupée Parish, surrounded by railroads and rivers. The Texas & Pacific Railroad tracks straddled the town. The town sat at the junction of Lower Old River and where the Mississippi River joined the Red and Atchafalaya rivers to the east.

Founded in 1902, the town was named for a young Spanish planter named Joseph Torras, a pioneer who immigrated from Barcelona, Spain, in 1820, eventually settled in Pointe Coupée Parish in 1845. Torras and his brother has envisioned that the town would develop into an important shipping and rail center. The flood of 1912, however, dashed their expectations when the levee in front of the town gave way and Torras and many other communities were virtually destroyed. Some 17,000 residents of Pointe Coupée Parish were forced from their homes and at least 28 people drowned.

The Red River Landing remained, thanks to a father and his son who operated a flat-bottomed pontoon ferry, a barge attached by ropes to a little gasoline-powered tugboat chugging its stern wheel indoors. If the two men happened to be on the other side of the river when passengers arrived, the passengers only had to holler across the river to get their attention. Passengers sat or stood on the tugboat. But the flatboat was for buggies and wagons, two at a time—or, in this case, one wagon and a coffin.

Halie, Peter, and the grown-ups climbed into the tugboat, the engine cranked to a roar, and at the end of the ropes, across the rushing waters they began the final journey. It was a long, lonely trip for Halie who watched the flatboat behind them carrying Charity. It was her mother's final journey home. Mahalia would talk later about the little white skiff that carried her mother's body back home, but she never talked about her grief.

Finally, returning to the house and the white wooden church nearby—St. John the Baptist where she had found religion and been baptized—Charity would join her mother, her two siblings, and three generations of Fiendleys and Clarks in this very courtyard.

When they started back home to New Orleans, Uncle Porter began singing: *"I'm so glad, I'm so glad, I'm so glad I've been in the grave an' rose again...."* Then the whispered conversation began to take shape on the subject of who would take responsibility for the orphans: Peter, now 10 years old, and Mahalia, age 6. Aunt Duke spoke up, settling things then and there. "I'll take them both. It's what Charity wanted." And that was that.

Of course, it made sense for Charity to want a second mother for her children, especially her little girl—a mother who would hold the precocious child straight, protect her from her own demons. Mahala "Duke" Paul was the power in the Clark family. Dark brown skin Duke, tall and erect with piercing gray eyes—Halie's eyes almost to a tee, except for the gray. Duke was what they called a high-class cook, first rate. She worked for a white family in the part of St. Charles Street where the real bluebloods lived. She ruled her kitchen in the white folks' house, and all the other help, too. When other Black help was getting half as much, Duke demanded, and got, $10 a week.

The tall Black woman was somebody in her neighborhood. Everyone knew how much Duke disapproved of the sinning that took place around her. She complained often about the so-called sporting life—the gambling lottery and games of Cotch and Georgia Skin, and the saloons only a block away from where she was trying to raise young children. She'd sometimes curse and turn over when she woke to the sound of arguments or fights outside her window. Sometimes, she'd go to her door and throw out a few threats if they didn't leave her premises.

Duke wouldn't think of leaving her neighborhood, though. She loved the community because the community loved her back. More than that, they respected her. Besides, where would she go with two orphan children to raise, a husband, and siblings who so often needed her. Then, there was Mt. Moriah Church. No, she'd never leave.

A Different Kind of Love

With all her pluses, Duke was a long way from Charity. In young Halie's eyes, Duke was nothing like Charity, who had brought light and warmth into every room she ever entered, who had a smile to share with her daughter even when she wasn't feeling so good, who would listen as Halie tried to explain why she didn't do exactly as Charity had directed.

Duke's was a different kind of love, an invisible love shrouded over by her need for order and structure and obedience. Mahalia had been "Little Halie" the pet, when it was just her mother and Peter. When her mother got sick, Halie sweet-talked her ailing mother and sashayed out the door to freedom, becoming a street urchin, running the streets as she pleased.

Everything changed when Duke took over Halie and Peter's lives. She put a stop to the wild freedom to which the girl had become accustomed. She aimed to raise the children right, and she would do it her own way. Unlike with Charity, the affection from grown-ups came sparingly. Duke wasn't one for showing affection. The Bible didn't speak of it, so it must not be godly. Duke believed in the church, hard work, and keeping her two wards on the straight and narrow.

Halie would learn, and learn fast, to tow Duke's hard line or feel Duke's wrath. There was no sparing the rod. Duke would often get out her cat-o'-nine-tails, and when she hit one lick, she was hitting nine times in different places.

Uncle Emanuel was the only source of affection little Halie could count on now, and every so often her father, who she sometimes snuck around the corner to see. Halie would later share stories of her moments in her father's barbershop, how he'd sit her on his lap and call her his "chocolate drop." Though this was not often, it meant so much to Halie because he never scolded or whipped her. And, when he could, he slipped her a few coins to take to Aunt Duke—a thank you for keeping the girl.

Mahalia Jackson's foreparents, grandparents, and parents lived through generations of racial and social atrocities: slavery, Jim Crow, floods, hurricanes. Then came the flu pandemic of 1918, also known as the Spanish Flu, one of the most tragic moments in New Orleans' legacy.

Charity, the light of the Clark family, died just four months after the deadly flu arrived in New Orleans. Her illness lingered for weeks before she finally succumbed to it. While she suffered female ailments most of her adult life, and she was never diagnosed with the Spanish Flu, there were mumblings that it could very well have been the cause of Charity's death.

Halie was exactly four months shy of turning 7 years old when her mother passed. September 1918 marked the month that the first death was officially attributed to this new influenza outbreak in New Orleans. Little did anyone know the country was on the precipice of one of the worst health pandemics in U.S. history. By the time the pandemic was under control, an estimated 500 million people worldwide (one-third of the world's population) became infected with the virus. The flu killed at least 50 million people worldwide, including about 675,000 in the United States.

Mahalia was three days past her 7th birthday, when the hopeful whispers were that the New Orleans' epidemic might soon be over. New Orleans experienced so many new influenza cases at one point that Charity Hospital officials turned their facility completely over to the care of influenza victims.

By early February 1919, the number of new influenza cases in New Orleans finally had slowed to a trickle; and on February 7, city health officials declared the influenza epidemic was officially over. The epidemic was a devastating one for New Orleans. Between October 1918 and April 1919, the city experienced a staggering 54,089 cases of influenza. Of these, 3,489 people died—a death rate of 734 per 100,000. Only Pittsburgh (806 per 100,000) and Philadelphia (748 per 100,000)—the two cities with the worst epidemics in the nation—had higher death rates.

The night after her mother's burial, Mahalia became an undocumented ward of Aunt Duke and her husband Emanuel Paul. Peter, her brother, was four years older and already prone not to show his grief, while Mahalia cried throughout the night.

When she would later talk about her childhood, Mahalia sometimes said that during much of her life she felt rudderless, though she had a family and a home. That sense of displacement remained throughout her childhood. It helped some when she got to know Grandmother Jackson who lived just a few blocks away.

Halie was a fast learner, and she learned quickly how to be the child that Duke expected her to be when she was home, in church, or working with Duke in the white folks' home. There, she was shy, obedient, and a hard worker. Duke showed her and often told her that life was hard and she should expect little from it, in spite of the voice she offered up to God each Sunday. In spite of Duke's harsh admonitions, Halie dared to dream, believing there was something waiting for her out there. Those dreams wouldn't die the way Duke hoped they would, they only grew.

Some neighbors had a phonograph next door to Aunt Duke, and they would often play Ma Rainey or Bessie Smith records. Uncle Porter said Bessie Smith had learned the blues from Ma Rainey. As Mahala worked and pretended not to hear, she listened attentively to Bessie Smith's popular song "Bo-Weavil Blues," about the boll weevil insect that destroyed the cotton crops.

As she did her chores at home, Mahalia would close her eyes and shape her lips around the words as she heard the music in her mind. She imagined the blues singer standing on a stage with her eyes closed and her hands clasped in front of her as she sang. The tune stayed with her that night as she lay in bed, finally drifting into a dream where she was singing, and her voice was Bessie Smith's voice, and Charity was there, smiling. In the background, though, was Aunt Duke, with a stern face and pressed lips.

Church people—the saved—don't sing the blues, she heard Aunt Duke say. Mahalia woke from her dream, sad and conflicted, the way she'd feel for most of her life about the music she loved and the music she vowed to sing.

Part 4

HALIE'S HARD CHILDHOOD

TOP: NEW ORLEANS SHANTY TOWN (NEW ORLEANS HISTORICAL ARCHIVES). **BOTTOM LEFT:** CHARITY AND THE CLARK SISTERS OF POINTE COUPÉE PARISH (TULANE CREDIT). **BOTTOM RIGHT:** JOHNNY JACKSON, SR., MAHALIA'S FATHER, CIRCA 1960 (TULANE CREDIT).

Hard Work Never Hurt Nobody

Aunt Duke didn't believe in waste, or frills. Everything she owned had a purpose; if it didn't, what was the point in having it? She had two uniforms for work—a blue one and a white one. She switched them up each week for her job with the white family on St. Charles Street. She also had a Sunday dress that she never wore any other time except for church. It wasn't fancy, but it was a proper Sunday dress. She made sure that Halie had a nice dress and a pair of good shoes for Sundays. The rest of the week, Halie might have been taken for a barefoot ragamuffin like most other children in the neighborhood.

Like most families in the community, full baths were an extravagance they saved for weekends, mainly for church. Duke and her family took turns taking their baths in the kitchen where the water was heated on the stove during the winters. During the summer, buckets of water were left outside to let the sun do the heating. Their bathing vessel was a No. 3 tin washtub. After their baths, Halie and Peter were directed to rub their legs, arms, and faces down with Vaseline® to make them shine.

In later life, Mahalia would not talk much about the hard times of growing up in "Nigger Town." Only those closest to her knew that she never had a toy or store-bought doll growing up in Aunt Duke's house. She would make herself a rag doll from pieces of old clothing and braid up grass to use as the doll's hair. She never saw a Christmas tree except at church. During the Christmas season, she always wished they would remain at church even longer so she could stare at the tall tree with home-made dolls and sparkling stars for decorations.

Many years later, Mahalia would decorate evergreen trees around her house with as many Christmas lights as they could hold. She could leave the lights on as long as she wanted and spend the night staring out her window at the twinkling colors.

Even more than most places in America's Southeast, New Orleans' summers were mercilessly hot and humid. You sweated all through the night, and once you started moving around during the day, the sweating never stopped. Most people rose early to get as much of their work done as possible before the morning sun turned scorching hot around noon.

Aunt Duke rose before sunrise every day to prepare to get off to the white people's homes and children. Uncle Emanuel usually cooked a breakfast of eggs, cornbread, and syrup. After breakfast, Halie would join him in the garden, pulling weeds and planting vegetables, beans, potatoes, and other crops.

By the time he was 10, Peter was already working as a yard boy for a white family Aunt Duke sent him to. That left the home chores to Halie. Before she turned 10, Halie was cleaning house the same as Aunt Duke, scrubbing the floors with a red brick and lye until the cypress wood was bleached pale blond.

Halie stuffed and sewed mattresses, filling them with corn shucks and soft grey Spanish moss that hung from the trees. Every summer, she gathered baskets of the moss and corn shucks and ticked them into mattress covers made from bleached cotton cement sacks with heavy twine and a long needle.

Halie was smart, with a quick and agile mind. None of her aunts could figure out where the girl got her ways. Though Halie could be quiet, they knew that was only because she was thinking all kinds of thoughts inside that head of hers. Other times, she would talk a mile a minute, asking the strangest questions about life and people.

Queer, different, strange, was how the family described little Halie. But she was also clever. She was able to create just about anything she put her mind to. Aunt Duke would take Halie to a nearby sugarcane plantation to collect cane stalks and palm fronds, and set her to weaving them into cane chairs. It took the girl only one day to learn the craft and learn it as well as her Aunt Duke, plaiting the two plants into the split-bottom cane chairs.

When Duke needed firewood for the kitchen stove, Halie took a wheelbarrow and ax along the river levee or into the swamps, picking up driftwood and splitting planks off old barges that were sinking into the mud. She'd use a long pole to fish floating snags and logs out of the river and lay them up on the bank to dry while she sat in the sun and watched the steamboats go by.

In New Orleans, the Mississippi River was as much a part of the community as anything. For whatever reason, children were drawn to the dangerous muddy waters filled with alligators and snakes. There was something mystical, magical about the Mississippi. For Halie, though, everything about her childhood in New Orleans was magical.

When she turned 8, the child was sent off to work with her aunt Bessie at the Rightors' home. Bessie took over the role Charity held before her death. Bessie was only 12 years old at the time. Halie, still in elementary school, started out just doing odd jobs Bessie would give her to keep her busy. Eventually, she began babysitting the Rightors' children.

Bessie and Halie would leave home each morning after breakfast, in time to help get the white children ready for school and get the family's breakfast dishes washed, before the girls left for school, themselves. In the afternoon, they would go back to the Rightors and help out again—all for $2 a week.

Even as she continued to take on more adult responsibilities, Halie found time to be a child, and sometimes a wayward child. Between Duke's home and the river were the railroad tracks where the New Orleans Public Belt Railroad train ran. She later recalled how the white trainman called "Hot Lips" would slow his train just enough for the neighborhood children to hitch a ride on his caboose. Halie and her friends would travel on the train from the neighborhood to the sugar district. There, they'd take sugar cane stalks from the warehouses, hide away, and consume the sweet nectar to their hearts' delight. That fun expedition ended around 1920, when blights of mosaic disease, root rot, and bad weather caused a series of weak harvests that led to the eventual end to New Orleans sugar dynasty.

Before the New Orleans winter would settle in, Halie would take baskets down to the railroad tracks to pick up lumps of coal behind the train engine, filling the coal bins.

There were children everywhere in Halie's neighborhood, and no one loved playing more than she did. She played with white children as well as Blacks. Back then, she said, it didn't make a difference; they all rode together on the merry-go-round in Audubon Park. They lived next to each other in the neighborhood and often played in each other's yards.

The largest white population in the community were Italians. When Halie found herself having to defend herself against the boys, she gave as good as she got. Sometimes she'd go home with a scar. More times than not, it was the feisty Italian children who did.

Halie spent most of the time working, either at Duke's house or at some white family's home. She and Peter knew at an early age that they were responsible for contributing to the household. One of her chores was to pull "peppergrass" for her family's supper. This edible weed was also called "Poor Man's Peppers" and "Virginia Pepperweed" and could be found along roadsides and in fields. The entire plant, which has a pepperlike flavor, was edible. The leaves were also sautéed or used fresh in salads or as potherb. The young seedpods were often used as a substitute black pepper.

Uncle Emanuel taught Peter how to take care of lawns, shrubbery, and flower gardens, while Halie was taught very early how to take care of the home, as well as the garden patch that was planted and cultivated beside their home. She was taught how to weed rows of okra, green beans, red beans, tomatoes, pumpkin, and corn. She was also responsible for feeding the chickens and the goat penned in one corner of the yard. Halie had to gather fruit in season—peaches, figs, bananas, oranges—and pecans, from which Aunt Duke taught her to make pralines, a candy made mostly of sugar, corn syrup, butter, and pecans.

When the hot sun made outdoor work too much, Aunt Duke found indoor tasks for Halie. She taught the sturdy child how to make mattress covers of the cloth cement sacks, often saying: "Hard work never hurt nobody. You're never too young to start."

Everyone knew that Mahala "Duke" Paul was a hard taskmaster and strict beyond belief. When she'd send Halie on an errand, Duke would forewarn her about dawdling.

"I'm going to spit on this hot stove, and if you ain't back by the time the spit dries, I'm gonna whup you till you think I'm Robert Charles," referencing the quasi-mythical African American who was killed and lynched by New Orleans police after being accused of killing six people in 1900.

Aunt Duke knew little Halie had hung her star on singing. While she sang like a bird in church, Duke had seen the girl standing still in the middle of her work, listening to the devil's music coming through the window from somebody's jukebox. Duke prayed that in time, the girl would grow out of her obsession with devil music, and God's music would win her over. Even so, she didn't give it a second thought that Halie might be able to make a living from her singing. And she faulted Hannah for filling the child's head with crazy dreams of becoming somebody great.

As far as Duke was concerned, singing was no way out for a Black child. Halie needed to know how to work with her hands to make a living for herself. That's what Black people had to do to survive in the South.

Sometimes, work crossed over into fun for Halie and Peter. Uncle Emanuel, likely sensing that the young people needed some time away from Duke's strict raising, took Halie and Peter to hunt turtles and alligators in the nearby swamps to cook for dinner. One of his and Duke's favorite meals was baked alligator tail, smothered with onions and garlic and herbs. Now and then, Duke went along with them on fishing trips. Sometimes, he could talk Duke into not rushing back. When they had caught enough fish, they would build a fire, fry the fish right there, and eat it on the spot. Besides singing in her church choir, these were the times that Halie would remember with fondness.

While Uncle Emanuel was teaching Peter bricklaying and garden work, Aunt Duke began Mahalia's instructions in cooking and housekeeping.

Mahalia learned quickly that she wasn't to ever throw out lard from the pork they cooked. Just about everything they ate was cooked with a dab of lard for the flavoring. A tin can of melted fat sat on the back of the stove for as long as Halie lived in the house on Water Street. All the drippings from fried bacon and roast pork went into that can for later use to season collard and mustard greens, and even cornbread. Aunt Duke even showed Mahalia how to make soap from the drippings.

Halie saw her Aunt Duke at her softest during the mornings they worked together in the kitchen or fishing with her uncle. Duke became a substitute mother, not simply her guardian. Duke would hum as she worked, songs like, *"Before I'd be a Slave, I'd Be Buried in My Grave," "Children, We Shall Be Free,"* or *"Walk Together Children, Don't You Get Weary."*

If Duke had a passion for anything, it was for her church, her faith. She taught Halie that the two most important things in life were work and church. And not only on Sundays, but each evening after Duke made it home from the white family's house, and the children finished their chores, they'd make their way down to Mt. Moriah for prayer services. Halie figured God certainly knew them all by their first names by now.

Saving Halie from the Music in Her Bones

Little Halie and her family resided in the most musical city in the land. New Orleans had Mardi Gras, Cajun music, street music, and jazz, which was born in the city but didn't gain its wings until the rest of the country accepted it. Halie would hear many of New Orleans' most prominent Black musicians on Sunday evenings as they performed at the Place Congo, just blocks from where she lived and attended church. When she was lucky, she actually saw and heard street musicians as she ran errands for Aunt Duke, or on her way to school.

The city was also home to great operas and concerts in which highly trained Black musicians performed. For years, the emotional and powerfully rhythmic African music of the slaves had stood in sharp contrast to the European music of the cultured free Blacks. By Mahalia's time, the two traditions were merged. And out of them came a new music with new sounds, a modern music that voiced the life of the 20th century.

While running errands along Water Street, young Halie would be immersed in the sounds of New Orleans. It was then that she was introduced to the sounds of the incomparable Bessie Smith, who was called the "Empress of the Blues" and an early *protégé* of the great Ma Rainey.

Halie would linger longer than she should, listening to the sounds from the phonographs wafting through windows on Water Street. She heard Bessie Smith's smooth, smoky singing of songs like W.C. Handy's "St. Louis Blues"—*"I hate to see that evenin' sun go down."* It was these songs, this music that drew little Halie to the music her family wanted to keep from her. She couldn't help but fall in love with Bessie Smith's smoky voice and imagine herself singing just like her.

When Halie walked downtown with Aunt Duke, the child would try mumbling Bessie's tunes under her breath as she heard it drifting out of the homes. Aunt Duke would stop in her tracks. She'd warn Halie about the cat-o'-nine-tails and where singing the blues would land her. Duke threatened to find the neighbors playing the devil's music with the moaning voices. She'd hold even tighter to the girl's little hand, praying under her breath to God to deliver the child from a future in hell.

At their regular prayer meetings, Halie sat beside Aunt Duke, watching her every move. She watched as her aunt rose to testify about the goodness of God and about the troubles she'd endured during the week. When Duke would ask forgiveness for her sins, Halie wondered if she was referring to the cat-o'-nine-tails she'd used on Halie and Peter that week.

Church for Halie was more than the experience of paying homage to God. She loved the feeling of church, and even more so, hearing the old songs the church members used to worship God. She also loved the feeling of being a part of a family, the security she felt from the adults who loved and protected her—a motherless child. This unconditional love was so important to Halie's spirit and soul.

Beyond anything, though, Halie's little heart leaped at the pure, raw songs of hope and faith in tomorrow. There were no recorded music or prepared songs during the weekly meetings. The songs came straight from the hearts of the women and men who experienced much of the same lives of impoverishment and oppression.

It was during these times, in the midst of these half-church, half-family gatherings that Halie fell in love with church. This love would never leave her and would direct her life in sometimes inexplicable ways. While Aunt Duke prayed, the child would squeeze her own eyes closed and offer up her own little prayers.

Aunt Duke regularly shared with Halie and Peter that money was scarce, that the children were "eating her out of house and home." She often complained that the way the children were growing, they needed new shoes and clothes just about every six months. Everything costs a lot, these days, she'd complain, and Halie's father's little contribution wasn't anything they could depend on since his work on the docks wasn't regular and his earnings from preaching and weekend barbering was just enough to keep his own house and family fed.

Aunt Duke wanted her godchild to get an education. She believed in its power. With a little schooling, she believed, Mahalia might become secretary to the many lodges, burial societies, and church organizations to which Aunt Duke belonged. Being a realist, however, Duke knew Halie would eventually have to work and that meant they didn't have the luxury of her attending school. There was no other way. Every person in the Paul house had to contribute.

The Rightor Family of New Orleans

When Halie was just 7 years old, shortly after finishing first grade, she began working when she wasn't in school, joining her Aunt Bessie, who was just a few years older than Halie, at her job. By the time Bessie had turned 12, she was already experienced in taking care of white children and doing domestic work. Duke made sure Bessie taught Mahalia all she knew.

The aunt and niece worked for the white Rightor family of New Orleans, for whom Charity had worked before her death. Mahalia made the beds, helped the children to dress for school, put away their clothing, served them their breakfast, and washed their dishes—all before she left for school herself.

The Rightor family was drawn to the young woman's bright and happy personality. She was a hard worker, and honest. From all reports, they were especially accepting of Charity's decision to bring on her sister Bessie to work in their home, and even to bring her young son Peter to the job when she found it necessary. Charity's sister Rhoda also worked there when needed. When Papa Paul Clark visited, he often stopped by the Rightor home to see his girls.

The Rightors lived in a prominent white neighborhood on Millaudon and Macarty streets. Henry Rightor was a writer and historian who wrote the book "Standard History of New Orleans, Louisiana." His wife, Ella, did not work outside the home, the norm at that time.

The Rightors' only son, Henry Jr., was one of Charity's charges. He and Charity's son, Peter, often played together when Charity brought Peter with her to work. The three Rightor girls were much older than Halie. When Charity began bringing her to work, Halie played with Henry and Peter.

One of the Rightor daughters, Marguerite Rightor Ellis, recalled the Clarks as sweet, outgoing, gentle, and good-looking. She recalled Bell and Charity's wonderful personalities and how quick they were to laugh. "Little Halie," she recalled, was a delight, though she was "very skinny, very black, very homely—and still bowlegged." Peter laughingly called his little sister "Fishhooks," and the other children in the neighborhood would follow suit, joking that when Halie walked, her feet scissored across each other.

Much later, it would come to Mahalia Jackson that the Rightor family was her first white audience. They accepted her in spite of what others called her—homely, black skin, and fishhook legs. It was during this time she would learn how she could delight audiences with her singing and dancing and somehow forget her bowlegs and homeliness.

Though Halie kept a smile on her face, there is little doubt that the children's taunting hurt. She would rarely speak of those hurtful times, not wanting the pity it would ensue. She did share it when she believed it would do good, like the time she shared it with a group of disabled students in New Jersey. *"When I was little, I was terribly deformed. My legs were crooked and bent. Your young hearts don't understand what has happened to you."*

Halie's work at the Rightors included walking the young Rightor children to their all-white school, before rushing off to her own Blacks-only school. She earned $2 a week and received the family's leftover food and clothing the children had outgrown. Sometimes, when no one saw her, Mahalia hugged a doll belonging to one of the Rightor girls. She had never owned a real doll.

Despite the harsh work at home and at her part-time job at the Rightor home, Halie somehow thrived on work. Her two favorite things were singing in the church choir and learning at school. She was an apt student who quickly learned to read, write, and do sums. She was especially good with math which helped make her understand early on the importance of saving money. It was her Aunt Duke's emphasis on how hard money was to get and keep that helped Halie make up her mind to save every penny Duke let her keep, for her future.

Whether Halie was dreaming of Chicago long before it became a reality for her is anyone's guess. What is certain is that her aunts, Bessie and Hannah, shared fascinating stories about the place they lived. Halie dreamed about a future where she was singing. The other dream she had was becoming a nurse.

Though Halie loved school, she was forced to leave when she was just in fourth grade. It was a hard decision for Aunt Duke, but a necessary one for the family. It helped that Mahalia was tall, towering above just about every girl or boy at her church or school. At 9 years old, she could have easily passed for 12. Duke hired Halie out as a laundress where she washed and ironed white families' clothing for 10 hours a day.

Halie was both fast and skillful, taking just three minutes to iron a man's shirt; though embroidered napkins and fancy linen took a lot of doing. Halie's body soon caught up with her big voice. Starting work at such an early age had given Halie an unusual maturity that had even impacted her already mature voice.

Fighting the Pull of New Orleans' Music

The Jacksons were sanctified, Holy Rollers, unapologetically expressive Christians. In their holiness church, there was laughter and joy, shouting and dancing in their worship. New Orleans claimed twice as many churches in any given block as there were barrooms. Pastors were rarely full time. Like Halie's father, they worked elsewhere during the week and took whatever salary the church could offer. Most met Wednesday, Friday, and four times on Sunday. Some mustered three choirs—adult, youth, and a children's choir.

More than anything else in the world and as early as she could remember, singing gave Halie unconditional joy. It came as natural as speech for her. Her first song, "Oh Pal, Oh God," was a hymn taught to her by an old man who sunned himself on the levee. She was not allowed to sing rowdy songs because of her family's devoted faith. While most Black New Orleanians were Protestants, there was a large number who were solid Baptists, which meant no jazz, no card playing, no high life.

When Mahalia began singing at 4 years old, her repertoire included songs like "Jesus Loves Me" and "Hand Me Down My Silver Trumpet, Gabriel," which she sang in the children's choir at Plymouth Rock, the

Jackson family's church. All of this holiness took place inside the church's wooden doors, while right outside were the sounds of the strawberry lady, the scissors man, the blackberry lady, the charcoal man—all selling something. But more importantly, they were all singing their own unique songs to lure their customers.

New Orleans had a song for every job, for every action—the men working on the docks, on the river wharf, on the levees, on the railroad tracks, even the serious gamblers in the alleyways.

Music was as natural to the city as the muddy Mississippi River. New Orleans was full of music—on the showboats on the Mississippi river; in the cabarets and cafes where musicians like Jelly Roll Morton and King Oliver played. Ragtime music and jazz and the blues were played all over. Everybody was buying phonographs, the kind you wound up on the side by hand. Everybody had records of all the Negro blues singers, most notably the great Bessie Smith, Ma Rainey, Mamie Smith, and some others.

There were also the famous white singers, like Caruso, you could hear coming out of the homes of whites and Italians. But in the colored houses, it was the blues—through the walls, through the open windows, up and down the streets. Everybody played it loud.

Duke, the staunch Baptist Christian that she was, bristled to think that this was what colored folks spent their money on, and spent their time doing. She was adamant that no decent colored person, no church-going colored person, would be caught dead down in Storyville where all the saloons and sporting houses used to be. Storyville was where one found the brass bands for funerals when a popular person—a lodge man or a sporting man—died. No brass band would be paid to serenade a common man, not even a minister.

Halie's trips to the store for Charity, and later Aunt Duke, were her opportunity to drink in the sounds of New Orleans—nothing she'd ever hear inside their home. It was in the air they breathed, all along the sidewalks, drifting out of every window. The street workers—whether shoeshine boys or vegetable vendors—had a tune they'd share. A special treat was when the bands came down the street in open cars; their music advertising their evening activities—dances or fish fries. Black musicians could be heard down several streets, from Water to Magazine, standing or sitting in the back of trucks with the tailgate down, playing ragtime jazz.

The Jackson Family of New Orleans

The first time that young Halie set eyes on Johnny Jackson, the man whose name she carried, she couldn't take her eyes off him. He was the best-looking man she'd ever seen, and she immediately fell in love with him. While Johnny Jackson was no talker, he talked with his smiles and his twinkling eyes. What he did say was in a calming voice, with a kind demeanor.

Because she was hungry for the affection of the man who was her father, Halie made excuses to stop by the barbershop where Johnny worked. There is little indication that a genuine father-daughter relationship developed during her childhood, though one would evolve later in life. The nice man, with the nice smile, was kind, but not terribly interested in his daughter. Halie would often leave the barbershop depressed. The next time, she always hoped, would be different.

In time, Halie would get to know her paternal grandparents—Johnny's mother Fannie (Henrietta) and his father John Andrew Jackson—and Johnny's sister Jeanette Burnette. She didn't know yet about his other family, and children.

Halie's paternal grandparents had been truck farmers in Kenner, Louisiana. Her grandfather John Andrew was drawn to the New Orleans waterfront. After arriving in the city, he had worked his way up to longshoreman straw boss at the Walnut Wharf. As a straw boss, he was able to hire and fire his own crew. His word was law on whether a nonunion man was bumped when a union man applied. Halie ingratiated herself to the Jackson family, even her paternal great-grandmother Sarah Lemore, who lived just blocks from Mahalia's home.

Saturdays became special for Halie after she learned about her father. She couldn't wait to spend a few minutes with him. Aunt Duke had nothing so sentimental in mind. Like clockwork, on Saturdays after lunch, Aunt Duke would send Halie off to visit her father's barbershop, directing her to tell him that his daughter would be attending school barefoot unless he supplied her with money for shoes.

This was always a doubly exciting day for Halie. Not only was she getting to see her father, but she was able to soak in the feels and sounds of New Orleans' streets on her way to the barbershop and back. She would often dawdle beside the children playing craps or another game in the streets. She loved watching the washboard band, usually just a few men who made music through the mouth of an empty glass gallon jug, while the band leader brushed a nail against the corrugated face of a washboard that Southerners called a "Jew's Harp."

Farther along the route would be the Eureka Brass Band, the pride of New Orleans, leading a funeral march to the cemetery. Halie and other youngsters would follow the band as far as they could before dropping off for their destinations. The burial societies supported the Eureka Band, and the church people forgave them for playing for sinners in dance halls. The sinners didn't like them any less for playing in the churches. Sooner or later, the brass band followed church members, sinners, backsliders, unbelievers, the saved and unsaved, to the graveyard and returned blaring "When the Saints Go Marching In."

When Halie finally made her way to her father's barbershop, he was usually busy and didn't see her. She was content just to sit quietly and watch him work until he finished. She was certain that Johnny Jackson was the handsomest man in New Orleans. The only place she could visit her father was on the job.

"How's my little chocolate drop?" asked her father as the customer got out of the chair. Mahalia smiled. She hungered for his embrace, but his smile and acknowledgment were all he usually had to share. She would commence to repeat Aunt Dukes message. "Aunt Duke sent me for shoe money, Papa." He'd look down as she showed her shoes, filled with holes, to him. Rarely did he have money to spare, but he would search his pocket and come up with a dime and a nickel. Mahalia thanked him, tightened her fist around the coins, and said goodbye as she left for home, taking the long route back. She hoped her aunt wouldn't scold her for not bringing home enough money for new shoes.

Thanks to her paternal and maternal families, Mahalia grew up under the influence of both Baptist and holiness churches. She would often join her paternal great-grandmother on Saturdays, when she traveled clear across town to 2400 Delachaise Street to attend their weekly church service at Ephesus Seventh-day Adventist Church. It was one of the few Seventh-day Adventist churches in New Orleans, where Catholic and Baptist churches reigned. Halie would later learn that her great-grandmother was an ex-slave. She would live to be 104 years old.

Halie recalled that church was practically an everyday affair. But she wanted more than anything to sing in the choir. She would learn, in time, that some of her father's family were in show business. Mahalia's aunt and uncle—Jeanette Jackson Burnette and her husband Josie Burnette—traveled with a "Butterbeans and Susie" comedy act that was part of Ma Rainey's tent show. Back then, Blacks were not allowed to play in theaters. They would set up tents wherever they could and charge nickels and dimes for the entrance fee.

When the Burnettes learned Halie could sing like a bird, they wanted to sign her up and take her on the road. But as much as Aunt Duke complained about money, she wouldn't hear of Halie joining such a wicked show. Excited, young Halie just wanted to sing. She imagined she'd be able to sing to her heart's delight. That was years before she realized God had something much bigger in store for her. She would later thank Duke for holding out, despite knowing that the money Halie would bring in could contribute to the household.

The Clark family members were workers and good at it. They were also devout Christians who shut everything down from Friday until

Monday. Either you were a Christian and acted like it, or you were put out of church.

Halie's paternal grandmother stayed busy with her house, the church, and taking care of her two grandchildren—her daughter Jeanette's children. Jeanette was still mostly in vaudeville. She would later become half of the comedy act "Camp and Camp." Her son, Edward, would brag to Halie about his mother's friends—Ma Rainey, Bessie Smith, Mamie Smith, Jack Wiggins, King Rastus Brown, and Stove Pipe. He gloated that he had met them all at one time or another. Mahalia was jealous but told herself God had something more in store for her.

The Jacksons attended Plymouth Rock Baptist Church on Hillary Street, but Mahalia learned about a different kind of church from her mother's family.

Halie would sometimes spend part of her time playing with her Jackson cousins Edward, Celie, and Jack in Audubon Park when she was sent to pull peppergrass. Sometimes they'd slow down long enough to roast acorns.

Only on Sundays—Jim Crow in New Orleans

"If I owned a home in hell and one in New Orleans, I'd rent out the one in New Orleans and live in hell" was a common joke in New Orleans, but a serious allusion to the history of racial segregation, discrimination, and oppression. Mahalia and her family rode in streetcars for Blacks only. Twenty-one years before Mahalia was born, the state of Louisiana adopted a law requiring railroads to carry Black passengers in separate cars, so-called Jim Crow cars, or behind partitions.

In 1892, Homer Plessy challenged the law when he bought a first-class ticket in New Orleans for Covington, Louisiana, got on the train, and took a seat in the "whites only" car. The conductor ordered him to move to the Jim Crow car, but he refused and was arrested. At the trial, Plessy's lawyer argued before criminal court Judge John H. Ferguson that

Jim Crow law was unconstitutional. It violated the 14th Amendment to the Constitution of the United States, which said no state could make a law depriving a citizen of his equal rights.

Judge Ferguson ruled against Plessy and declared him guilty of breaking the separate car law. Plessy fought the case all the way to the U.S. Supreme Court. In 1896, however, the high court's majority decided against Plessy, ruling that segregation didn't discriminate against Negroes. The ruling gave birth to the historic "separate but equal" law, which gave states the right to label their citizens by race and self-claim public facilities for Blacks as equal to those of whites.

The ruling authorized Jim Crow, giving Southern states the green light to effectuate racist Jim Crow policies and laws openly and publicly. "Whites Only" or "Colored" signs began to pop up everywhere—at water fountains, toilets, waiting rooms, ticket windows—all were tagged by race to keep whites and Blacks from meeting on equal terms. These openly racial inequity laws heightened during this period throughout the South, and it was no different in New Orleans.

Though Halie didn't know the name for it, she surely would have been constricted by Jim Crow laws. Yet, her neighborhood was a true melting pot. Blacks, whites, French, Italians, and Creoles living side by side. The children played and fought together on Water Street. Their fathers worked side by side on the docks and ports and the sugar warehouses. Halie never considered it was different in other parts of the city.

Halie attended a segregated school. Her schoolbooks were stored separately from whites. She couldn't attend the circus on the same dates and times as white children. The circus set aside one day for Blacks to watch the clowns. Blacks couldn't attend white churches. They couldn't make an oath on the same Bible in certain courts—Jim Crow demanded one Bible for Blacks, another for whites.

If Halie's father, Johnny Jackson, wanted to go fishing with a white friend, they couldn't lunch together. The law made them put an oar across the middle of the boat and sit with the oar between them while they ate.

During slavery, Blacks couldn't fraternize or congregate in a public space without suspicions from whites and policemen. The one place they were able to congregate was Congo Square, but only on Sundays. The square had significant history for Black New Orleans. It was the place where African men, women, and children were herded off the boats, like cattle, and traded and sold into slavery to new masters.

Congo Square is just as well remembered as the one place in New Orleans where Black slaves could gather on Sundays and holy days to make music, dance, and experience one moment of freedom. All, however, under the vigilant eye of the police.

On those music-filled Sundays, a few thousand whites and Blacks would gather to listen to the music and watch the dancers assembled in groups in different parts of the square. Each group had its own orchestra—drums, rattles, and stringed instruments made by themselves. The music and dancing lasted as long as five or six hours.

Sundays would play an inalienable role in Halie's childhood, too. It was the most significant day of her week. On Sunday mornings, Halie walked to church with Aunt Duke, Uncle Manuel, Peter, and her other aunts. She looked forward to seeing friends she'd missed seeing at church, or other family members visiting. Her Sundays didn't change much during the 11 years she lived with Aunt Duke, except that as Halie became more accepted as "the girl with the voice," she grew to love church more and more.

Even as Halie settled more and more into her role as the girl with the voice at Mt. Moriah Church, singing mournful spirituals and upbeat gospel tunes, she could never quite rid herself of the music of New Orleans' streets. It was in her blood, there to stay no matter how she tried to hide it.

Mahalia beautifully strung together the two sides of music in every song she sang—be it gospel or spiritual—whether she admitted it or not.

Though she would keep her word to God to stay with the gospel, the street would be right there, and her audiences were drawn as much to that part of her performances as the godly part.

Aunt Duke was sure she had successfully turned the girl off from trying to follow that sin-filled music. Halie accepted that the church was where she belonged, where the music came with the warm hugs, the sobs, the nods of approval from the church ladies—and, most importantly, from Aunt Duke.

There was something transformative in the old church spirituals that allowed Halie to forget the harsh realities of her life, the fears and doubts Aunt Duke pressed on her. She could forget that she was no longer allowed to attend school, forget that her days were filled mostly with work for white families and their children, followed up by even harsher work under Aunt Duke's watchful eye.

On Sundays, Mahalia was the center of attention at Mt. Moriah church. The role brought more than simple enjoyment, it instilled confidence and gave her a reason to dream. That's what Sundays meant for Halie. She woke up on those days with a smile, knowing it was another chance to imagine being something besides what she was. Dreams of being somebody one day filled her head. Hannah had said it, and Halie believed it. She'd said Halie would one day sing for queens and kings. But how? How could something so big ever come true for this child washerwoman? Her dreaming never gave her the answer to that.

Halie's tug-of-war, though, never ended. The enchantment of New Orleans' music was as real as if she could touch it, feel it. It fed some part of Halie she didn't understand, didn't want to understand—the part of her that Aunt Duke scared her into denying. Duke's fear put the fear of the worldly music in Halie, likening it to a hot stove she dared not touch.

Yet, she couldn't completely avoid it. Not in New Orleans. Halie would be sprinkled like dew or mist with the sounds as she ran errands for Aunt Duke or made her way to her grown-folk jobs. The child couldn't have known it then, but the music was an undeniable, unavoidable part of her world and her deep, rich history—like the slave market; and the red-light district; and the voodoo queens; and the child street dancers; and the gamblers; and the honky-tonks that never closed, spitting out devil music and drunks around the clock.

Somehow Aunt Duke tied it all together. That fool music, she swore, was part and parcel of the sinful goings-on in the New Orleans streets. Like the women and men sitting on the stoops laughing or singing along with the languid sounds drifting out of the windows left open to cool their homes. Aunt Duke cursed the music, and the fools who enjoyed it. They all knew better than to darken her steps or her yard with that devil mess.

When Halie wasn't acting like a prim-and-proper church girl, she was a tomboy who loved to play rough with the boys in the community. When they played, it sometimes turned ugly. Mahalia was a hard fighter who gave as good as she got.

One Saturday, she was accosted by a gang of boys—Italians, who jumped down on her from a tree. After a tussle, Halie got loose, kicked two of them, and choked the other. Another boy ran away after he got the hardest lick in. Halie found him the next day and beat him with a stick. If you'd asked her about race, she wouldn't have understood. It was just children playing rough with each other. A week later, they were friends again, playing like nothing had happened.

Mahalia didn't focus on race growing up, even when she was taken to the homes of the white people who employed her mother and her Aunt Bell. In Halie's mind, they were simply nice folks who happened to be white. They gave her the best clothes she ever had growing up. They always treated her nice.

The Rightors, like many white employers, gave their food extras, called "the pan," to their house servants. What wasn't served up during the meals was put into a big pan for the servants and their families. Halie would say later that "the pan" helped many a colored widow woman to bring up her family. But the pan was also a treat because the Clark girls were excellent cooks, and now they would get to eat the good food they'd cooked for the white family. The pan was an important part of the New Orleans human food chain.

Cooking and sitting down to eat with family were something Black families did when they could. But work came first because eating together was a luxury that all families couldn't enjoy. Food, though, had such an important role in New Orleans life, much like the music did.

Halie and her friends often went out on the river to fish, catching buckets of fish, crabs, and shrimp. Very few families bought their food from the corner stores or grocery stores, except for the basics like flour, meal, salt, and sugar.

Foods like okra, pumpkins, peas, corn, green beans, red beans, tomatoes, and mustard greens were grown in gardens and truck patches. Most meat was even home grown—chickens, goats, hogs, and some cows. Fish were caught in the river or ocean, and the swamps provided turtles and alligators. Then, there was food from the woods—raccoons, rabbits, squirrels, and possums. Fruits such as apples, peaches, figs, bananas, and oranges, and various nuts were eaten straight from the trees or cooked as desserts.

In most New Orleans homes, it wasn't just cleanliness, but also good cooking that was considered near godliness. Cooking was taught very early in Black households. Children were taught that it was important for their health and that preparing it properly was a matter of pride. Halie, like most young people during the early 20th century, learned to cook on wood-burning stoves. Duke was a hard, but meticulous teacher. Some of Halie's earliest meals were red beans with salt pork and green beans with pig tails.

Halie learned to bake the hot breads—hot-water corn bread, butter cake, biscuits, and spoonbread. Duke would tell her that hot-water corn bread—made with water, corn meal, and a little grease to fry it—was the food that poor Black folks had eaten since slavery. These foods provided strength to work and stuck to the ribs when Blacks couldn't afford anything else. Corn bread was usually eaten with boiled greens or beans—or with syrup in the mornings.

Finally, Halie was put in charge of cooking Sunday dinners, preparing bowls of sliced tomatoes, potato salad, yams, gravy, and roast pork.

Hogs, since slavery days, played an important role in the Black kitchens in the South. Duke taught Halie how to clean, prepare, and cook hog chitlins—the stomach and intestines of the hog. This was one of Mahalia's least favorite parts of food preparation. She would never forget Duke's lessons: scraping the waste from the hog guts until they were no longer gritty, rinsing them at least 10 times, then boiling them for two hours. But before boiling the chitlins, they had to be seasoned with garlic, onion, bell pepper, salt, parsley for taste and to kill the strong, unpleasant odor. The dish was usually served with greens or potato salad.

Halie also learned how to prepare hog head cheese or souse. It was made with the whole head of a hog, stewed in a variety of seasonings on the back of the stove in a big iron kettle until the juice turned to a clear jelly, then poured into a mold and chilled.

For breakfast, Uncle Emanuel sometimes prepared baby alligator that was captured by one of the children—usually Halie or Peter—while it was sleeping or sunning itself on the riverbank or in the swamp. He would bake the tail like smothered chicken with onions and garlic herbs.

On winter mornings, the children were served orange tea made from orange peelings dried in the sun, then placed in a bag and crumbled into a powder. One teaspoonful in a cup of hot water sweetened with either sugar or syrup created a strong and healthy morning tea.

Christmas dinners were the most festive and enjoyable of the year in the Paul household. Halie enjoyed it mostly because Aunt Duke always cooked Christmas dinners all by herself. It was one of the only times of the year that Aunt Duke took over the kitchen. She dared anyone inside her kitchen during her three days of Christmas cooking.

Duke's meals were always perfect and delicious. She cooked roast goose, roast pork, and plates of vegetables. Sometimes she cooked a big raccoon stuffed with sweet potatoes. She would be up all night, baking hot breads, pies, and spice cakes. Christmas Day was the only day in the year that Aunt Duke served wine.

School—An Unaffordable Luxury for Young Halie

As Halie lay sleeping each night, trains rumbled by between the river levee and the poor community where Charity and Aunt Duke and so many other Black households were huddled together. The train tracks were near enough to the Clarks' home that the house would rock and shake, the windows rattling until the train was miles down the track. It wasn't long after the child's birth that Halie was sleeping through the noise and undulating floors. It was just one more sound that made up Water Street.

The families of "Nigger Town" were different and the same, all scratching out a living. Most of the Black men in the community, including Halie's father Johnny Jackson, worked around the river, on the docks or the steamboats. Her father was a stevedore who moved cotton on the boats during the day, and also barbered at night, and preached on Sunday.

Growing up on the Mississippi levee, Halie learned early on what was meant by the haves and have-nots. While most families she knew had hard-working men and women, few ever rose above just surviving, never quite able to get past their needs. Work was for sustaining, not moving up another notch in life.

Life was hardscrabble, and no one was more aware than Duke, who woke one morning and told Halie school was a luxury they couldn't afford. While Mahalia would pretend for years that she graduated from eighth grade, the fact was, she was often pulled out of school before entering fourth grade. When one of Halie's aunts fell sick and couldn't continue her job with the white Rightors family, Duke took the opportunity to replace her with another family member—her 8-year-old ward, Halie.

Halie loved school. She loved learning. It was the one part of her childhood that made her feel good about herself. She felt safe and hopeful when she arrived at McDonogh School 24 each morning. Unlike other parts of her life, Halie really shined in her classrooms. She was good at numbers and writing. Her teachers took to her fast mind. But, according to Duke, there were more important things to consider than the child's education. They didn't have the luxury of the childhood experiences that other children took for granted. Halie had to contribute something to the household.

McDonogh 24 was one of 30 public schools funded by a trust left by wealthy slave owner and businessman John McDonogh, who made his fortune trading human beings into slavery. The schools were the penance he paid for what he'd finally decided was wrong. McDonogh's trust underwrote and built the schools for poor children—specifically, poor white and freed Black children in both New Orleans and his native Baltimore, Maryland. Although during his life McDonogh was an infamous miser, he left the bulk of his fortune—close to $2 million—to the two cities for the purpose of building public schools for poor children.

The former slave trader eventually supported the American Colonization Society, which organized transportation for freed people of color to Liberia in Africa, and he organized the self-purchase by slaves in his control. When McDonogh died in 1850, he requested that he be buried alongside his slaves in the McDonoghville Cemetery on his plantation in present-day Gretna, Louisiana. In 1860, however, his remains were exhumed and reburied in the Green Mount Cemetery in Baltimore.

Part 5

GOODBYE NIGGER TOWN, HELLO PROMISED LAND
(1927)

CHICAGO DURING THE GREAT DEPRESSION
(CHICAGO TRIBUNE HISTORICAL ARCHIVES).

Halie's Giant Leap of Faith

Halie turned 16 on October 26, 1927. It was a Sunday that defined the rest of her life. Aunt Hannah was visiting from Chicago and joined Aunt Duke and the rest of the family at Mt. Moriah Baptist Church for Sunday school and morning service. Halie was fidgety all morning, sad and excited all at once as she thought about this being her last Sunday at the church, in Aunt Duke's orbit, in New Orleans.

Aunt Hannah's visit was short. She had traveled home with one goal in mind, to convince Duke to let Halie return to Chicago with her. Duke was dead set against it. The sisters argued back and forth. Duke insisted Halie wasn't mature enough to live in a place like Chicago; besides she wasn't convinced the place kept its promises to Black folks. Emanuel had told her the other side of the story. Hannah argued that, even so, there were opportunities that sure weren't available in New Orleans.

Aunt Duke wasn't giving an inch. She wouldn't agree to Halie going off to what she imagined was a "wicked city." The girl was her responsibility, and she'd promised Charity she'd take care of her. The girl had said she wanted to become a nurse, Hannah reminded Duke. There was no opportunity for that in New Orleans. She also reminded her sister that New Orleans had just one hospital for Blacks. There was nowhere for Blacks to gain nurses' training. Duke complained of Chicago being a cold city and so far from home.

Halie sat in her room, listening quietly to her aunts' loud whispers. The visions of Chicago played in her head, but right along beside them, she was imagining what it would be like to leave New Orleans behind, her community, her family—Aunt Duke, Uncle Emanuel, Peter, her aunts and cousins; her church and the choir members; her friends; and yes, even her father though he'd never been a close member of her family.

The girl was feeling torn. There was a tug-of-war happening inside her—between her dreams of Chicago and nursing school and staying ensconced inside the security of Duke's familial web. There was a pit in her stomach as Halie kept hearing Duke's questions to Hannah. What guarantees did she have that the girl would be able to get into this nursing school?

After dinner, Hannah asked Halie if she was ready to move to Chicago. Halie hesitantly nodded. When Hannah asked her whether she was changing her mind, she told her aunt that she was just thinking about how Aunt Duke depended on her to do all the letters for the church women's club and to accompany her during her visits to the sick and shut-in.

Hannah reminded her niece that she wasn't the only girl who could help Aunt Duke write letters and visit the sick and shut-in. There were other girls at the church who could help. Halie knew it was true, but she didn't like the feeling that she was leaving Aunt Duke high and dry. Just as she always did when she ran into problems too large for her, Halie prayed in her heart for the right decision.

She went back and forth in her head long after the conversation ended. As she sat in church the next morning, Halie realized that nothing seemed as simple as she'd always thought. This was all so troubling. Aunt Duke needed her, but there was also the need inside herself to do more with her life, to try and see what she could make of herself. She needed to follow her dream of becoming a nurse; and if she was honest, she wanted to see if she could be a singer up North. Aunt Hannah was returning to Chicago on Monday. Her nerves were on edge that Aunt Duke still stood solidly against her going.

For years now, Halie had hidden away a little bit of her earnings each week—money she'd made taking care of white people's babies and washing and ironing their clothes. All of her savings had been given to Aunt Duke for safekeeping. Would Aunt Duke give her the money if she decided against her aunt's wishes to go to Chicago with Aunt Hannah?

As she sat in the church choir that morning, Mahalia was waiting for a song that would direct her, help her resolve her problem. She looked out at all the faces she knew so well. Some were still schoolgirls with some promise of a future. Others, like her—who had left school early to work full time as house servants or laborers such as nursemaids, laundresses, cooks, domestic servants—had been working since grammar school, and none earning much more than a few dollars a week. She realized these girls' lives would likely be the same for the rest of their years, even after they married and started their families. By then, they would be too old and too connected to the community to leave.

Mahalia's throat constricted. As she lowered her eyes, she prayed for God's direction. But Aunt Duke hadn't given an inch, she cautioned herself. Why was she asking God for directions before Aunt Duke gave in? Something inside her made her know that her will to leave was stronger than Aunt Duke's will to keep her here. She didn't believe God wanted her to spend the rest of her life being somebody's babysitter or washerwoman.

God had put a chance for something different in her path, and only he would keep her from taking it. She prayed Aunt Duke would accept that this was her one chance at following her dreams of becoming a nurse, and the other dream that she talked less about, of becoming a singer. She wanted a chance to prove herself at one or the other, or both.

Halie sat in the choir stand waiting for the older choir member to select a song. That was the way, the young deferred to the older members' selections. She knew there had been some who said she was "putting too many frills on the spirituals." She had to be careful, wait for the song, and for God's answer. She didn't want to leave New Orleans in disgrace.

A moment passed before the song took shape. Halie could feel God's presence building in the song. She was taken to that place that singing always took her and always made her forget Aunt Duke's strict warnings about singing for her own glory rather than for God's.

This song deserved all of her, no holding back. The first few words were whispered so low that no one could hear it except Halie. They could see it coming up out of her, in her face. She was in that place. *"Sometimes I feel like a motherless child"* was her own personal admission of her many sleepless nights she'd grieved for her mother's warmth, her smile, her kind touch.

The older choir members followed the girls lead. Young Halie's powerful voice circled the church, pushed its way into the rafters and buttressed the closed storm windows. In time, it made its way outside into the narrow churchyard. It wasn't long before the tears, first quiet, then louder, began. The song overflowed into Water Street. Passersby stopped and listened, and found themselves singing.

As she sometimes did, and it always brought a small frown to Aunt Duke's face, Halie found herself carried away by the spirit and sank to her knees with her face turned up toward the heavens. Just 16, and she could out-sing any grown-up in the church, any church in the city, some would say. The Baptists jokingly called Halie a "church wrecker."

Even after the song ended and the choir was settled back into their seats, Mahalia stayed for a while on her knees, eyes closed, head bowed. Only God could fix things before Hannah left tomorrow morning.

After the service, Halie and Aunt Hannah waited outside the church for Aunt Duke. Hannah was quiet, Halie was praying. Duke always stayed a little while to speak to her club members or to settle some church affairs. "Beautiful song, Sister Halie," one member whispered.

The passing congregation members heaped kind words and compliments on Halie. "Lord sho' gave you a gift, Halie," they whispered as they hugged the girl. She smiled and thanked them. Just in that moment, she wondered if she really wanted to leave New Orleans. Leave everything she knew and loved, and all the people who loved her? Leaving Water Street for the cold "Windy City" was a huge step, Halie knew—just as big as her mother and aunts moving off Gumpstump plantation to New Orleans.

"What's keeping Duke?" Hannah complained.

Halie laughed. "Don't you remember? She never feels right till she sees that everyone's out."

Finally, Aunt Duke and Emanuel walked toward them, and they all started for home. As they neared home, Halie caught a whiff of the collard greens and salt pork Aunt Duke had left on the back of the stove.

Aunt Duke hurried to the kitchen, lifting the lid on the stove and putting in a log of firewood. Halie didn't stop to change clothes, but hurriedly put on her apron. She needed to talk to Aunt Duke all by herself. God had given her the answer she was waiting for.

Restless. That's the word Duke and the others used to describe Halie, shaking their heads in exasperation and a little fear. As much as the city of New Orleans had to offer, it couldn't constrain the girl's spirit—a spirit filled with wanting more, always looking for more, or reaching for something more.

Halie had been an observant child from the moment she could focus her tiny, bright eyes on one thing at a time. She watched and learned from her elders, gleaning every little bit of understanding she could. And, there was so much to see and hear in New Orleans. So much to learn, but for Halie, never enough.

In 1927, something began to stir inside Halie. Maybe it was the curse or the blessing of being part of the Clark sisters of Pointe Coupée Parish. Each one of them carried a small magic inside them, the ability to steal a glimpse into tomorrow. Halie had a very narrow glimpse, something more akin to an uncontrollable yearning that was mighty and ever growing. She had a yearning that brought with it its own bit of fear; not fear of change in itself, but of change without foreknowledge or control.

Halie had always sought control of the big and little things in her life. She wanted to see it before it happened. At 16 years old, she couldn't see very far in front of her, as hard as she tried.

Hannah would know. Hannah's seeing gift was the most powerful of any of the Clark girls. She could help Halie. "Never you mind about anything, Halie," Aunt Hannah told her. "Honey, you will one day walk with kings and queens." As much as she wanted to, Halie couldn't accept this as truth right away. Did Aunt Hannah get her future mixed up with someone else? A white girl named Halie?

Though she'd heard both good and bad stories about the North, somehow, she had it in her mind that Chicago was the answer to the question. Hannah had lived in Chicago for some years now, and Uncle Porterfield had moved up North to Ohio, working with the trains after spending most of his youth working on steamboats. Uncle Emanuel had brought back stories about the North—namely Chicago—from his trips there.

The saddest story about the North was how it took away the cousin she loved like a brother and admired more than any New Orleans musician. If Halie took after any of her relatives, it was Fred, who everyone called Chafalaye. She had his same independent streak, that restlessness she couldn't contain.

But Chafalaye's restlessness had killed him. That was Halie's saddest childhood memory, not just his death, but witnessing Aunt Duke, the strongest person she knew, crying to the point of making herself sick. Fred was her only son, and the one person she loved more than life itself. Against her will, he had moved up North to Kansas City, bent on realizing his dream of becoming a famous musician.

Oh, how Halie mourned his death, more than she'd mourned him leaving for Kansas City; more than she'd missed him dancing and singing in his room at night; more than introducing her to Bessie Smith's records; and more than sneaking to let her listen to her favorite Bessie Smith song, "St. Louis Blues," that included the words *I hate to see that evening sun go down… 'Cause it makes me feel like I'm on my last go-round.* They both knew Aunt Duke would skin them alive if she found out they were playing the devil's music in her house. Halie's sadness was the knowledge that there was so very much she still needed to learn from him.

Though Fred's waywardness kept Duke on her knees begging God to keep her son safe, Fred was loved by everyone. His smile and laughter and wicked jokes drew folks to him like bees to honey. His death sent both Duke and Halie spiraling into a deep depression. Duke didn't have it in her to soothe the child's grief, and Halie would be too afraid to dare try assuaging her aunt's sorrow.

Halie hadn't experienced grown-up grief before. Neither had she lost someone so close to her, except her mother when she was too young to fully grasp that death meant goodbye forever. But Fred's leaving was something tangible. She understood it was truly goodbye, and she knew what all she was missing out on by not having him in her life.

But, then, there were the good stories from up North. Uncle Emanuel went up to Chicago and worked as a bricklayer, making enough money to take care of the household back in New Orleans. He would tell stories of how, in Chicago, colored people could go shopping in white people's stores. Negro women, he said, could try on dresses that white women tried on, too!

By 1928, colored men, women, and young people were leaving New Orleans for the North at a steady pace. Many of them came home and told how Negroes lived better up there, rode in buses and trolleys with white people, and many had their own automobiles. Uncle Porter was one of the Northern migrators who moved from the fancy steamboats in New Orleans to the railway trains up North. He later said he hadn't missed a beat; didn't lose anything by the change. His coworkers nicknamed him "Coal Oil Johnny," dubbing him the fastest second cook on the line. Halie had never imagined colored people could live any other way than the way they did in New Orleans, as second-class citizens, separate and unequal.

Halie Joins the Black Migration

The Illinois Central Railroad's Big 4 train sat on South Rampart Street. It was an express train that ran from New Orleans straight through to destinations up North. It was the Big 4, Halie would later say, that transformed her from the tall, awkward 16-year-old girl into the Mahalia Jackson the whole world would know.

It was just a few days past Thanksgiving when Hannah and Halie left New Orleans. Halie jumped when the explosion of steam escaped the locomotive. She hurried with her aunt to the end of the line at the closed Jim Crow ticket window. Her heart was pounding. This would be her first-ever traveling experience—except for a few Sunday school excursions in the city.

Hannah wasn't doing much talking, still fuming that Duke held them up until the last moment, fussing and giving forewarnings about what Halie would find in Chicago. Too mad to cry, Hannah knew she was more scared for the girl than mad, but still. Her sister had a soft spot somewhere inside her for Halie, but Duke just never understood that the girl needed to see that softness every once in a while. Halie needed to realize that all Duke's hardness was for the girl's own good.

Uncle Emanuel had hugged Halie and wiped tears from the side of his eyes. He promised they'd be praying for her every day, and he warned her that she'd better write, or else. Of course, Duke was sad to see Halie go. She'd raised the girl since she was 6 years old; had been her mother for the better part of her life. Now, that role was being snatched from her. She was a hard woman. She had to be to make it in New Orleans on her own all those years. Yet, she loved the girl, in her own way. She was scared for her. Halie was flighty, bull-headed, always needed someone to reign her in. Nobody else saw that the way Duke did.

Hannah thought back on the scene at Duke's. The woman never gave an inch. Never agreed that Halie could go. Halie had made that final decision, promising Duke she'd remember all she'd taught her and find a church home as soon as she got there. Hannah had looked from Duke to Halie, sensing the girl's sadness in going against Duke for probably the first time in her life. But Hannah sensed that Halie's will to leave was just as strong.

Hannah blamed her sister. She could have made it easier for the girl. Poor Halie would carry Duke's disappointment right on into Chicago with her. It would haunt her from now on. Why couldn't Duke give the child her blessings and send her on her way?

Even if they got their tickets in time, they would have to hurry to get to the Jim Crow coach at the far end of the platform. The ticket agent, it seemed, was manning both the white and colored ticket windows, and the lines were getting longer. When the white lines dwindled down, the agent moved to the Black window. Halie watched a young mother with three small children, and a baby in her arms, trying to keep them in line. Halie, with her heart the size of New Orleans, was feeling sorry for the woman and was about to ask if she could help her when Hannah urged her forward in the long line.

Lord knows, Halie had nursed enough children and adults, too, for almost nothing a week to entitle her to make a living at it. All kinds of thoughts were running through Halie's head. *Lord, how many miles will I have to travel to get where I want to be? To get rid of this scared, cold unwanted feeling? Will I always be like that little boll weevil, looking for a home?* She wanted a home—or at least a room of her own. She longed to have some privacy where she could listen to Bessie Smith's records and sing when she felt like it and as loud as she wanted to without someone reminding her that she was doing something bad.

For the most part, even with the growing crowd of travelers, it was quiet in the colored section of the train station. Quiet enough for Halie to think back on her goodbye to Duke. Hannah looked over, caught Halie's eye, and shook her head. She saw the tears welling in the corner of the girl's eyes and knew she was having second thoughts. But Halie was young. She would be fine once they got to Chicago and settled in. Duke would be fine, too.

They were finally standing in front of the colored ticket window. The young man looked every way except in their faces as he asked where they were going.

"Chicago," Hannah told him.

"Round trip or one way?"

"One way." Hannah's answer was short, hurrying.

He gave Hannah the two tickets as if Halie wasn't standing there, then looked questioningly as if he wondered if either the woman or girl could count. Without a word, Hannah placed the bills and coin in front of him. He spit a brown liquid into the spittoon.

Hannah nervously smiled over at Halie, mumbling under her breath.

Tickets in hand, they picked up their luggage and lunch basket and hurried to the colored coach. Hannah looked back at Halie and whispered that white folks called this train, the "Chicken Bone Express," on account of all the greasy bags and scattered chicken bones littering the floor by the time the train reached its destination.

Finally, all the passengers were boarded. Mahalia saw that the overburdened mother and her children had found seats at the very back of the coach near the door. She followed her aunt to an empty seat, helped load the bags into the overhead rack, and sat down. Finally taking a load off, she thought.

Halie listened for the locomotive's warning whistle and the clanging of the bells. The train jerked forward, a sign that they were on their way up North. She could hardly believe it. She was actually on her way to Chicago.

Halie breathed a long, heavy sigh of relief. She'd been holding it in since she'd left Aunt Duke's. Lord, she'd miss Aunt Duke. She'd pray every night for forgiveness for any harm she'd caused the woman all these years. She knew she could never live up to her aunt's expectations, but Lord knows she'd tried. And she would have kept right on trying to be the Halie that

Duke wanted her to be if she stayed in New Orleans. Surely, God wanted her to find out who Halie was for herself.

The girl was tired and sleepy, but she couldn't sleep with so many things going around in her head. So much to dream about, to see, to pray about. She took the advertisement for nursing school out of her sweater pocket. She had clipped it from the Chicago Defender newspaper that one of Duke's friends read, then stowed away. It was she who had complimented Halie on her healing hands and voice, and slipped the girl the paper, quietly pointing out the ad about nursing school when Duke wasn't looking.

Halie had read it so many times she knew it by heart. It was as if the woman knew how Halie had told the Lord that she wanted to be a nurse and help make people better. But it was Duke who had planted the seed in Halie about helping people. She had been Duke's shadow during the hundreds of home visits to sick family, church members, and neighbors. Duke, hard as nails, had a heart of gold when it came to the sick and ailing. And Halie was there with her, assisting with the care they needed, offering what she had, her songs and her prayers.

Halie read the advertisement again: *Provident Hospital and Training School for Nurses offers young colored women a three-year course in the practice and theory of nursing. Graduates eligible for registration from any state. Classes now forming. For information, apply to Superintendent, Provident Hospital, 16 West 36th Street, Chicago, IL.*

Halie put the clipping back in her pocket, next to her train ticket. She knew in her heart that the clipping was another kind of ticket, an opportunity for her to become someone different, someone better and special—a way to improve her lot. Still, there was a niggling of worry at the back of her mind. Would the school take her, a school dropout before she entered fourth grade? She would say she went to eighth grade. People looked at that differently.

Hannah watched the girl out of the corner of her eye. How much thinking could there be in a 16-year-old girl's head? The child never stopped. What kind of thoughts rattled around in that mind of hers?

"You got to get some decent clothes, Halie. You can't let those Provident people see you looking like a field hand."

The girl looked down at herself, at the sweater she'd worn for the last few years. She had a light jacket packed in her suitcase. She didn't own a winter coat. How could she have forgotten the stories her family had told them about the cold up North? She'd make do somehow until she got a job and saved enough money. She didn't fool herself. Hannah couldn't help her with extras. She knew without asking that they were just scraping by. Halie was thankful for a place to lay her head and meals to eat. The rest, she'd have to get for herself.

Yes, Hannah was right. She did look like a poor country girl. She remembered the times she and her friends had giggled and whispered about the country girls moving into the neighborhood off the plantations. She would be that country girl, now in a big place like Chicago.

Her heavy working shoes sure didn't help any. She was sure no one wore shoes like hers in Chicago. She sighed and tried to keep a positive outlook. She'd get herself a part-time job and go to nursing school at night. Somehow, she'd make enough money to buy new clothes and shoes before the Chicago winter set in for good.

The first thing she had to do, she remembered, was find herself a church home and a choir that would let her try out to sing with them. When they heard her, she was sure they'd invite her to join their choir. She smiled a little. Everything would work out just fine once she could sing. She'd write Aunt Duke and tell her just that.

Hannah bumped her shoulder, interrupting her daydreaming. "You hungry, now?"

Before Halie could answer, Hannah took the cover off the basket of leftovers from Aunt Duke's Sunday dinner. Halie and Hannah had packed enough to last them the day-and-a-half it would take to get to Chicago. At least they'd have a full belly when they arrived. Her first bite of Duke's crispy, brown fried chicken let Halie know she was indeed hungry. It made her miss Duke, too. There were baked yams in the basket and Duke's delicious biscuits, too.

"Lord, have mercy, the biscuits are still warm!" Hannah laughed.

Halie blessed the food the way she did at Duke's house, and they ate in silence while the train chugged northward. She eyed the Mississippi River out the window.

Good bye, old Mississippi, Halie half-smiled to herself, tears already dribbling down her cheeks.

She looked away from Hannah while she finished eating. She erased the tears with the back of her hand, then helped Hannah tidy up around them. The Clarks was a neat and tidy family. Halie couldn't imagine who would leave chicken bones or greasy sacks on the floor of the train. They packed the basket away and sighed with the satisfaction of a full stomach.

When darkness fell, it seemed the train picked up speed as it rumbled over the cold rails. Halie closed her eyes. She gained comfort from the lowered voices in the car. No sooner had she begun to drift off to sleep, she heard the soft twanging of a guitar followed by a man's soft voice. Peeking behind her, she saw an old Black man pulling a knife blade across the steel strings of the guitar. As many strange songs as she'd heard on the streets of New Orleans, Halie couldn't place this one.

> *I'm tired of this Jim Crow, gonna leave this Jim Crow town*
> *Doggone my Black soul, I'm sweet Chicago bound*
> *Yes, I'm leavin' here, from this old Jim Crow town*
> *I'm goin' up North where they say money grows on trees*
> *I don't give a doggone, if my Black soul leaves,*
> *I'm goin' where I don't need my BVDs.*

Halie wouldn't sleep as long as the man was playing and singing. As foreign as it was, there was plaintiveness about it that made her sad. The song, though, was suddenly interrupted by a baby's loud wails. When she turned back again, she saw the woman with her four children. One of the children wailing and coughing as if she was sick. Halie peeped over at Hannah and knew she was dozing by her soft snores. Halie made her way down the aisle to where the family sat.

"Can I help?" Halie asked, smiling down at the woman and her baby.

"Naw, child. Don't bother yourself," the woman responded. "She's just fussy, not use to trains. We'll make out." The woman didn't look much older than Halie. Halie wondered, but didn't ask if she was on her way to *the promised land,* too.

Halie patted the baby's head. "Isn't she cold? She don't have on much." Halie thought about it for just a moment before taking off her sweater and putting it around the baby. She ignored the woman's words of gratitude.

"Bless you, honey. God sure gone bless you." The mother smiled, with a hint of curiosity on her face.

Mahalia scurried back to her seat and tried to sleep. Now, the cold kept her awake, but she knew they'd be in Chicago before too long. She could stand the cold until then. She watched the reflections and shadows as the train raced down the track passing eerily etched images of lopsided shanties with tin roofs. Most had a chicken coop in the back, a little vegetable garden, and some chickens, pigs, or cows scattered nearby. She was surprised to see that the shanties were so much like theirs on Water Street.

It was morning before she knew it. Halie had slept after all. The mother had brought the sweater back and laid it in Halie's lap.

Hannah frowned and shook her head. "Halie, you can't go 'round Chicago giving away your stuff to strangers."

Halie smiled and nodded. They ate the leftover biscuits and chicken from the basket for breakfast. The ticket agent walked through the cabs announcing they were almost in Chicago. Hannah turned to Halie, looking her directly in the eyes, now.

"Listen, Halie. Chicago's different. With different kinds of strangers. Take New Orleans, for instance. You get the notion that all those whites worry about is how to keep Blacks down and out of sight. In Chicago, whites are so busy getting ahead they don't seem to worry about Blacks.

That is, until a Black tries to buy a home in a white neighborhood or tries to get a good job beside a white man.

"A lot of folks come up here thinking they found heaven, but it ain't even close. We're still coloreds, and coloreds is a long way from white. They just not looking for ways to make sure you know it."

Hannah reached up and pulled their baggage from the rack above them. Halie's small eyes grew as she looked out the window at what looked like hundreds of railroad tracks and trains and box cars. The railroad station seemed as big as a city all by itself. So, this is Chicago!

Chicago—Halie's New Home

It was the eve of December when Halie arrived in Chicago. She got a taste of what winter in Chicago was like when she and Hannah walked from the train into Union Station. She watched as Hannah looked around as they walked into the station.

"A friend said he'd pick us up. I got to phone him," Hannah said. "Watch our bags. You got to keep your eyes open at all times, or someone will steal your stuff. You're not at home, Halie. You're in Chicago."

Soon, Hannah was back. She started toward the lunch counter.

"We'll get a cup of coffee." It wasn't a question. Everybody drank coffee down in New Orleans, starting a lot earlier than Halie's 16 years.

Halie followed. She noticed that there were no colored people sitting at the counter. Did Hannah know what she was doing? Would they be served by that white woman behind the counter? That would never happen back in New Orleans. A colored person could get arrested for asking for a drink of water in a New Orleans coffee shop. She prayed Hannah wouldn't get her arrested her first day in Chicago.

"Here, let's take these two seats. Put your bag down and sit."

Halie nervously sat beside her aunt, praying she knew what she was doing. On the other side, a white woman sat without paying a lick of attention to the colored woman and teenaged girl. She kept drinking her coffee. Hannah signaled to the white waitress.

"We'd like two cups of coffee," Hannah told the waitress. Just like that—no please or ma'am or anything.

Halie's mouth dropped open. She looked from the waitress to her Aunt Hannah. She had never in her 16 years seen a colored person ask anything of a white person without saying *please, sir,* or *ma'am.* There was so very much for her to learn, and it was still early morning.

"Black or white?"

The waitress looked back at Hannah as she filled the two cups. Mahalia was puzzled. Black or white? Couldn't the woman see they were colored? Hannah's mind seemed somewhere else, as she mumbled, "white."

This was Halie's first time eating or drinking in a public café, and certainly the first time being served by a white person.

"I couldn't reach my friend. I guess something came up. We'll have to get a cab."

Hannah guided Halie outside the station door. Cabs were lined up as far down the street as she could see. One quickly drove up beside Hannah, and the driver jumped out to grab their bags and place them in the back. A white cab driver picking them up?

As they ducked inside the taxi, Halie couldn't help but shake her head. Down in New Orleans it was against the law for a Black person to ride in a cab driven by a white man. When the driver climbed back in the car, Hannah gave him her address.

Off they went. Halie drinking in the picture she was creating in her head about this new home of hers, Chicago. People rushed along the sidewalks as if fleeing from the devil. Why was everyone in such a hurry, she wondered.

They were silent for what seemed like a long time, before Hannah spoke.

"Halie, I've been thinking a lot on our way up here—about things, about your wanting to be a nurse and all. I think that's a real good thing to go after...."

"Uh huh?" Halie could hear Hannah's hesitation, the pause to add a "but" in there.

"I was thinking…you're just 16, Halie. Maybe this is something you can do next year, after you get yourself settled in here."

Halie's face fought against the frown she was feeling. "But, Aunt Hannah, that's why I came with you up here."

Hannah was silent, looking out the window, as if she hadn't heard her niece.

"You know, us Clark women have never done anything but work for white folks, Halie. Wash their dirty clothes, take care of their brats, cook their meals, and scrub their floors."

Halie turned from Hannah and looked out the window, too. The cab made a sharp turn throwing the girl and the woman together. They both grinned. Halie noticed the scene outside the window was different. They were in a different part of Chicago.

"You know, there's ways to make a living here in Chicago, Halie, but you got to work. Just going to school don't pay no bills," Hannah said. "Young women, up here, make a good living in the hair business. Washing and straightening Black women's hair is a good business. It don't take long to learn, I hear. A lot of young women even setting up their own shops."

Halie looked down. Aunt Hannah hadn't breathed a word of any of this before she left New Orleans. Had she and Aunt Duke talked about it? They both knew why she'd come. All she'd talked about was the nursing school.

Halie sighed. She was here, and she wasn't turning around and heading back. She wasn't going to ruin her excitement by crying over what Hannah was telling her. In truth, it had piqued her interest. She loved fixing hair. Aunt Duke had even let her press and curl hers sometimes.

"Don't you have to go to school before you can open a hair business, Aunt Hannah?"

"Some, not as much as nursing. Course, if you don't take to hair, maybe you'd like to go into embalming."

"You mean messing with dead people? Getting them ready for funerals?"

"Yeah, girl. Nowadays, Black undertakers are hiring women to do embalming and preparation for funerals—especially women."

Halie was shaking her head. She couldn't believe Hannah was suggesting she dress dead people! Never in a million years would she leave New Orleans and Duke to dress dead people in Chicago.

"I want to help heal live people, Aunt Hannah. That's why I want to go to nursing school."

When Hannah didn't answer, Halie resumed studying the fading streets as the car whizzed by. There were colored people walking the streets, fast, like they had somewhere to go, a purpose behind them.

"You know, rich colored folk live over that way, where you see the doormen in front of the apartment."

"Rich colored people, my goodness. How did they get rich? Are they friendly-like?"

"Same way everybody gets rich…work like a dog," Hannah said, smiling. "And, yeah…they friendlier than rich white folks."

Hannah thought for a while, then added, "Some of them got rich from saving all their life; some from owning their own business; and of course, some from the policy banks."

"Policy banks is gambling, Aunt Hannah! That's devil's work."

"Yeah, it is. But you asked me how some of them got rich, didn't you?"

"What's that I smell, Aunt Hannah?"

"The stockyard, girl. A lot of white folks got rich off that funky stockyard. Lots of colored folks help them get rich, working there. That's where they kill hogs and cows and prepare them for selling to shops and restaurants."

The two rode through a park and come out on the street again. Hannah leaned slightly forward and pointed out.

"That's Provident Hospital over there."

Halie looked. Her heart beating rapidly. Then she looked away.

"So, you think if I work and save up my money, I can look to go there next year, Aunt Hannah?"

Hannah couldn't ignore the sadness in the girl's voice. She smiled over at her niece and nodded.

"Sure, you can, Halie. You know there's a Black doctor there. He operated on a man's heart and saved him."

Halie looked hard at her aunt. Why hadn't she mentioned that before? A Black doctor working at Provident Hospital, and now she wasn't sure she'd ever get to meet him.

"He must be a mighty smart man, and a good one."

"Now, look over there, Halie," Hannah said, pointing. "That's the Regal Theater where Bessie Smith sings when she's in Chicago."

Now, the girl's ears were wide open, to match her wide-open eyes. Halie looked directly in her aunt's eyes.

"Aunt Hannah, is that the truth? Bessie Smith sings over there?"

Hannah laughed, nodding. "She sho' do, girl."

"Oh, Aunt Hannah. I just got to hear Bessie Smith, if that's the last thing in the world I do. I just got to! How much the ticket cost?"

"They a dollar."

Halie nodded. Oh, she would see Bessie Smith, one way or another.

South Side Chicago, a place with rich colored folks. A place second only to Harlem in the boom days of the late 1920s. Some of the apartment houses where these wealthy colored folks lived even had doormen.

Halie wouldn't have dreamed this was possible. There had been talk of wealthy Creoles and coloreds in New Orleans, but she had never come in contact with any of them. Here, they seemed to be right there for all to see, living finer than some of the wealthy white folks in New Orleans. Mahalia was all eyes as her aunt pointed out the Bronzeville district and some of the big churches owned by Black congregations, including Greater Salem Baptist Church, where Aunt Hannah and Aunt Alice attended.

"Alice and me want you to join us at Salem, Halie."

Mahalia said she would, but she wondered about the church's singing program. She wasn't looking for any fancy singing, like she'd heard about. The Southerners who moved up North changed their singing style, ashamed of the church music they were raised on.

"What kind of singing at your church, Aunt Hannah? Is it fancy singing?"

"Church singing, Halie. Same as church singing anywhere."

Hannah pointed out Black-owned businesses. Some were prosperous, like the Chicago Defender—the world's leading Black newspaper. Hannah told her there were plenty of Black business offices in Chicago. Doctors, dentists, lawyers, undertakers. A Black policeman directed traffic right there at a busy intersection. A Black cop! Mahalia had never seen one before.

"Lots of Black women work in the hotels, here," Hannah said. "They get $12 a week, Halie, along with two hot meals and tips."

The South Side even had elected the first Black congressman from the North, Oscar De Priest. His family was also from down South, in Alabama. Halie thought if a colored man from Alabama could be sent to Washington as a congressman, anything could happen. Anything.

Finally, they arrived at Hannah's apartment building. When they went into the building, Mahalia noticed the smell of something strange cooking. She looked up and down the dim hall as Hannah searched for the key to her apartment.

When they walked in, Hannah told her she'd show her around and where she would sleep. Their first stop was Aunt Alice's bedroom, then on to the tiny living room where the couch served as Hannah's bed. Hannah hurried past a closed door.

"That's our renter. He's a waiter on the railroad dining car, where your Uncle Porter works."

Halie frowned in surprise at this new thing Hannah hadn't mentioned. When they arrived at the dining room, Hannah told her this was where Nathaniel, Alice's young son, slept.

Finally, Hannah and Mahalia arrived at an enclosed sun porch. A much-used couch sat in the corner of the room.

"This is where you'll sleep, Halie. We'll make sure you have plenty of cover to keep you warm."

Halie didn't know what she had expected, coming to Chicago, but this wasn't it. She stood in the middle of the small room, then walked to the couch and set her suitcase on top. Hannah left to start dinner. While Halie was putting her clothes away, she heard Aunt Alice come in. She rushed out to greet her aunt with a big smile. As they laughed and hugged, Halie noticed there was a hesitance in Aunt Alice's usually warm hugs. There was something wrong.

"Sweet Halie, it's so good to see you. That old mean Duke actually let you come," she laughed. "Hannah and me are real happy you here."

Later, Halie would learn what caused Alice's hesitation earlier. She'd received the news that her boss was letting her go.

"I lost my job. Here we go again. I'll have to start right away searching for another one."

Halie's heart dropped, yet again. What else could go wrong, she wondered. When they sat down to the simple meal of hot dogs and corn meal mush, they ate in silence.

"Halie, I don't want you worrying. We always make out," promised Alice. "My friend gave me some leads, a list of white folks needing laundresses. I'll check out most of them…. I was thinking, though, Halie…I thought you might look into one of them. If between the two of us, we get enough laundry work, and Hannah keep her job, we'll definitely be fine."

Hannah and Alice smiled weakly. Halie couldn't force a smile. This wasn't her plan, but she couldn't argue. She wondered how long it would be before she'd be able to apply for the training program at Provident. This year? Next Year? Five years from now?

Hannah and Alice looked at each other, knowing the girl's disappointment.

"We sorry, child, but our rent is $50 a month. For a time, at least, we'll need you to help us with that."

"Fifty dollars?" Halie knew that was a lot of money.

"Fifty dollars, honey. Our lodger's rent just pays for the gas and electricity."

Halie ducked her head, then offered her aunts a weak smile. "I'll pay my share, aunties."

Chicago Washerwoman—Halie's Dreams Deferred

Halie was in Chicago less than a month and already knew she'd never get used to the cold. Hannah had told her it was as much a part of Chicago life as the stink of the stockyards or the railroad trains that ran all day coming from and going to Lord knows where. It was a natural part of the place she now called home. It was a gray, bitter cold morning, but the city paid it no mind, kept moving straight ahead.

Alice and Halie got up early, drank coffee, and ate toast before leaving out for the train several blocks away. There wasn't much morning talk. Alice woke Nathaniel and helped him dress before he ate his breakfast. Hannah would drop the boy off at school on her way to the white family's home. Alice rode with Halie on the train until they arrived at her stop. Halie got off, too, to catch a different train. Halie listened intently as her aunt went over the directions to the white woman's house.

"Now, count 15 stops, then get off and take a crosstown train for five more stops. You got that, Halie?"

"Yes, ma'am. I got it. Bye."

Halie stepped onto the second train and looked up and down the length of the car. Most of the passengers were white men on their way downtown. She spied a handful of colored passengers. No one had been clear whether it was fine to sit beside white folks here. Never in New Orleans would that be okay. She hesitated, wondering if she should walk to the back and look for the colored section. No one seemed to pay much attention to her at all. Finally, she took a seat next to a young white man. She held her breath, expecting to hear protest, but the man seemed to have other things on his mind, namely the newspaper in front of him.

Halie was wrestling with all her feelings, some she had no words for, as she rode the train this morning. She didn't come back to herself until she heard the screech of the train. She looked up, terrified to realize she hadn't kept up with her stops. Had she already passed the fifteenth stop? The first streaks of morning light grayed the train's dirty windows, and she could barely see outside as the train came to another stop. Thankfully, the engineer called out the stop and she realized she had more stops to go.

She hurried to stand by the door once she saw how people inside pushed to get out as those on the outside pushed forward. She counted each stop under her breath. Finally, the train stopped at the station Halie believed was the right one. She nervously hurried closer to the exit as she saw others do in anticipation for the door to open. Once outside, she looked up to read directions. There was the crosstown train she needed to catch. She was almost there.

Halie hurriedly stepped onto the crosstown train and found that it was almost empty. She found a seat near the door, all to herself. As the train left the station, she breathed a long sigh of relief. After five stops, she got off and walked down the street. As cold as it was, the slip of paper with the woman's name and address had dampened in her clenched hand.

Herndon Avenue. Finally, there it was in front of her. She realized the morning coffee and toast hadn't filled her. She could only hope that the people would offer her something to drink or eat before evening like the white people often did in New Orleans.

She rang the doorbell. While she waited, the smell of fresh coffee made her mouth water. When a plump, tired face appeared in the crack of the door, Halie smiled and said she was there for the laundress job.

"Oh. Go down there, to the basement. I'll be down there in a little bit."

The woman pointed to a door leading to the basement. Mahalia let herself into the cold laundry room. There, in the far corner, sat a mountain of soiled clothing. Sheets, pillowcases, tablecloths, children's clothing, and what not. Halie imagined it would have taken a small family at least a month to soil that many clothes.

She had just walked over to the pile of dirty laundry when the door at the top of the stairs opened. The woman with the plump, tired face walked halfway down the stairs, leaving the door open. The pungent breakfast smells made Halie know the door led to the kitchen.

"I'm Mrs. Smith. What's your name?"

"I'm Halie. Mahalia Jackson."

"Mahaila…that's a mouth full. I think I'll call you Halie. I'll pay you a dollar a day and carfare. The tubs, washboards, soap, and boilers are over there behind the furnace."

Halie saw that everything she needed was there. She nodded at the woman, took off her sweater, and rolled up her sleeves.

"When you come tomorrow, Halie, I'd like you to do the ironing. It's my day to play bridge with the girls."

"Yes'm."

"While you're ironing, you can also keep an eye on the children. I just got two little ones." The woman turned and went back up the stairs, closing the kitchen door behind her.

Mahalia filled the tubs and set to work. It had been some months now since she did laundry work. The coarse soap bit into her flesh. The work felt harder than it used to be, but in time it got easier. Her body remembered the laundry woman's work tempo.

As she fell into the work, Halie tried to remember her favorite laundry song. It didn't come. She figured the cold basement and the growling in her stomach kept her memory from working.

Finally, minutes later, it came to her. She worked, closed her eyes and opened her mouth and sang "His Eye is on the Sparrow." She sang the song over and over, until she didn't feel the cold in the room or the empty hunger inside her stomach. She sang in gratitude, and yes, in sorrow.

This wasn't at all what she'd thought she would be doing in Chicago. Not being a laundry woman, again. But, the singing, yes, the singing would always be part of who she was, and always who she wanted to be.

"Will you sing another song, please?"

Halie stopped quickly. She felt someone watching her. Looking up, she saw a child sitting on the stairs. How long had the child been there? Quiet as a mouse. Mahalia smiled up at her, and began another song, one she thought a child might like.

"Jesus loves me, this I know, for the Bible tells me so…."

"What on earth are you doing on them cold steps, child?" It was the mother, standing in the kitchen doorway, one hand on the door and the other on her waist.

"Just listening to the colored lady sing."

"Well, you gone catch your death of cold, child. You come on back in here in a little while."

The woman cocked her head slightly as she looked down at Halie who had resumed scrubbing the clothes.

"You do have a real pretty voice. And those are some mighty nice songs you singing."

"Thank you, ma'am. I been singing all my life. Started singing in the church at 4."

The woman nodded, half smiled, then walked back up the stairs. Right around noon, Mrs. Smith walked back down the stairs and gave

Halie a plate of food—fried chicken, green beans, and cornbread. And not a minute too soon. Halie's stomach growls had gone from puppy growls to bears. Once she stopped singing, the hunger had come back full force.

After finishing her lunch, Halie set the plate on the stairs and resumed her washing and rinsing. She was nearly halfway through the mountain of clothes by then. She would have to hang every piece up before she left.

Her first day went pretty much the way work went in New Orleans—from sunup to sundown. She earned 25 cents more than she had in New Orleans.

As she walked from the elevated train to Hannah's apartment that night, Halie was surprised by the number of churches she saw. She thought she'd better settle for one soon, to make Aunt Duke know she wasn't playing around with God. Hannah and Alice wanted her at Greater Salem, and maybe that's where she'd end up, but she wanted to see the other churches first. She needed to feel at home at church. She needed to be able to praise God with her voice, the only way she knew how. That very day, she decided if she saw a poster with a gospel choir outside the church, that was the right one for her.

Hannah said most churches in Chicago had two choirs. The gospel choir was made up of men and women with untrained voices. They sang the old-time spirituals the way their parents had sung them, and when they got happy, they weren't ashamed to clap, pat their feet, or shout. Halie guessed that was the choir she would join.

During one of her walks home, Halie saw posted outside a record shop all the most popular songs of the day: "Bo-Weavil Blues," "Back Water Blues," "Blue Devil Blues" "Black Snake Blues," "Basin Street Blues," "Jobless Blues," "Eviction Blues," "Landlord Blues," "Howling Cat Blues," and "St. Louis Blues."

She was ashamed that here she was looking for a church choir, and she could sing most of those songs from front to back. It was as if the devil music was following her. She wouldn't give in. Much as she idolized Bessie Smith, she wouldn't sing the blues. She would sing for God. She'd promised

God, Aunt Duke, and herself she wasn't going to be no boogie-woogie singer. That was Aunt Duke's biggest fear of her coming here.

Halie dreamed of saving enough money in a year or two to get her a place of her own. She could buy herself a phonograph and listen to all the music she wanted to—any kind of music, and not feel bad about doing it. Nowhere in the Bible did it say it was a sin to listen to blues music—as long as you didn't sing the blues. No, God would be fine with that because listening didn't mean she'd sing it. Halie had to admit, though, some of the blues sounded mighty fine. And even God understood that church people sometimes feel blue…as blue as she had felt most times since moving to Chicago. Not blue enough to head back home, though. She knew it would pass. Aunt Duke always said it was people with idle minds who ever had time enough to study 'bout being sad.

Though it was almost time for winter to turn to spring in Chicago, the seasons hadn't completely changed, and most days were still marked by gray skies and freezing nights. It bothered Halie that of all the people she passed on the streets going to and from the trains, not a one seemed to have time to stop and ask how you felt or say good morning or even offer a smile. These were the things that made her miss New Orleans. She missed Aunt Duke and Uncle Emanuel. She missed all the church friends and the children in the community. She missed the Southern ritual of smiling and saying hello, even to complete strangers. Never in her wildest dreams did she think she would be pining for what she left behind in New Orleans.

Halie stopped outside a church, peeking through the windows. She saw that people were gathered inside, and she could hear faint singing. She shook her head. No, this wouldn't do. The singing seemed cold. Maybe Chicago's cold did something to colored people's voices.

She hurried her steps, wanting nothing more than to be inside Aunt Hannah and Aunt Alice's apartment. She'd keep looking for a church until she felt God gave her the message. Entering the apartment building, she searched for the key Hannah had given her. But there was Aunt Alice standing inside the opened door, crying.

"Oh, Halie. I was waiting for you. Your Aunt Hannah done had a heart attack. The ambulance on the way." Alice had also called Hannah's doctor, and he would meet them at Provident Hospital.

After the doctor spent almost an hour with Hannah, he told Alice to let her sleep. He'd given her some medicine to help stabilize her heart and would find out tomorrow if something more was needed. Alice shook her head and began crying all over. She knew what something more meant, surgery.

When they walked in, Hannah was fast asleep. Halie could see in Aunt Alice's eyes how afraid she was for Hannah's life. Alice was quiet, praying under her breath. Halie joined her. Finally, they caught a street bus back home. They prayed together, again, before they went off to bed. Before going to bed, Halie fell to her knees and prayed again through tears that God would spare her Aunt Hannah.

Halie Finds a Church Home

Halie had settled on Hannah and Alice's church, after all. The aunts were ecstatic to have their niece joining them at the church they'd joined shortly after their arrival in Chicago. For Halie, Greater Salem Baptist Church was the closest thing to New Orleans, offering her the same feeling of being among family that Mt. Moriah had given her all those years.

She knew the only thing she had to offer the church was her voice. It seemed she could never hold onto any extra money after she paid her part for living to Hannah. But she had always been told that hers was a mighty voice, and she would give it freely and lovingly.

The day the choir leader asked Halie to try out for the choir, Halie's smile could be seen from the front of the church to the back where Aunt Duke always said only the backsliders sat. Greater Salem had an impressive choir, made up of over 100 members with an equal number of men and women. Most had sung together for years. Halie was coming in as the outsider and would have to prove herself.

Halie noticed the choir sang from the songbooks. She thought some of them might have even taken professional training the way they held themselves as they sang. She sat quietly, nervous and anxious, as the choirmaster put the singers through their paces.

Halie had never learned to read music. Nobody down in "Nigger Town" thought she needed it. She knew nothing about harmonizing or the structure of chords. Her singing came out of her heart and her gut. It was all part of the free spirit she'd felt at Mt. Moriah Church, and the secret place inside her after Charity left, and the joy she felt in just living and dreaming. She always wondered what Duke meant when she complained, "The girl is in her own world half the time!"

While Halie would never say it out loud, her love of music wasn't restricted just to gospel church music. She loved all kinds of music, including the blues and jazz and the Mardi Gras music of New Orleans that was belted out from the juke boxes, from the street vendors, and from her cousin Fred's little record player.

Duke would just die to hear her say that Ma Rainey and Bessie Smith, two of the world's greatest blues singers, deserved some of the credit for the sound and the spirit that became distinctively Mahalia.

Halie looked down, frowning. Of course, she would never share that truth. She didn't believe God thought she was a bad sinner because she liked all music. As she waited for her tryout that night, she prayed God wouldn't punish her for learning to sing his songs of praise about goodness and right living, while listening to the songs of the unsaved and the wicked.

Halie saw the choir members locking eyes with the pianist. She had never depended on anyone, certainly not a pianist to help her sing. Mt. Moriah didn't have a piano in the church. She believed every singer had her own special way of tackling a song, and it was all about how that song fit her journey.

She believed that if she put her mind to it, she could sing most anything, but God wouldn't be pleased just because she could sing it. It had to be singing his praises. At 17, Halie had developed a unique sense of hearing. She learned every song by ear, and it came out exact, but unique, with a special tinge added. That was her faith. Her worship singing. She felt always that she had to give God something more.

Miss Mahalia Jackson!

For maybe the first time since she was 4 years old standing in front of the old people at Mt. Moriah, Halie found herself petrified. She asked God for strength. Somehow, God had shown her that her future wasn't at Provident Hospital, but in this, singing, because her voice could do the healing when hospitals couldn't. She could make people see God's goodness in her songs. Her singing now included her prayer that Hannah would get well, soon. If only God would give her the healing voice tonight!

Miss Jackson!

Halie stood and hurried toward the choirmaster. She could hear Aunt Duke: *"Ain't no place for that daydreaming in this house, Halie Jackson!"*

She stopped beside the piano and waited. The choirmaster gave her music sheets. It was the song that opened the door for her at Mt. Moriah Church when she was just 4 years old, "Hand Me down My Silver Trumpet, Gabriel." She looked at the pianist and nodded her head.

Though she stood very near the pianist, it was as if the sound was far away. She closed her eyes and whispered the words to herself before singing. She visualized how her voice would bounce off the ceiling, against the four walls, travel all the way to the front of the church.

Her eyes remained closed as she began the first verse. By the time she had finished, the room was filled with people who had come from all parts of the church. Her voice had, indeed, traveled throughout the building and beckoned listeners to her. There were visitors inside the door, and others peering in from the streets.

Now, comfortable that God hadn't betrayed her, the tall girl pressed her hands lightly to her stomach and began another round of the song. Her voice a summons to the faithful, the sinners, and even the fence-sitters.

Though she had won a place in Greater Salem's choir soon after arriving, Halie would later audition as a soloist. It was the second time she'd been tested to prove her voice. She often joked she passed the test because she sang louder than anyone else.

Her invitation to sing with the Johnson Gospel Singers, a quartet was the happiest day of Halie's short time in Chicago. With Halie joining them, they became the Johnson Singers quintet. The members included the church pastor's three sons—Prince, Robert, and Wilbur Johnson—herself, and another girl named Louise Barry.

Finally, 17-year-old Halie was enjoying her new life in Chicago. The teenagers at Greater Salem sang and put on skits to lighten the church's more somber program of saving souls. Soon they were singing all over the South Side and even at churches in downstate Illinois and Indiana. They never dreamed of earning a lot of money. And they didn't. Like Mahalia, they all scrambled for work to keep eating. For this was a time of great trouble.

The Great Depression—Chicago's Hoovervilles

Halie turned 18 in October 1929, the same month the Great Depression hit America, and the world, and millions of people—Blacks and whites—lost their jobs and experienced hunger and being without across the country. It was the year that banks lost their deposits, rich men went bankrupt, city treasuries went broke, and Chicago and other cities across the land stopped paying their schoolteachers. Tens of thousands of children stayed home from school—most were too hungry and cold to learn anyway, since their parents had no jobs to go to and no money to feed them or buy coal for their heaters.

The Depression pummeled Chicago worse than any other city. Joblessness was worse. Evictions were worse. Homelessness was worse. Families left the city in droves looking for work. By the time President Herbert Hoover realized just how bad things were, it was too late for him to do much good. Some people began their campaign right away to kick him out of office in the next election.

Finally, Chicago's civic and political leaders started acting, rather than reacting. Soup kitchens were set up around the city, as well as temporary shelters for those who had lost their homes. The landscape of this most impressive city changed overnight.

The hungry lined the streets all hours of the day, and each day more and more homeless families walked the streets. The Great Depression would hit America's most vulnerable citizens first, and hardest. In less than two years, half the country's Negroes were without jobs, a much higher rate than whites. And where public relief was granted, Blacks got less than whites. The lives that Blacks had tried to build for themselves in the city of promise fell apart.

Before Chicago factories laid off their white workers, they fired Negroes who had been the last to be hired. These were the same poor Negroes who had fled the hand-to-mouth life of sharecropping in Southern cotton fields. In Chicago, for the first time, they had felt hard cash in their pockets on payday. They had made more money than they ever had before. They were proud of their work and were some of the hardest workers in any industry.

They instinctively understood the importance of saving for a rainy day, but no longer were these former field hands and sharecroppers and manual laborers able to save. The cost of living and raising families took everything they earned. The Depression would strip them of their dreams, and for some, there would never be an opportunity to dream again.

Out of desperation, the homeless found themselves settling into the poor outskirts of the city in make-do homes that were poor substitutes for housing. These crude shelters were made out of tar paper and tin or old wooden crates or cardboard boxes—materials that were useless as a deterrent to Chicago's freezing cold, harsh winds, or rain and snow. These shantytowns sprang up all around Chicago and cities across the United

States. They came to be called *Hoovervilles,* as a back-handed homage to President Hoover who everyone blamed for the drastic national event. For as long as they lasted, soup kitchens fed the hungry for free.

A large Chicago Hooverville sprang up in the city center at the foot of Randolph Street near Grant Park, which also claimed its own form of government with a man named Mike Donovan, a disabled former railroad brakeman and miner, as its "mayor." Donovan told a reporter at the time, "Building construction may be at a standstill elsewhere, but down here everything is booming."

Another large Hooverville was situated along the banks of the Mississippi River in St. Louis, Missouri. Supporting some 500 people, it consisted of four distinct racial sectors, though the people integrated to "support" their city. They, too, had an unofficial mayor by the name of Gus Smith, who was also a pastor. The community, which depended primarily on private donations and scavenging, created its own churches and other social institutions. It remained a viable community until 1936 when the federal Works Progress Administration allocated slum-clearance funds for the area. Hoovervilles existed all over the United States—at the edges of Portland, Oregon; Washington, D.C.; Los Angeles, California; and everywhere.

In the latter half of the 1930s, the number of homeless people increased as factories closed and farmers were displaced. Far worse than Chicago was California, designated the "hardest hit" by transients during the Depression years. Having only 4.7% of the population when it began, the state would wind up with 14% of the nation's transients.

Overwhelmed officials tried to figure out how to absorb as many as 6,000 migrants crossing its borders daily. Also feeling the effects of the Depression, California infrastructures were already overburdened, and the steady stream of newly arriving migrants was more than the system could bear.

Halie was still doing laundry work in Chicago's northern suburbs when the Depression hit. She watched like an outsider as most Negroes spent every waking hour looking for food or work or both. Though she had long ago given up her dream of attending nursing school, she was now hopeful that her voice would save her from the drudgery she witnessed each day.

The colored churches in Halie's community were hard hit. Without jobs, members could no longer support their pastor or keep the churches open for services. Halie recognized the irony in that. In her eyes, as people lost everything, including their hope and faith, the church and the ministers were needed more than ever in the cities.

Religion, some thought, was a luxury for those who could comfortably allocate their Sundays to prayer and church when times were good. Nothing came easy in the middle of the Depression, not even praying. The Depression was unrelenting and didn't discriminate. The suffering didn't stop at the people at the bottom of the rung, but like a tideless flood, it rose to the top rung where mostly white folks resided.

Reverend Leon Jenkins at Greater Salem Baptist watched his congregation suffer for as long as he could before he decided his church had to do something. He didn't need to look on the next corner to witness suffering, just look inside his own flock. The families he ministered to and prayed for each and every Sunday were suffering. He implored the more fortunate members to give and help feed, clothe, house, and nurse those that couldn't help themselves. They did. And for months, Chicagoans inside and outside the neighborhood found ways to help the people of South Chicago.

The Depression didn't bypass the Clark sisters' household. They suffered along with the rest of Chicago and the rest of the country. They would wait it out just like the rest of the city. While they could barely afford to live in Chicago, they couldn't afford to return to New Orleans.

Halie found herself dreaming a lot about New Orleans, Mt. Moriah Church, and so vividly about Aunt Duke and Uncle Emanuel. She awoke with Aunt Duke's last words ringing in her ears: *"Look out, you ain't jumping out of the frying pan right into the fire."* Chicago, the city of promise for so many Southern Negroes, was now more akin to that trap.

Working to Live; Living to Sing

It was 1931 and the Depression was still going strong. Thank God, Halie had a job. She even had a half of a job singing with the Johnson Gospel Singers at Greater Salem. After she was invited to sing solo with the choir, she'd become something of a celebrity at Greater Salem—the tall girl from New Orleans with the big voice, and pretty in a country kinda way.

Now, Halie's days were divided into the number of buckets she had to carry to fill tubs. She soaped soiled clothing on a corrugated washboard and rubbed the dirt out, rinsing the clothes in water doused with bluing. Some of the more soiled things had to be placed in boiling water. The clothes were then put through hand-operated wringers to remove the water. And then, Halie would hang the clothes on the line to dry in the harsh wind blowing off Lake Michigan.

Tomorrow, God willing, she'd return and iron the rough-dry laundry. Now she was getting $1.50 a day—twice what she had earned in New Orleans. It was good money she thought as she boarded her train, even though it cost twice as much to live in Chicago.

With her share of the free-will offering she got for singing with the Johnson Gospel Singers, Halie was doing better than some Black men who still hung onto piddly jobs and had families to support. But would she be stuck at a washtub the rest of her life? After giving Alice and Hannah her share of the food and rent money, she still had a few dollars she could squirrel away for herself.

Halie had learned from Duke that poor folks didn't have the luxury of wallowing in regrets. You had to take life as God gave it to you and try your best to make something out of it. There was no place for regret here in Chicago. In fact, Halie had a lot to be grateful for. Besides, there was something in this Chicago air, even in the midst of the Depression—possibility. That was akin to promise and hope. She felt God was still guiding her steps, and she was full of hope about her future. While Chicago wasn't the promised land she'd imagined as a child, it wasn't a dead-end street, like New Orleans.

Her mind took her back to how she'd arrived in the cold, dark city still filled with so much hope, confidence, and wonder. She had told herself it wouldn't always be cold or dark, and the spring would come. It did, but even with some still dark days and some expectations dashed, she was slowly building up her confidence.

It took a lot for her to keep believing, but she always found a way to pick herself up out of her depression and plaster on her Halie smile. She didn't come all this way to fail, Halie told herself over and over.

That was the hardest difference to swallow, how the grown-ups back home had always embraced her, pushed her to always do her best. There were just a handful of people here that seemed to care enough to push her. Halie sometimes wondered about Aunt Hannah and Aunt Alice, whether they still believed her voice held any value. She was especially hurt that Hannah—who had encouraged her to follow her dreams, to come to Chicago and work until she got her singing noticed—seemed to have forgotten all about that long ago dream Halie had shared with her.

It didn't take Halie long to learn the lay of the land when it came to church music here in Chicago. More than a few churches, though they were made up of people who came from the South, now turned their noses up at the country ways of talking and singing.

Alice and Hannah hadn't forewarned her that her kind of singing might be looked down on in some of Chicago's Black churches. Though her feelings had been bruised, Halie wouldn't be Duke's adopted child if she didn't find a second way to skin that cat. She had connected with tent churches outside the city that welcomed her into their folds with open arms.

Some of the choir members at Greater Salem suggested that if she wanted to go further than singing in the church, she might want to take voice lessons. Most places expect singers to read music, these days. Halie shrugged, still not convinced she needed lessons. God had given her all she needed.

One day, one of the Johnson Gospel Singers, the group she sang with, told her about a voice teacher. "There's that Professor DuBois 'round the corner who used to be a concert singer."

Robert Johnson, the leader of their group, told her that, with her voice, she could sing just about anybody under the church. She was so good, he said, that he was sure she would end up singing for some of those snooty places she always complained about.

"They'll come knocking on your door one day, Halie. I know they will…and you want to be prepared, to make sure you can sing your own natural way, but also the snooty way, too."

They all laughed. But Halie was thinking more seriously about what Robert had told her. She didn't want to miss out on singing opportunities because she didn't at least try. There was something some folks expected from a singer that she sensed she didn't have. Robert said this teacher could help her get that extra thing and prepare her for anything.

Halie's feelings were hurt, but she knew her friend meant it for her own good. Though she would take his advice, her mind was against it. If her friend Louise Barry hadn't agreed to go with her to take lessons, too, she was sure she wouldn't go through with it.

A promise is a promise. She and Louise went for their first lesson that very night. Halie had her $4 for the lesson. She sighed as she clasped the bills in her hands. Four dollars was a lot of money.

Their train roared into the South Side station and stopped long enough for Halie to step off, right along with the suds-busters and range breakers—Black women who, like herself, counted themselves lucky to have domestic work during the Great Depression's dark days.

When she reached the main street, she found it jammed with people. The crowd was silently staring at the hunger marchers. Her heart beat faster as she watched row after row of colored men, women carrying babies, children moving slowly down the middle of the street. Their shabby clothing looked even shabbier in the gray evening light. Police mounted on skittery horses rode alongside the marchers, who carried handmade signs reading: "Join the Hunger March," "Protest Firings of Blacks," "Give Us Food," "Protest Evictions of Our Families," "Don't Buy Where You Can't Work."

Hannah had said police had shot some hunger marchers, killing five men. Mahalia fought her way through the packed pavement toward Greater Salem. She made some progress till she came to an eviction in progress.

The sheriff's deputies were taking the furniture out of a house and putting it in the street. As quickly as the deputies carried the battered furniture into the street, members of Marcus Garvey's United Negro Improvement Association carried it back into the house. Garvey's men outnumbered the white deputies, as did the crowd watching. The Garveyites won the contest. The tenants could stay another night. But what about tomorrow?

Mahalia continued on her way, getting madder and madder at herself with every step. Why was she giving $4 to a music teacher when there were people starving in the streets? Four dollars could help a family pay their rent.

She argued back and forth to herself. She decided the music lessons might help her make a larger contribution to many more people later on. She felt better as she recalled how she had helped raise money for the poor when she sang solo for Greater Salem and with her singing with the Johnson Gospel Singers in the little storefront churches. Anyhow, Halie had already made the appointment with Professor DuBois. He'd charge her whether she came or not.

When she got within sight of Greater Salem Baptist Church, Mahalia saw a line of people standing at the basement entrance to the church cafeteria. They were waiting until the earlier group had finished eating, making room at the tables. She went to another entrance, and once inside, found Robert, Wilbur, Prince, and Louise.

Mahalia took off her coat and joined her friends behind the steam table loaded with cooked food. Mahalia's mouth watered at the sight of the food. She felt as hungry as the poor marchers looked, but she wouldn't eat until she helped with the serving.

That was their job. Some of the church members went from market to market getting donations of food from sympathetic merchants. Some delivered the food to the church in their trucks. Some cooked the food. Some washed the pots and pans. No one got paid. Greater Salem had become a busy relief agency that brought Blacks together.

Tonight, the very sight of the cooked food made her so hungry she could hardly talk. She swallowed as she looked at the pig tails in sauerkraut, sweet potatoes, red and white beans, rice and black-eyed peas, and bread pudding. The smell of freshly brewed coffee was almost her undoing.

Louise was watching her. "Something wrong, Mahalia?"

Mahalia shrugged. "Oh, I'm fine."

Prince chimed in, "No, young lady, you don't look like your usual happy self. You the one usually picking us up."

For the longest, Halie didn't respond. Then she stopped serving for a minute.

"It's just that I saw the hunger marchers on my way in, and it just makes me so sad to see them. In the South, all we had to do was keep out of the way of whites and fight hard times. We usually had a little garden of collards, some chickens, and maybe a pig to help us stay alive. We could eat all the fish and wildlife we wanted. As bad as we thought things were, there wasn't many people going hungry. Something about all this just don't seem right."

Prince spoke up. "Halie, what it all boils down to is that this Depression proves once again that colored folks better learn how to take care of their own. The government and white people got their minds on themselves."

Everyone nodded and seconded Prince's statement.

Louise frowned and looked over at Prince. "You know, there should be a way that we add some kind of message like that in our songs when we go around the city."

Wilbur smiled, and they all nodded in agreement.

"With a few verses thrown in on how we ought to begin our own businesses to give our own people jobs, so we won't have to depend on white folks!"

Halie laughed, "Well, let's make sure God don't have a problem with mixing marching songs with church songs…if he okay with it, I am, too."

Prince looked at his watch, then back up at Louise and Halie. "What time do you two prima donnas have to take your music lessons, tonight?"

Louise looked over at Halie. "Eight. And we'd better go on and eat our dinner so we won't be late."

Professor DuBois' Music Lesson

Mahalia and Louise put food on their trays and went to a nearby table to eat. Mahalia looked over at her friend and sighed. "I might as well go into the lion's den with a hearty meal under my belt." The two girls laughed.

"Oh, you not the one who need to be worrying, Halie. You'll for sure become Professor DuBois' star student."

"Hmmph. I don't know about that," said Halie, adding, "Louise, I'm scared. I never let nobody tell me how to sing before."

"Scared? Why in the world? You're the Johnson Gospel Singers' star. People come out just to see you, Mahalia!"

Halie didn't seem appeased.

When the teenagers arrived at Professor DuBois' studio, he was finishing a lesson with another young woman. When she left, he turned to Louise and Halie. "So, which one of you is Miss Jackson?"

Halie put her hand up, shyly. "That's me, sir."

The music teacher nodded over at her. He was a tall, light-skinned man who stood proper-like as if he slept on a board, and he used extra-proper speech. Halie didn't have a good feeling. Something told her this might not be for her.

"And, you're Miss Barry?"

"Yes, sir. Louise Barry."

He nodded and sat down at the piano.

"Miss Jackson. What would you like to sing, Miss Jackson, to show me what sort of voice you have?"

"I'd like to sing one of those songs we used to sing down home when I was a kid."

Mahalia took her place near the piano. Oh, how she longed for a pipe organ! Since she'd been at Greater Salem, she'd fallen in love with how the organ matched her singing so well, accompanying her while letting her do all the little improvisations she loved to do.

"Where in the South are you from, Miss Jackson?"

"New Orleans."

"Oh, I see," he said, staring down at the piano keys. "One thing I find I have to work on with colored singers who come up from the South is… you can get them out of the South, but it's a job getting the South out of them when they come up North." He offered a small laugh.

"Here's something you're probably familiar with, 'Standing in the Need of Prayer.' " He handed Halie the sheet music. She stared at the black notes, too embarrassed to tell the professor she couldn't read music. Maybe she wouldn't have to, since she knew the song. She had sung it many times at Mt. Moriah Baptist Church, down in New Orleans.

The teacher began playing. Halie watched the long, thin fingers play the music before she took a big breath and closed her eyes.

"It's me, it's me, O Lawd…."

Just as she began the next line, she heard the man groan. Opening her eyes, she saw him shake his head. He continued playing, and she kept singing.

"…standin' in the need of prayer."

The music stopped. She opened her eyes to see the professor sitting stiffly at the piano, his hands on his thighs.

"Miss Jackson, you're over-singing, getting in the way of the song. Look at me." He clasped his hands in front of him and began rolling out the song slowly, like sweet cane syrup, with a hangdog look on his face.

Halie tried it his way…over and over and over.

"Let's let Miss Barry try it, now," the professor suggested, as he took the sheet of music from Mahalia and handed it to her friend. As he began playing, Mahalia watched as her friend clasped her hands together just as the professor had.

Louise looked up into the clouds when she sang. She didn't close her eyes. She sang each word distinctly, imitating the professor. Halie had to admit the girl had a sweet voice.

"Alright. Thank you, Miss Barry. Very well done," the professor said. "Do you hear what I mean, Miss Jackson? She's not fighting with the song; she's letting the song lead her. That's what I need you to do. Can you do that? I think you can, with proper training, but you have to be willing to become a cultured singer and leave the country singing down there in the country. Now. Are you ready to try again?" he asked, this time with a softer tone.

Not waiting for her answer, he began playing. Halie clasped her hands before her as he'd suggested and began to sing. She even tried slowing down her natural singing tempo, but something inside her wouldn't allow it. Slowly, but surely, the song picked up the beat as she continued to sing.

When she opened her eyes just a little, she saw the professor again shaking his head. Again, he abruptly stopped playing. This time, banging out the final note.

"Please stop, Miss Jackson. I really need you to slow down, and I need you to try pronouncing the words so cultured Negro people and white people can understand you. Please don't sing in a way that a lot of people won't appreciate."

If Halie Jackson could have turned colors she would have. She was embarrassed, but even more so, hurt. Such hateful words, and in front of her friend, too. She couldn't make herself respond. The man looked in her face and must have realized how deeply his words had cut.

"I'm sorry, but you are doing everything wrong, Miss Jackson. I'm sorry that no one has told you this before, but I can barely understand your words. You breathe in and out at the wrong time, and you hold your notes too long…and that bounce. Lord, you have to get rid of that bounce!"

"Yes, sir. I'll try."

The practice session didn't get easier for Halie, and she knew it wasn't easy for Professor DuBois. He was trying all he knew to try.

"Alright. Thank you both for coming. I expect to see you back here next week at the same time."

Both girls nodded. Mahalia walked over and got her coat, took the $4 out of her pocketbook and handed it to Professor DuBois.

On the way home, Louise was quiet, listening to Halie grumble about the professor. When Halie said she was through with singing lessons, Louise was crestfallen.

"Please, Halie, let's go at least a month, then see how you like it." When Halie said she wouldn't, Louise turned quiet and remained quiet the rest of the way to the train station. Before Louise left the train, she looked at her friend and smiled.

"I do understand. He didn't have to be so hard. But I'll keep taking lessons for a month, because I really do need lessons more than you, Mahalia. I don't care what he says. Even if he don't like your singing, everybody else sure do!"

Mahalia didn't agree or disagree. If that was what Louise wanted, then she should do it. It wasn't for her. She was a Negro from New Orleans.

Why should she sing songs the way white folks or proper colored folks liked? She could never sing in that formal style he suggested for more than a minute, before her real style came bubbling out. She could never be happy singing the way someone else wanted her to sing. And that was that.

Still, it was the put-down by the professor that really hurt. She'd had to deal with his kind of put-downs from proper Black folks ever since she came to Chicago. It hurt, but not enough to make her change. She had enough people who loved her singing to feel confident in her way of singing. She wouldn't change unless God told her to…and she knew he wouldn't. He was the one who blessed her with her singing.

Chicago Skies Turning Blue / Grandpa Clark Visits Chicago

The Depression was in its fifth year and still going strong in Chicago and around the world. Mahalia was learning the truth about hard times; that if you braved through it, you came out stronger.

It had been three years since the music teacher tore down her self-confidence and made her doubt the value of God's gift. After the hurt had finally subsided, and it took a few weeks, she found that his harsh assessment brought out her bull-headedness that she'd inherited from Aunt Duke. Yes, she'd wallowed in self-pity for a while, but once it was over, she was ashamed of herself. What right did she have to question God's gift because some proper teacher didn't like it?

No, no more thoughts about changing her singing or her style for the music teacher or anyone else. It was this brave and bold new Mahalia who walked into Decca Records in the middle of the Depression, taped a song, and walked out with $25, a lot of money in 1934. Halie had sung and taped "God's Gonna Separate the Wheat from the Tares," the very same song she performed in churches around the city and during tent meetings outside the city. It had always been a favorite because it was from her favorite chapter in the Bible: Matthew 13:25-30.

As she walked out of the recording studio, Halie's smile changed her whole face, those small narrow eyes almost closed. She was humming the song that just netted her $25:

If you never hear me sing no more,
Go, and meet me on the other shore
God's gonna separate the wheat from the tares,
Didn't he say?

Halie decided that part of the money would go to her savings. The other she would use to help pay for Papa Paul Clark's train trip to Chicago. As she made her way home, she still couldn't believe it. Twenty-five dollars for singing one song. When she sang with the Johnson Gospel Singers, they were happy when they had $5 to divide among themselves.

When Mahalia looked back at her first weeks in Chicago, she found it hard to admit it had been eight years ago. As she walked home, she wanted to fall down on her knees and praise God. *Look at what he done for me!*

Halie was most surprised that it was a white British-owned company who heard something in her voice and thought it was worth that kind of money. She would later learn, though, that they produced both Black and white artists, including the Andrews Sisters, the Black big bands, or jazz orchestras, and the Arkansas-born blues musician Louis Jordan. But hers was Southern-style gospel, completely different.

Whatever their reasoning, Halie knew they would make a lot more than $25 from the taping. She knew that when they insisted on paying her a flat fee, no royalties would be forthcoming, no matter what happened with the record, they said. She wasn't in a position then to fuss. She really wasn't anybody, in their eyes. She rolled her eyes when they told her they were doing it because they wanted to encourage other Blacks to sing. Aunt Duke didn't raise no dummy.

She was too poor to squabble, Mahalia thought. She had been gifted with a keen business instinct even without a formal education. Business was business. The white folks weren't giving away nothing to no Black woman. They were about making a profit.

What she didn't know, she knew how to learn. She asked questions. After talking to other Chicago musicians, she learned there was profit in so-called race records, Black music for Black audiences. Once such a record as Mahalia's came alive, Decca salesmen would go door to door in the Black neighborhoods selling it.

People who might not have running water or electricity in their homes somehow scraped up enough money to buy a hand-cranked phonograph. Negroes were often willing to spend their last dollar for a record made by a Black singer or musician. Halie knew that was the power of music. It had that kind of power over her growing up down in "Nigger Town."

Halie entered the bank and took her place at the end of the line. She got out her bank book, something she had never had before coming to Chicago. If she'd had her own account in New Orleans, she wouldn't have had all the fuss over the money Aunt Duke had been saving for her. Getting it from her aunt had been like pulling hen's teeth. It taught her a lesson, and a good one. Never in this lifetime would she ever lean on someone else to take care of her money.

Halie looked at the first entry in her bank book. That dollar came from babysitting. Another dollar below it came from singing with the Johnson Singers. Here was a $3 entry. Yes, she got that for singing at a funeral at Bob Miller's undertaker parlor. Funerals weren't as fancy in Chicago as they were in New Orleans, and instead of having a marching band for the trip to the cemetery, the family sometimes had a soloist to sing the deceased person's favorite hymn.

Mahalia was happy to have this sometimes-job, something to fall back on if the Johnson Gospel Singers broke up. Not if, but when. She could feel that it was time for her to move on. She was getting invitations to churches to sing solo. While they wished her well, they loved having her being part of the group. It wasn't just her singing. They loved her spirit, and she was funny, too. They all admitted, though, nothing was forever.

After making her deposit, Mahalia hurried home to the dinner she knew was waiting for her. Hannah would outdo herself, putting the big pot in the little pot as Aunt Duke used to do down in New Orleans.

Hannah had bought a 10-pound pail of chitlins, the cheapest meat they could eat. There was nothing fancy about the hog guts, but when Hannah got through with them, they were something else! Halie had begged her aunt for her recipe for years. Hannah had finally relented and shared the recipe with Halie only after she promised not to go passing it around.

Hannah's Chicago Ruffles (Chitlins)

1. *Scrape the chitlins good under running water to clean them.*

2. *Parboil chitlins in a cup of vinegar and water in a large pot for an hour. Throw the parboiled water away.*

3. *Add two cups of fresh water, a mess of garlic, onions, hot peppers, and parsley in the cooking pot.*

4. *Let the pot simmer for an hour or so.*

5. *Eat while piping hot!*

When Mahalia let herself into the apartment, she quietly closed the door behind her and stood for a moment to get a good look at the old man sitting at the head of the table as royally as an African king. Grandpa Paul Clark was telling his daughters about how slave masters married the slaves back in those dark days of bondage.

"When a couple found out they were in love, they went up to the "Big House" to get the master to marry them. And the master and his wife took them to the kitchen. The master put a broomstick on the floor and told the couple to stand on one side of it. The master didn't have a Bible or nothing in his hand when he mated the couple. We kids knew what was up. We'd heard the old folks talking about it in Slave Row where all the Blacks lived.

"Well, we're peeping in through the kitchen door to see the couple jump over the broomstick. And that was what the master told the couple to do: 'jump over the broomstick—now you man and wife.' That's the truth. That's the truth," said Grandpa Paul, who they also called Papa.

"And, that's why they call getting married jumping the broom?" asked little Nathaniel, Alice's son. Mahalia went into the dining room to join the laughter, and Papa let loose a sound of sheer delight.

"There's my girl. You didn't think Papa was coming up here to visit you, did you?" He wrapped his arms around his favorite granddaughter. "We still missing you down there in N'awlins, Halie."

Halie basked in her grandfather's adoration. "I miss you and all my folks every day, Papa. And I pray for God to protect you, too." She loved it that Papa had finally agreed to come to Chicago to visit his daughters, his granddaughter, and his grandson. He brought with him all of Mahalia's favorite memories of her childhood home.

Hannah and Alice had been trying for years to get him to visit Chicago. Ever since she'd arrived here, they'd put Mahalia up to asking, thinking that surely he'd say yes to his sweet Halie. Now, they swore it was only because Halie asked that he'd found a way to come. But, no matter. He was here, and they'd enjoy every minute of his visit.

Halie was admiring the spread on their table and was so thankful for her family there with her—Grandpa Paul, little Nathaniel, Alice, and Hannah. She wouldn't be surprised if one of their neighbors smelled their dinner and found an excuse to stop by just as they finished the blessing.

Halie was delighted to see that Grandpa Paul hadn't lost his appetite. He enjoyed food the way it was meant to be enjoyed. The way most folk down in New Orleans enjoyed food. She sat back after dinner, ready to listen to her grandfather's stories. She learned so much about her history that the teachers never taught her in the schools.

Grandpa Paul was born into slavery, way back in 1856. He was a child when President Lincoln made freedom the law for slaves. For a man of 78, his memory was still good. He remembered the good, as well as the bad.

Something came to Halie as she sat there listening and looking around at her family. There needs to be a way to remember this moment, after Papa had gone back home and the rest of them were back to what they did every day.

She remembered the photography shop not too far from the apartment building. Why couldn't they all go down and get a photo made? She knew a lot of colored families with family pictures on their walls. Some had pictures up all around the walls, made with their parents sitting proudly in the center. No, it would be best to have one picture made of Grandpa alone and then one of him with the aunts, Nathaniel, and Halie. Whichever way would be fine, but the first thing was to get Papa up from the table before he yawned and took a nap. By the time he woke up from that nap, the photographer would have closed shop and gone home for his dinner.

After they finished the blackberry cobbler, Mahalia saw her chance. "Papa, I think it would be wonderful if you come round to the photographer with me and have your picture taken. It'll leave us something to have around when you're back in New Orleans."

The sisters and Nathaniel had stopped talking in the middle of the sentence, looked at Halie, then at Papa. Alice spoke what Hannah was thinking.

"Halie, it's awfully hot for your grandpa to go out so soon after eating a full meal."

"Auntie, it would only take a few minutes, no more than 20 minutes at the most," Mahalia responded.

"But pictures take extra money, Halie. Where we gone get the money to take pictures?" Hannah asked, a furrow deepening in her forehead.

"I'm sure that would cost at least $5, Halie," Alice said, nodding toward Hannah.

"Well, I was wanting to make it a surprise, but I got a few extra dollars from my singing, and I wanted to spend a bit of it on pictures with Papa," Mahalia said, now smiling broadly.

She hadn't really meant to tell them about the record. She was always nervous about how her aunts felt about her trying to make a career out of her singing. They were comfortable as long as she was singing in the church, but selling her voice for the money sounded like something else, they might well have told her.

"Oh, daughters, I don't mind going and taking a picture with Halie. She's trying to do something nice for Papa, and I appreciate it. Tell you what, Halie, I'll go if you sing my favorite song." Papa was smiling over at his granddaughter.

Mahalia jumped up from the table as fast as she could. She knew Papa's favorite song, and didn't mind a bit singing it for him.

Steal Away, steal away
Steal away to Jesus
Steal away, steal away home
I ain't got long to stay here.

Halie's aunts seemed to be enjoying her song as much as Papa, and Nathaniel, too. When Mahalia opened her eyes, though, Papa Paul's head was resting on his chest. They all looked and tittered behind their hands. Papa had eaten a full plate of chitlins and all the sides, plus a plate of cobbler. He was losing the battle to keep his eyes open.

Mahalia gently touched his shoulder and his eyes fluttered open. "Papa, you ready to go take that picture?"

He stood and grabbed his hat. "Let's go. I'll take me a little nap when we get back."

Finally, they were heading to the photographer's office.

At almost 80 years old, Grandpa Paul Clark was still a fine upstanding sight and hadn't lost one bit of his cantankerous spirit when he wanted to be. The good-natured photographer made his best efforts to humor the old man into a smile, but Papa wasn't accommodating him.

"Young man, I don't really feel like smiling; just take the picture while I'm in a good mood." As Papa grumbled, his daughters and Halie hid their laughter.

Mahalia, more than either of his daughters, could usually lighten Papa's mood. She tried, now, but it just wasn't working. He continued to grumble and frown. As Mahalia turned to the photographer to ask him to give them a little time, she saw the man's face turn to one of horror as he hurried over to where Papa sat.

She followed his eyes and saw that Papa Paul had a terrible grimace on his face and was slouching further and further down in the photographer's chair. Mahalia's first thought was that he'd fallen asleep again. As she moved closer and peered into her grandfather's face, chills ran over her body.

"Papa!" the sisters, niece and nephew yelled at the same time.

Everyone was rushing over at once, but the photographer quickly shushed the women and took control. He directed them to lay Papa on the floor, remove his hat, and loosen his tie. He wouldn't know that Papa never left his house without a jacket, tie, and hat.

"Please don't move him, now. Wait there while I call an ambulance. Looks like the heat might have gotten to him. He'll be okay." The photographer left Paul Clark and his daughters and grandchildren hovering over their kin, while he ran to the phone on the wall.

Twenty minutes later, an ambulance screeched to a stop in front of the studio. The paramedics rushed in and loaded Paul Clark onto a stretcher and carried him to the ambulance, then off to the hospital.

"Where you taking him?" Halie yelled.

One man turned and told her "Provident Hospital. You know where it is?"

She hesitated just a second, before saying, "Yes, we'll be there soon as we can."

It was all just too much for Mahalia. Her nerves could never stand up for sickness in the family. She imagined Papa was already dead, and the ambulance was a hearse. She ran out to flag a taxi for her and her two aunts and Nathaniel. Did they need two? No, they could squeeze into one. By the time they arrived at the hospital, the doctor had already examined Paul Clark. The doctor came out long enough to say Papa wasn't fully conscious, yet. He'd have someone let them know when he was.

Mahalia looked at her Aunt Hannah for comfort. But Hannah was wrapped up in her own fear and grief. She knew they would never hear the last of it if Papa got really sick, or God forbid, died up here with them. Duke would blame them for it forever.

"Lord, Halie, why you have to push Papa into going to that studio in this terrible heat? I wish you'd have listened to me. Lord…you just had to have some pictures." That was Hannah, still worried about Duke's hard words when she found out.

Aunt Hannah's words were worse than a slap. Mahalia was too hurt to say anything. She went into the hall and walked until the tears blinded her, and she just had to stop somewhere. She saw an empty room, went in, and closed the door. She immediately fell on her knees. It seemed all the tears she'd ever held in were flowing now.

Yes, there was no way around it. This was all her fault. Papa had wanted to take the pictures, but it was because he wanted to please Halie. She saw the smile on his face as she sang his favorite song. Why didn't she just leave it at that? Let him sleep through the afternoon? Halie, with her penchant for reading signs, should have felt something when she sang the song "I ain't got long to stay here." It should have been a warning.

If God would only let him live! She couldn't go around the rest of her life feeling guilty about killing him. What could she do to keep her grandpa alive?

Mahalia prayed. *God, if you will only let Grandpa live, I'll devote the rest of my life to the church and doing your bidding.*

Mahalia sat quietly, listening for God's answer. She was thinking, *What is it that I should give up for God's blessing, if he will do this one thing for me?* She would forever count it as one of God's divine miracles if the old man lived. She didn't drink liquor or smoke or dance. She didn't gamble or visit honky-tonks.

Halie did love the movies, though, watching all the actors like Charlie Chaplin, Norma Shearer, Clara Bow, Bing Crosby, Cab Calloway, the Mills Brothers. But she'd give all that up, she vowed, if God would give Papa back to us, whole.

When she went back out to the waiting room, the woman at the desk said her aunts had gone back to her grandfather's room. She gave Halie the room number. Papa was still asleep. The doctor said it was a coma, and most times patients came out of it.

Mahalia repeated her vow to God the next day, and the next. For nine days she repeated her vow and prayed for her grandfather's recovery. On the ninth day Paul Clark came out of the coma. It wasn't long before he walked out of the hospital well and strong.

He never blamed Halie for his heat stroke; said he needed to take better care of himself. He said the next time he came he'd come in cooler weather. Then, they'd take that picture that Halie wanted.

Paul Clark never returned to Chicago, but he lived out a full life in New Orleans.

Part 6

LOVE AND HORSES
AND FISH AND BREAD

Mahalia's Lesson in Love

Mahalia turned 24 the year she had her first experience with love. As far as most people knew, Mahalia hadn't had much experience in the love department. Only she could tell folks any different, and she chose not to address it either way.

Truthfully, the young woman hadn't had time for love since moving to Chicago. Every waking hour was spent working two to three jobs at a time, or spending hours rehearsing, worshipping, or performing at her church. And, during her free time, she traveled with the Johnson quintet to churches throughout the Midwestern region.

Oh, there were a few young men who caught her eye, and she'd spend some time thinking about them later that night or the next day. There were a few instances of flirting that took place during her singing trips. The Johnson boys would tease her about this one or that one. But Halie had long decided she was going to wait for God's directions in the love department. He'd tap her on the shoulder when it was time to accept a man into her life.

Mahalia didn't dream about the kind of man God might send her. Whoever he sent would be the right one. Her male friends all agreed that whoever decided to make Mahalia his wife, they better have some special powers because it would take that to stand up to Mahalia. She was a serious young woman who knew exactly what she wanted and how she needed to go about getting it. She had a mind of her own and wouldn't accept just anything from a man just because he was a man.

Still, in 1935, when the man she was sure God sent showed up, Halie wasn't so sure God hadn't made a mistake. Not a bad mistake, but a strange mistake. The man he'd sent was educated, mature, and well-spoken, with not a hint of country in his demeanor. Her friends wouldn't admit it, but they were more than a little surprised as well.

Halie's surprise, however, didn't make her question God. No, it was because she was sure Isaac "Ike" Hockenhull was sent by God that she gave herself over to his adept courting.

Duke's warnings played like a record in the back of her head the night she first met Ike Hockenhull. *Watch out, up there. There's a lot of wolves in sheep's clothing, girl.*

She was on program to sing that night at Greater Salem Baptist Church. She had been waiting rather impatiently when she heard her name called by the emcee. Halie was a naturally impatient young woman. She quickly made her way to the front of the church because she never learned how to move slowly. Aunt Duke had always disparaged slow walkers, saying they moved *like they had dead lice falling off them*—moving so slowly that they're already dead, and any lice on them have starved to death. Halie never wanted to be that person.

When Halie looked back at how it happened that Ike came into her life, instead of a different kind of young man, she decided it was the vow she'd made to God—that she wouldn't go to the movies or to the theater or to dances. She didn't drink or gamble. She shunned parties, even the ones with no alcohol, because she was scared it fit into one of the things she'd vowed she wouldn't do. She hedged her bets.

Halie thought of herself as a 24-year-old good girl, spending most of her spare time singing either at Greater Salem or at some storefront church. Even her aunts said she was married to the church.

Mahalia reached the front of the church and nodded to the pianist who played a short introduction. She cleared her throat and looked out at the congregation. Before closing her eyes, as she always did, she noticed a man sitting alone in the back of the church, staring at her.

People always stared at her when she stood up in front of the congregation. She didn't think that was too odd. She was a tall girl, skinny and tall. Her skin was dark, real dark, and some people for some reason thought that was different. Some people said she had a regal baring. She had to ask around to find out what that meant. She decided it was a compliment. She'd even been told by a few men that she was a pretty girl…a pretty, dark girl.

But the way this young man stared at her was different. Her heart fluttered. She didn't know nothing about falling in love. She would just ignore the rude man and keep her mind on her singing.

"God's gonna separate the wheat from the tares," began Mahalia. She kept her eyes closed while she searched around inside for the right sound that let her know she was singing her best. The right sound made her feel happy. She couldn't sing a song unless it did something for her. When she kept her eyes closed, she found the right music, and in the darkness, she concentrated and put all her feeling into her voice.

Isaac Hockenhull, the man staring at Mahalia, was 34 years old and worked part-time as a postal clerk. Like most young men during the Depression, his work was irregular. He was on call 24 hours a day in case extra workers were needed to handle incoming mail. Substitutes earned about $20 a week, and if they were lucky, they might become regulars.

Before the Depression, a job in the postal service was one of the best jobs available to colored men. They weren't hiring colored women for postal workers then. Many postal workers were able to buy homes and send their daughters and sons to college. Though the federal postal service provided good jobs and high status in the community, during the Depression it became the graveyard for a number of college graduates like Hockenhull. Dentists, lawyers, teachers, even doctors found they were stuck in the postal service for the rest of their lives. The pay there was more than they could earn in their chosen profession.

Before coming to Chicago, Isaac Hockenhull had attended Tuskegee Institute in Alabama where he studied chemistry and mathematics. After finishing at Tuskegee, he went to Fisk University, planning to join his family's cosmetics manufacturing company. But the family firm went bankrupt, the way a large number of businesses did during those bad times. Isaac Hockenhull moved to Chicago.

When Mahalia finished her song and opened her eyes, the man was still sitting at the back of the church, and still staring at her. He joined the rest of the church in applauding, maybe a little louder than the rest.

He smiled up at Mahalia as she began her encore. After, she'd finished, he walked up, standing behind the others clustered around her and congratulating her on her singing. When the others finally left, he stood before her staring much like he had from the back of the church.

Ike Hockenhull's first courting words to Mahalia were:

"I remember seeing you one time in a little storefront church. I was passing by when it seemed your voice reached out and pulled me in. There you were, a big green-as-grass girl from down home, singing in that rundown place cold as a refrigerator. You were up there in front, telling them to clap their hands or they'd freeze to death—and finally you got some heat in there, though there still wasn't any fire in the stove."

Mahalia didn't know how she should respond, but she enjoyed hearing him talk. She could have listened to him talk all night, until he said the worst thing he could say to Mahalia.

"Why do you waste such a wonderful voice?"

Waste her voice? What did he mean? She worked hard so that she could sing when and where she wanted. Mahalia's eyes narrowed, and her face froze over when the wrong things came out of people's mouth. Ike quickly realized he had hit a nerve, spoken out of line. For the rest of their conversation, he treaded a lot more lightly.

Mahalia, by then, was singing fairly regularly in and around Chicago. Her name had gotten around, and she was fast building herself a fan base. She'd lost her laundry job because singing out of town made her miss a day's work. She had packed dates for $7 a week, but decided the money wasn't even enough to keep her in a job she hated as much as she hated working in the date factory.

Now she was working in a hotel, cleaning 33 rooms a day for $12 a week. She turned and walked to the refreshment table for ice cream and cake. For the rest of that evening, she tried to avoid Isaac Hockenhull.

"Look, it's your business where and what you sing. Still and all, I can't get over how humiliating it must have been for you that night." Ike had walked up behind her while she was talking to a church friend. Halie thought he'd left. Hockenhull didn't know how to stop when he was ahead, Mahalia thought.

"Just, what do you mean, humiliating for me?" she asked

"I mean hanging around till the collection plate was passed around. I saw they were collecting nickels, dimes, and pennies mostly. How much do they usually give you?"

"What did you put in the collection?" she asked, with a half-smile.

He laughed. "I wasn't able to put a thin dime in the collection plate tonight, but I'll make up for it next time. I hope you'll let me walk you home."

Why should she? she asked herself. But for some strange reason, she did.

Becoming Mrs. Mahalia Hockenhull

Mahalia and Ike dated for about a year. He never relented after that first night, always trying to convince her to give up the "humiliating gospel racket" and become a great concert artist. When he asked Mahalia to marry him, she realized it wouldn't be a perfect union given he was already trying to change her, and they were both poor. Yet, she was sure Ike had been sent by God, and in time she realized she was in love with him.

Ike was 10 years older than Mahalia, sophisticated and educated. And, in spite of all that, she was convinced after their year of courting that he truly loved her. Ike loving her wasn't what scared her. It was his unapologetic obsession to make her into someone he thought she should be.

Mahalia had never been in love before, and God had never sent her someone to love before. She didn't know she could ask for a redo. That if there was an inkling of doubt about her and this man being spiritually yoked, she could pray to God to send a substitute.

Mahalia found his gentlemanly demeanor irresistible, as well as the pretty way he talked. He talked prettier than anyone Mahalia had ever known, even Papa Paul Clark. Ike must have been the most dignified postman they ever had. He took himself and life very seriously and had a speaking voice that called for you to listen to him even if he was only telling you to pass the potatoes.

Mahalia was warily happy about the marriage. Everyone told her she had made a good decision with Ike. He failed to tell her up until a few days before their marriage that he'd been married before, to a Marion E. Smith. They had married in Chicago just four years earlier.

Ike Hockenhull and Mahalia Jackson were married in Hannah's apartment by Pastor Leon Jenkins of Greater Salem Baptist Church. They moved into the small apartment with Hannah, Alice, little Nathaniel, and the roomer. It was a mistake. Halie's family complained constantly that Ike locked himself in the only bathroom to experiment with his cosmetics and hair ointments. He argued that this was how he would contribute to the family. Once he perfected them, he and Mahalia would sell the beauty products during Mahalia's singing engagements.

The more time Ike spent locked in the bathroom, the more resentful Halie's aunts, Hannah and Alice, became. It became more and more urgent for Mahalia and her husband to move into their own apartment. Money from the cosmetics would make this possible, he said.

Mahalia noticed that her husband spent an inordinate amount of time at the public library. She assumed he was doing research on his cosmetics. She was wrong. Hockenhull spent his spare time studying the pedigree, speed, and endurance of racehorses. He knew the size and design of every important racetrack in the country. He dreamed of owning a racehorse the way Mahalia dreamed of becoming a famous singer and owning her own home.

In time, Mahalia realized Ike's weakness for horses, betting on the horses. She couldn't believe she hadn't realized what he was up to before now. She'd prided herself on having discernment, but when it came to relationships, she learned she had a blind eye. She prayed about her husband's sinful habit and came to the conclusion that it was up to her to help save her husband.

Ike detested the name "Halie" from the beginning, saying it didn't suit her at all. He never called her anything except Mahalia. The things she would learn about Isaac were far more than she knew about him before they married.

Isaac Lane-Gray Hockenhull's parents were from Arkansas and Mississippi. He had spent most of his childhood in Pine Bluff, Arkansas, with his mother Martha "Mattie" Hockenhull. He had also spent some time in Hot Springs, Arkansas, where he must have gained his love for the horses.

Ike and his mother moved up North around the same time that many other coloreds decided there had to be something better. His mother, though, was a beauty culturist and wrote books about beauty and hair. His parents were divorced, and he was cited as a stepson to Robert Hockenhull of Arkansas. Ike told Mahalia that his mother had studied under the great Madam C.J. Walker and learned about hair products and the beauty culture.

Mahalia was working as a hotel maid when she wasn't singing in church. She couldn't understand how this educated man who was 10 years older was really interested in a girl who never knew any school after the fourth grade. But Ike was serious about everything in life. He believed Mahalia had a voice made for great concerts, and he wanted to help steer her toward her destiny.

A year later, the young couple scraped together enough money for an apartment, but the dark times of the Depression dogged Ike so much that he could never get ahead. He'd have regular work for a time, then be laid off again. He was always looking for a way to make money.

Ike's mother was living in St. Louis and had a cosmetics business there, before everything came crashing down. She made up lotions and creams, and put them out under the name "Madam Hockenhull," and they sold really well. Ike knew the formula, and from his chemistry training, he knew how to mix up the batches of powders and oils. He and Mahalia often stayed up all night making up dozens of jars. And Ike would try to find ways of selling them in Chicago while Mahalia would pack a suitcase full of cosmetics to take with her on the road to sell at the gospel meetings.

Ike wasn't happy with Mahalia as she was because he knew she could be so much more. Specifically, he told her over and over that she was destined to be a famous concert singer. Mahalia told him that what he wanted his wife to be didn't make it so.

Mahalia sold quite a lot of Ike's cosmetics. Even that didn't make Ike happy. Mahalia would learn in time that he generally wasn't happy with his life and always saw how it should be different. He was unhappy that her traveling kept them apart, and he didn't like her spending so much time singing gospel songs. Ike didn't grow up in the church and only went on special occasions. If she begged him to, he would attend church with her.

An educated Negro, Ike saw gospel singing as unsophisticated, for uneducated people. He suggested Mahalia take voice training. She told him about the one time she almost took voice lessons and how that interaction had her dead set against ever taking voice lessons again. Come to think of it, she said, she could now see some similarities between that music teacher and Ike.

The couple often argued about Mahalia's singing as if it belonged to both of them. He tried to convince her that gospel was not art. He was incredulous that she would spend so much time on something that anyone could walk out of the cotton field and do. Rather than let Ike make her so mad she'd do something she'd regret later on, she laughed and told him that her music was art to her and God. She said it was part of her history, and she was proud to sing just the way she'd heard folks sing it down South during those great Baptist revival meetings on the Mississippi River when she was a child.

Ike was right, Mahalia could have been a fine opera singer. She could have been a blues or jazz singer. Earl "Fatha" Hines and Louis Armstrong heard about her and wanted her to sing with their jazz bands at the Grand Terrace Ballroom. She wouldn't. It wasn't the kind of life she wanted to live.

People were always encouraging her to become a blues singer. She'd come back with, *"What Negro couldn't become a great blues singer?*

"Blues are the songs of despair, but gospel songs are the songs of hope. When you sing them, you are delivered of your burdens. You have a feeling there is a cure for what's wrong. It always gives me joy to sing gospel songs. I feel better right away. When you get through with the blues, you've got nothing to rest on. I tell people that the person who sings the blues is like someone in a deep pit yelling for help, and I'm simply not in that position."

Mahalia and Ike's arguments about her becoming a popular singer came to a climax when they were both out of work. Ike had been laid off, again, and Mahalia had lost her hotel maid's job because of her traveling obligations. They sat down at the kitchen table one morning and realized they only had a few pennies between them. Ike had a newspaper clipping about the federal theater project casting an all-Negro company for "The Mikado" operetta.

They were holding auditions in Chicago that week to select a girl with an outstanding voice for one of the lead roles. "You can win that role," Ike told Mahalia. "You can have that part if you'll just go around to the theater and sing for them."

Mahalia said it wasn't for her and pushed the clipping back to him. She told him she didn't want to get mixed up with that kind of singing; wanted to stay with her gospel music. Ike was angry that she wouldn't even give it a chance—so angry he was pounding on the table telling her she was throwing her life away and missing all the opportunities. "The Mikado" would take her all over the country, he said, give her training and experience she wouldn't get any other way. Give her recognition all over the country, maybe the world.

Angry, he minimized her gospel singing, saying she'd never get anywhere running around to those churches hollering her head off with those gospel songs. He threw her own words back at her, "God gave you a voice, and you're not using it to become a great artist?"

Finally, they'd both run out of arguments when Ike said, "There's no money in the house, Mahalia. That theater job would pay you $60 a week. I'm going out to find work. You've got to do the same." He laid the clipping on the table and left.

Mahalia has often said that that afternoon was one of the most painful in her whole life. Everything inside her was fighting against the kind of singing she would have to do on the stage. Yet, she knew they needed the money. She'd have to try. She finally took the streetcar downtown to the Great Northern Theatre. She walked up to the side door and asked where they were holding auditions. A white woman on duty pointed her upstairs, but told her she had to bring her music with her. Mahalia held up her little book of Sunday School songs called "Gospel Pearls." That wasn't acceptable, the woman told her and sent Mahalia around the corner to a music store.

At the store, Mahalia found the music for "Sometimes I Feel Like a Motherless Child." It cost 25 cents. She walked slowly back to the theater and to the audition room where it was filled with girls there for the audition. The judges were up front, and a man sat at the piano.

While the other girls were excited, Mahalia was dejected, hoping against hope that they'd chose the girl before they got to her. She soon realized, however, that they were taking people by alphabet. Suddenly, her name was called. When she walked up and handed the pianist her music, she didn't tell him she couldn't read a lick of sheet music.

Most likely, not one girl in the room could have sung "Sometimes I Feel Like a Motherless Child" as Mahalia did. It all came from the heart. She was singing of her feeling of desertion by her husband, and of the loss of a mother she could not remember. She sang the way she felt. Mahalia left the theater knowing they had chosen her, and she couldn't have been more miserable.

She took the streetcar back to the apartment. Ike was already home, too excited to talk clearly as he shouted that she'd won, and they wanted her to come in for rehearsal right away. He seemed not to notice her despondency.

The four most beautiful words that whole evening came from Ike, when Mahalia asked him how his luck had been. "I got a job," he said. That settled it for her. She would not take the singing job. Her decision almost caused the end of their marriage.

Ike's Other Love

Mahalia learned about Ike's "other Love" by happenstance after a weekend singing trip in Buffalo, New York, that ended in her missing her bus home, costing her the hotel cleaning job she had. Now there was no one in the house working full time. How in the world would they eat and pay for the little two-room apartment they'd rented?

Mahalia couldn't go crawling back to her aunts asking them to let her and Ike return. Thanks to Ike, Hannah and Alice were only too happy to see the door close behind them. Wasn't any way to start out a marriage anyway, in a cramped sunroom, with one bathroom for six people, and Ike turning the bathroom and kitchen into his cosmetics lab. Hannah's small place had never been big enough for three people, let alone six. And now Halie was remembering how cold and drafty that sunroom got during the cold Chicago winters.

In their new apartment, Ike used one room for his laboratory, manufacturing cosmetics, and unbeknownst to Mahalia, for analyzing his racing forms, dreaming of the horse that would bring him fortune once he accrued the money to bet on it.

To make up for the money they weren't bringing in, Mahalia set up a part-time beauty parlor in Ike's cosmetics lab. She washed, pressed, and styled hair for church members and friends for a few dollars each. In her mind, this was temporary until they could pull enough money together for her to open herself a real beauty parlor.

Mahalia's long ago dream of becoming a nurse sauntered in from time to time, but it wouldn't stay long. She had to eat and live, and nursing school was taking, not giving, money. Hannah had been right, with not even a fourth-grade education and poor to boot, Mahalia had simply aimed too high. Now Halie was looking at things more realistically. Hannah was right, too, that there was a living to be made in Chicago's ghetto in the hair-dressing business. Even more, once she and Ike had enough money to invest in it.

Mahalia continued to sing wherever she could on Sundays and weekends, and she did hair dressing when she wasn't singing. She and Ike sold his cosmetics whenever they could. Wherever she sang, she took along a suitcase packed with jars of ointments and cosmetics to sell during intermission. Ike was the door-to-door salesman. Gratefully, the cosmetic business was good enough for them to buy groceries, but all too often there wasn't enough left to pay the landlord.

Mahalia and Ike laughed about the rumors going around in the church that they were actually selling conjuring herbs, not cosmetics. The rumors had them preparing voodoo concoctions made of roots and herbs for people who wanted to do harm to others. They went so far as to claim that the couple went out to the graveyard at night to get dirt to sell to people who wished someone bad luck. According to voodoo lore, the buyer of graveyard dirt rubbed it on a glove and shook hands with the unguarded one, bringing bad trouble.

Rent day was a blue day for Mahalia and Ike. Their faces were long, and there was little conversation as they unpacked the jars that they had filled with Ike's hair ointment. Ike put aside the newspaper the jars were wrapped in to read later. Mahalia looked at her husband with a worried look. How much longer would they have to live this way?

Mahalia was now 27, and at this point, she saw no way out of this life of poverty. She wondered about how different being poor in Chicago was from being poor in New Orleans. She hardly knew she was poor back then. There were things she wished she had, but there were few times Aunt Duke had to worry about rent or putting food on her table.

Halie shook her head. She had experienced being poor all her life, but she knew Ike's life had been different. He was used to living better. His people had had enough money to send him to college. She wondered if they'd ever get to that kind of place.

Mahalia never stopped dreaming, in spite of all they didn't have. She desperately wanted children, but first they needed a home where children could sleep and grow. She wanted a yard with flowers and a kitchen big enough for her to cook all the foods she loved to cook. She wanted to enjoy being married, but she saw the years creeping by, and she was afraid she may never see that in her lifetime. Besides, none of that would ever work if Ike didn't stop his gambling. She was still praying night and day for that. She believed that with God's help she could help save him.

Mahalia often wondered what if she'd taken the role with "The Mikado." Where would they be now? They might be doing well. For sure, Ike would be happy. Mahalia would be miserable. She was sure of it.

It was a pity that Ike could never understand that, for her, gospel singing was broadcasting good news. It was the salvation of Blacks. That was what gospel songs were. Good tidings set to music. Gospel singing connected the singer and listener in an outpouring of joyful emotion. And the joyful emotion came from the singer and the listener knowing that each would overcome.

Gospel music was helping Blacks survive the Great Depression. She admired the older gospel singers, the way they carried themselves. They sang while they lived in the ghetto's ugliness. She wanted to walk tall and upright like the older women who walked as though marching to Zion. She worried that Ike might never understand why she couldn't trade her gospel singing for all "The Swing Mikados" in the world.

While they were waiting for Mahalia's miracle to come true, Ike found himself hitting a lucky number at the horses. He had bet $20 on a 100-to-1 horse. The horse won, and Ike collected $2,000. He was more excited than

Mahalia had ever seen him. He came home that day and threw the $2,000 on the bed.

Mahalia's naturally small eyes grew as big as half-dollar coins. She immediately asked her husband where he'd gotten that kind of money. Ike said he'd won it on the horses. His gambling had finally paid off. He'd picked the right number thanks to all his studying.

As they talked through the night about what they should do, Ike suggested Mahalia hold on to the money until they decided where to buy a home. Mahalia fell on her knees thanking God for this miracle, but she worried about what to do with all that money.

She was afraid to carry it with her to Detroit, afraid someone would hit her over her head and rob her. And she was afraid to leave it home where Ike would come back looking for it. Finally, she got the idea of rolling up the rug in their bedroom and laying it under there, bill by bill, until the whole floor was covered with $10 and $20 bills. Finally comfortable that no one would guess the money was under the rug, she went to Detroit.

When she returned, the first thing she did before kicking off her shoes and throwing off her coat was check under the rug. It didn't take her long to realize that every last dollar of the money was gone. Mahalia knew in her heart what had happened. She was heartbroken. Why hadn't she put it in the bank? She should have known better. She checked her locks, her windows. She knew, no one had broken into the house.

When Ike arrived home, Mahalia was in tears. Ike comforted her, saying all wasn't lost. He had found the money and used it to buy a racehorse, a great investment for their future. Mahalia was beyond angry.

"Ike, that's a lot of money to pay for a horse. Especially since I don't eat horsemeat."

He'd laughed. Mahalia could be hilarious when she wanted to, he thought. "Silly goose. This horse is not for eating. He's a racehorse."

"And…when will you race him, Ike? I want to know. Because I don't want that money if you win."

"I'll race him in a couple of months," he answered nonchalantly.

151

"And, where are you keeping this horse of yours, since there's hardly enough room in this apartment for the two of us? And, what will he eat?"

Ike frowned. He'd had enough of the questions. "Look, Mahalia…I'm putting him in a boarding stable till I race him."

Mahalia looked at her husband. She didn't understand him anymore than he understood her commitment to singing gospel, even when they were starving.

Mahalia and Ike's relationship was never really the same after that. He had finally realized he would never change her. He'd pester her every once in a while, but he'd given up. While they remained married for a time, there would forever be the singing that sat between them, and his love for the horses.

Finally, they both decided the marriage was just a sham. Even after their divorce, the two remained friends. Mahalia would always believe Ike truly loved her and had nothing but her best interests at heart. When asked how it felt to be divorced given how close she was to the church, Mahalia answered that she was meant to give her life to God and the church, and she wasn't ashamed of that.

Mahalia took the brunt of the blame for their breakup, saying she understood that a man wouldn't want his wife running all around, even if it's for the Lord. But she said it wasn't something she could ever stop doing.

"When you have something deep inside of you, when you're torn apart by it, when you've got to express what's inside of you for the world, nothing can stop you—and I guess that's the way it was with me. I gave the other things up for the work I wanted to do."

Mahalia knew that Ike's horse gambling was part of the blame for their failed marriage. She had tried all she could to help him quit. She'd prayed constantly that God would take away his love for the racetracks. For whatever reason, God hadn't. It wasn't for her to understand.

Blues Dressed in Sunday Clothes

In the spring of 1939, Mahalia was finishing up her choir practice when she felt a pair of eyes directed at her. This time, it wasn't a tall handsome young man, but a slight older man with a different kind of intellect from the man who had come to her church staring at her before.

Thomas Dorsey walked into Greater Salem Baptist Church looking for her. He had an offer he hoped the 28-year-old Mahalia Jackson wouldn't refuse. Mahalia listened quietly to the song maker's proposal before asking, "What's a song plugger?" Dorsey patiently explained that it was a person employed to promote a composer's songs and induce people to buy them.

Dorsey told the young singer that he could write a truckload of religious songs, but if he couldn't get them sold, he might as well not go through the trouble. In 1939, Dorsey's music publishing house competed with five other firms headed by equally gifted Black composers.

Dorsey was at the peak of his musical life. It was just a few years since he'd returned to the church, getting baptized a second time and declaring he was saved again. Dorsey had lived a blues man's life for most of his adult life, creating blues songs—under the name "Georgia Tom"—that made many a good man want to sin, and many a sinner sin even more.

Recognized as a prolific songwriter and composer, Dorsey had gained his reputation at a cost. This musical genius had had two nervous breakdowns and lost his beloved wife and their infant son during childbirth. Dorsey was admired, but with skepticism, by Black churches where people knew his blues history and questioned the validity of his conversion.

But, since returning to the church, Dorsey composed religious songs as diligently as he had created the blues. Not surprisingly, even these sacred songs made the church people dance—a holy dance. Dorsey, the blues magician, became the church magician. But he was still looked down on by many proper churches as blues dressed in Sunday clothes.

Dorsey knew more about Mahalia Jackson than he let on. He'd followed her rise and listened to her from back pews more than once. He decided she was the woman and her voice was the sound he needed.

Mahalia Jackson was finally on the road to becoming somebody. Her musical career was finally smoothing out, and her reality was catching up to her dreams. Mahalia's voice was at its strongest. There was a confidence and poise in her performances. An indelible Mahalia style was forming itself.

Mahalia had earned a little money recording her gospel songs, even though her records, "God's Gonna Separate the Wheat from the Tares," "Keep Me Every Day," and "God Will Wipe All Tears Away," had been copied by other companies without her permission. She didn't complain too loud because they sold so well that she would eventually profit from their success.

It is little wonder that Mahalia Jackson and Thomas Dorsey's paths would cross. They were both accused of singing the same kind of gospel—blues dressed in Sunday clothing. Mahalia had been trying for more than 10 years by then to break into Chicago's churches. They all heard the blues when she opened her mouth, saw the writhing of her body as she sang, and declared her sacrilegious, at best.

The composer had introduced his first gospel hit in 1926, "If You See My Savior, Tell Him That You Saw Me." Mahalia knew it well. He told her he'd had 500 copies printed, borrowing money to mail the song to churches throughout the country. Three years passed before he sold a single copy.

When the National Baptist Convention—the very one that snubbed Mahalia for years—met in Chicago in 1930, Dorsey hired a girl to sing the song at the meeting in the coliseum. When she finished singing, he told Mahalia, everyone was crying. The musical director of the biggest Baptist organization in the land let Dorsey sell all the copies of the song he wanted to sell. That is what a song plugger can do, he told Mahalia.

Mahalia stared hard at this man she'd heard so much about and whose path she'd crossed a few times. Who was this Thomas Dorsey, she wondered? In fact, he was something nearing a male version of Mahalia—both of them uneducated, but with enough spunk and belief in themselves that they created their own success. Never saying never; never giving up their dreams no matter how many nay-sayers were in their path.

Dorsey was the son of an itinerant Baptist preacher whose wife served as organist on Sundays and worked in white families' homes during the week. The Dorsey family lived in Villa Rica, Georgia, a small town near Atlanta. Early on, Thomas Dorsey's parents realized they had a musical prodigy on their hands. The child had mastered several musical instruments at a very early age—all except the piano, and only because there was no piano in his home or in his father's church.

A music teacher who lived four miles away in the country offered to teach the child how to play the piano. Dorsey walked the distance from his home to the teacher's house for lessons four times a week. From his teacher, he learned to play ragtime, blues, jazz, and religious music.

In spite of the young Tom Dorsey's extraordinary capacity for learning and playing music, he fell in love with the circus and playing music with the circus band. He ran away with the circus in middle school. After a few years, he left the circus and began ghetto entertainment where he earned $1.50 a night stomping a piano at Saturday night dances.

Still a teenager, he fell madly in love with a beautiful girl who rejected him. Dejected, he stopped playing music for a time and joined the Great Migration, moving from Georgia to the Midwest. First, he worked in steel mills in Gary, Indiana. While he had left music behind, music wouldn't leave him. He eventually organized a five-piece band to play music at parties, including jazz arrangements that he created. He played in the Black communities of Gary and South Chicago.

Dorsey yearned to compose his own music. With the money he earned from his party entertainment, he signed up for composition lessons at a music school in Chicago. It wasn't long before he became a huge success in Chicago where he was known as "the whispering pianist."

Dorsey eventually joined Chicago's Pilgrim Baptist Church. It was there he heard a gospel song entitled "I Do, Don't You?" that he would later say moved him more than any music he had ever heard, even blues. That song propelled him to write church music that would give others the same heart-shaking experience he had listening to "I Do, Don't You?"

To earn a living, Dorsey took a job with a band, but he later organized his own band, which toured with and backed up Ma Rainey. The Ma Rainey's Rabbit Foot Minstrels followed the South's Black entertainment circuit from cotton plantations to sugar fields to turpentine distilleries—wherever Blacks labored. Thomas Dorsey became known as Georgia Tom, the blues pianist and composer.

It was in 1932 when Dorsey returned to the church and to writing sacred songs. He wrote thousands of songs in the course of his career. His most famous song was "Take My Hand, Precious Lord," which would later become Reverend Martin Luther King Jr.'s favorite.

Mahalia listened while Dorsey talked about the bright future for gospel music. He wanted Mahalia to sing his new songs. They could lift the spirit and inspire Blacks to carry on the unfinished fight for freedom. But, should she agree to go on the road with Dorsey? She was getting along in years— 28 now. She had to put something aside for a rainy day. Would this be the way to do it? Could she spend still more years living out of a suitcase? That was one of the reasons she and Ike had broken up. He wanted a wife in the home, not on the road.

Mahalia admired Dorsey. Like herself, he wasn't ashamed to admit he had been born in the South. Nor was he ashamed of his gospel music, the music some middle-class Blacks derided as "cotton picking" songs, calling gospel singers "nappy-headed shouters."

Mahalia considered her Chicago income in comparison to what she might make on the road with Dorsey. She was earning $10 a week singing at funerals. Occasionally, she earned as much as $50 a week from concerts, and the free-will offerings added something on top. Now and then, she got $25 for cutting a record.

Finally, after weighing all her options, Mahalia said yes, if Dorsey could promise they'd return to Chicago often enough for her to start her beauty parlor. He promised they'd return to Chicago often enough for her to keep a handle on her business.

Mahalia didn't see the need to tell Thomas Dorsey she needed to get out of Chicago until she could get past some of the pain of a failed marriage. Ike had left, and she was missing him. If she stayed here, she wouldn't stop missing him and would surely take him back if he asked. Even knowing their marriage wasn't working and wouldn't work. Neither of them was changing.

Dorsey hired Bob Jones, an old gospel singer who had lost his voice, as their driver. The only trouble with Bob Jones was that he dozed off sometimes while driving and often lost his way. The three of them headed south from Chicago early on a Friday morning to host an evening program in a Baptist church in Springfield, Illinois. Their gas tank was full, but for safety they carried an emergency supply of gas and oil in case they ran out and a white filling station attendant chose not to sell them fuel. That sometimes happened in this part of the country. Mahalia had prepared sandwiches and coffee so they wouldn't have to go to the rear of segregated restaurants to buy food.

Thomas Dorsey had traveled these roads before with circuses and jazz bands, or with Ma Rainey, or with his "Evening with Dorsey" gospel music concerts. As they traveled, he kept up a steady stream of stories of his checkered past. Mahalia loved stories and listened intently, until he began telling her how she sang. She was remembering how Ike had wanted to tell her how to sing, and she was losing her patience with Tom Dorsey doing the same. With a sweet smile plastered on her face, Mahalia told Dorsey she would sing the song the way she wanted to, and she always had to wait until the moment before she started singing to find out how she felt she should sing.

Shaking his head, Dorsey reminded the younger singer that he was a composer and had written and composed music for respected Blacks and successful white singers and orchestra leaders, and that he knew just about all there was to know about music.

Mahalia laughed when she realized that with all his knowledge and experience, Tom Dorsey didn't have much more sway with Black churches than she did. Many ministers still objected to gospel songs and gospel singers. They had to work hard to persuade Black middle-class congregations to listen and give gospel music a chance.

But the real obstacles were the Black ministers. It came down to this—if a minister let a gospel singer in his church, that gospel singer had the means to take over the spiritual leadership of the church. She could sing one song and set a church on fire with more spirited rejoicing than a preacher could with a two-hour sermon. And most gospel singers were, after all, women. Could a preacher stand to one side while a woman took over the leadership of his flock?

When they came to the little Baptist church in Springfield where Mahalia was to sing, she realized it was too poor to afford even a church mouse. The floor sagged under her weight. Through the cracks in it, she could see the basement below. No matter. They began their program. Dorsey played the piano, and Mahalia sang.

After a moment, Dorsey stopped to remind Mahalia he was playing one of his own compositions. He didn't like the way she was rearranging it, bending his notes, giving his lyrics her own phrasing. But he had to admire the young woman. Big, forceful, fiery, overpowering with her talent and presence. She was a real stretch-out singer, breaking all the rules, changing the melody and meter as the spirit dictated. Singing to that mysterious inner beat that would present difficulties to any musician who tried to accompany her.

When Dorsey and Mahalia finished, the audience's "Thank you, Jesus! Thank you, Jesus!" took a long time to end. In the back of the church, their driver Bob Jones checked the cash receipts. Dorsey and Mahalia would get

40 percent. The church took 60. Bob had traveled with Dorsey from the days when the converted jazz musician played for Ma Rainey and the unsaved. One of his last chores was to find out the best route to their next stop.

The gospel pioneers stayed long enough after the program to eat supper. That was why they were called "fish-and-bread" singers. "We sang for our supper as well as for the Lord," Mahalia explained.

Then the three of them would head on to Cairo, Illinois, and from there to Memphis, Tennessee, and on down to Birmingham, Alabama. They traveled over bumpy dirt roads, and Mahalia saw Blacks working the vast stretches of land. The trio drove through company-store country where, from one crop to another, the people lived on credit from the grocer. It was a land where the roof over the people's heads was rented to them by the same man who sold them the meat, molasses, and cornmeal on credit. Down here among these people, Mahalia felt she had come back to her source, and it renewed her. Here in the unhurried South, she was one with the people.

While they traveled, Dorsey began writing songs especially tailored to fit Mahalia's style. As she sang the songs written for her, she found that people began following her from town to town, from church to church. And she saw that it pleased Dorsey when his songs, his soloists, his gospel music were treasured by audiences above the gospel music of his competitors.

Birmingham was established as a gospel capital of America. But the nearby town of Bessemer tried to take the crown away from Birmingham with a gospel program that featured some of the most popular singers in the land. They called this program "Back to God Day."

When it came Mahalia's turn to sing, she saw more people than she had ever sung for—50,000 people! A crowd made up of Blacks and whites, separated. Some people were standing; others sitting in their shabby wagons behind their tired horses and mules. They were separated but equal in their love of gospel music.

This time, Mahalia could not sing with her eyes shut, for Dorsey had scores of new compositions for her to try. He handed them to her, one by one, and she read the words and sang. There were 20 songs by the time she finished, and he let her sing them her own way. The people who had come hundreds of miles to hear her went wild—some of them fainting, shouting (getting happy), and doing holy dances all over the place.

Mahalia traveled with Thomas Dorsey for five years. She sang his songs her own way, fighting most of the suggestions he made to "improve" her voice. Some of his advice she did listen to, such as how to "talk up a song" in between verses, how to protect herself from the crooked promoters, how to work out contracts for sharing in royalties from her recordings, and how to appraise her audience.

She told him, "When I enter a meeting, I don't know what I'm going to sing. I walk in, I get the vibration of the people in the place, and then the song comes."

This amazing music education and training continued for five years, and both Mahalia and Dorsey would become better because of it. Thomas Dorsey would eventually become known as the "Father of Gospel Music," and Mahalia Jackson would become known as the "Queen of Gospel."

Becoming Mahalia—The Birth of a Star

Mahalia, at 33, was closing one door and preparing to open others. Five years of bouncing over the country in automobiles with Thomas Dorsey—former known as Georgia Tom—and living out of a suitcase were enough. Thirty-three and feeling at least 10 years older, Mahalia needed a change from the endless one-night stands. It was time to settle down in Chicago. Time to find a husband—another husband—and have a family, if the good Lord was willing.

Now and then, Mahalia had interrupted her travels to return to Chicago to take lessons in beauty culture and flower arranging. With her touring now over, she did not come home without the means to make a go of it in business. She opened Mahalia's Beauty Parlor, which in time employed six people and was highly successful.

Once she realized the beauty shop could run without her full-time oversight, she left its day-to-day management to her most competent employee and immediately started another business—Mahalia's House of Flowers, which also proved successful.

Blacks bought flowers from her for weddings, parties, and funerals so they could engage her to sing at their affairs. She could have sold them weeds provided her voice went with the weeds. Mahalia sold a lot of flowers because she knew a large number of ministers and undertakers who were always trying different ways to get her to sing for them. As for her beauty shop, she knew all the gospel singers in Chicago. They came to get their hair washed and set.

Mahalia became a success in business. She bought property with her profits. First came an apartment building, so she'd have a place all to herself and where she could sing as loudly as she pleased.

Throughout her venture into business, Mahalia never gave up her singing. She still performed in and around Chicago on weekends. Not only would she sing at churches, but Mahalia was not above accepting requests to sing at tent revivals, jails, reform schools, and even hospitals. She would often visit—along with her pastor, Reverend Seal from Pilgrim Baptist Church—the bedside of the sick. While Reverend Seal prayed, Mahalia would sing. At tent revivals, she sometimes began singing at 11 a.m. and would continue through the last alter call the next morning. Many in the revival congregation would flock to Mahalia after the service.

During this period in her career, Mahalia began traveling to states with high concentrations of Black churches—Detroit; Newark, New Jersey; Philadelphia; and New York City. The congregations wanted her to sing the old songs of faith the way they had heard them sung in cotton fields, under revival tents, and at churches like Mt. Moriah. To these Blacks, her songs were like letters from folks back home.

Mahalia was the first gospel singer to sing and later record using the organ, along with the piano. When she recorded "God's Gonna Wipe All Tears Away" with Decca Records, the organ accompaniment created quite a stir in religious circles.

At the urgent request of New York gospel promoter Johnny Myers, Mahalia went to New York City to work with Elder Brodie in a 10-day citywide revival at the Golden Gate Theater. She set a record at a religious program, attracting two audiences of 5,000 persons each, on the same day.

Soon after, Mahalia received a recording contract with Apollo Records. While her first recording was not well received, her next—a two-sided version of "Move on Up a Little Higher"—was a huge success, quickly surpassing two million copies in sales nationwide.

Joe Bostic—a prominent Black New York promoter, disc jockey, and TV sportscaster—presented Mahalia in a sold-out gospel concert at the nation's famed Carnegie Hall in New York City on October 4, 1950. It was the first time Carnegie hosted a gospel event, and Mahalia's performance drew multiple encores and rave reviews from critics.

The next year, long lines of over 3,500 people waited to hear Mahalia. Busloads of fans from upstate New York, as well as the adjoining states of Connecticut and Massachusetts, were turned away. Some 300 folding chairs were placed on stage to help accommodate the overflow crowd, and the fans swarmed over the stage, intent on witnessing the performance. Every available space was sold out and late comers were turned away in droves. Mahalia mused about this turn in her life.

"Who would'a ever thought a little barefoot girl from Louisiana who played ball along the levee by the Mississippi River would someday stand on the stage at Carnegie Hall…. With God, all things are possible if we can just believe. From my childhood I was taught, 'In all thy ways acknowledge Him, and He will direct thy path.'"

Over the next few years, Mahalia was featured in five more sold-out appearances at Carnegie Hall, breaking the records of the legendary "King of Swing" Benny Goodman and the acclaimed Italian conductor Arturo Toscanini.

In 1951, in Dayton, Ohio, Mahalia wowed an interracial crowd of 50,000 people who lined the streets throughout the city for a "Welcome Mahalia Jackson" demonstration. Police said the demonstration exceeded a turnout for President Harry Truman several months earlier.

In 1952, Mahalia was invited to tour Europe, where she would make stops across the continent to share her unique brand of gospel, something most Europeans had never heard. The tour was a great triumph, even if the staid Englanders were not ready for Mahalia's style of down-home gospel.

In Paris, French jazz critic and record producer Hughes Panassié and French author and jazz expert Charles Delaunay paid a once-in-a-lifetime tribute to Mahalia Jackson. Panassié and Delaunay, heads of warring factions in the French capitol, both arrived at the airport at the same time to greet the gospel singer when she arrived in Paris. Mahalia laughed when she learned the two men hadn't spoken to each other in years. In Mahalia's presence, they had greeted each other warmly and posed together for pictures with her. Mahalia was dubbed "an angel of peace descending from the skies."

There was never a time during this period in her success that Mahalia was not courted by big production companies that wanted her to sing blues or jazz, or to sing in nightclubs or theaters—for more money than she'd ever make singing gospel. She continued to refuse, remembering the promise she'd made to God in exchange for her grandfather's life.

However, she always made clear that she had nothing against blues and jazz singers. "Some of our finest jazz singers were once church singers," she'd say. Mahalia, herself, once sang gospel next to the flamboyant, guitar-playing rock 'n' roll artist Sister Rosetta Tharpe. And blues and jazz singer Dinah Washington was once Mahalia's accompanist.

In 1954 and 55, the City of Chicago feted Mahalia at the Chicago Sun-Times Harvest Moon Festival. More than 25,000 people came out to hear her at each of the two successive festivals. She is said to have stolen the show that included performers with top-ranking theatrical names.

Mahalia's name was suddenly gold, and within five years, her voice, as well as her face, was known all over the world. The former fish-and-bread singer around the South was now being deluged with offers to perform on radio and television. Between 1955 and 1965, Mahalia's Hollywood schedule grew to include guest starring on others' shows, but also to be contracted to star in her own radio and television shows.

Mahalia co-starred on some of the greatest television shows of the times—"Red Skelton," "Ed Sullivan," "Arthur Godfrey," "Wake Up and Live," "Arlene Francis," "Dinah Shore," "Nat King Cole," "Studs Terkel," and her own "The Mahalia Jackson Show" on CBS. She also hosted her own radio show, also titled "The Mahalia Jackson Show," and guest-starred in dozens of other radio shows.

A Christmas Homecoming

The producer for Dave Garroway's "Wide World" TV series called Mahalia one morning and asked if she could sing for them. She said she'd love to, but was currently on her way home to New Orleans. She was spending Christmas at home for the first time in 13 years. That was fine with them, they said. They could tape from New Orleans with her singing in the little church where it all began.

Mahalia was excited to be going home. There were so many people she'd missed over the last 13 years. So many memories she wanted to revisit. She couldn't wait to walk inside the house she'd grown up in with her brother Peter, Aunt Duke and Uncle Emanuel, and all the aunts and cousins coming in and out.

She had to admit that she was also excited about Garroway's Christmas television show being shot down in her hometown—"in my old church where I first sang in the children's choir when I was 5 years old." She still had to pinch herself sometimes to make sure her life was real—mostly that God had blessed her beyond all her dreams.

Mahalia decided to split up where she was staying to keep the peace—first with Ida Beal and Elliott, then with Doodutz, then Ellen Blount. She was fussing when she arrived home. Just before she'd arrived in Jackson, Mississippi, the police stopped her, claiming she was going 90 miles an hour. When she disputed their clock, they became belligerent, warning her not to argue and fining her $100.

Mahalia and her entourage arrived about a week before Christmas Eve, but for Mahalia, it was like Christmas the whole time she was there. For the longest, she claimed it was the best Christmas of her entire life. Known for her generous heart, Mahalia shopped during the whole vacation for her family, especially the children, not wanting to leave anyone out. Then came the aunts and uncles from New Orleans and all around—most, she'd never met before. They had come along after she left New Orleans. And her father's other family—his wife, his children, and his siblings were the well-known secret in "Nigger Town."

It wasn't long before the big colored churches in downtown New Orleans learned about the Garraway program. The first night Mahalia was in town, ministers came calling to invite her to broadcast from downtown. They had big choirs with trained singers, they bragged. They were also sure they could present better music than little old Mt. Moriah Missionary Baptist Church on Millaudon Street.

Mahalia thanked them kindly for the invitation, but said she had already promised her little church. In fact, it meant a lot to her to film the show in her own little church where she was raised and received her first religious training.

One of the plans for Christmas was to create a Christmas party for Duke and Aunt Bell— one they wouldn't forget. Mahalia's grocery list was endless. The grocers thought they'd died and gone to heaven.

On her second day back home, Mahalia drove around the 16th Ward—the place she'd grown up—to see who from the old choir might still be around and willing to participate in the church filming. They'd had a dynamic sound back then when they were children. Many of her old friends, she learned, had never left town.

Mahalia knew that she'd need to convince them that she was the same old Mahalia before they agreed to be a part of the filming. She was amazed to learn that some of the old choir members didn't have television sets and didn't know that Mahalia Jackson was a name that most people around the country recognized, or what kind of singing she did. What they saw was the big car she drove, with the Illinois license plate. She could see in their faces they weren't sure how different she might be from the girl who'd left all those years ago.

Mahalia talked about the old times, the things they used to do as children. She hadn't forgotten, and she remembered it all with fondness. She needed them to know the part of her life that included them was a very important part of her life. "Can you remember playing out on the Mississippi levee, and all those songs we sang out there? The songs we sang out there, like "High Society" and "When the Saints Go Marching in?" The more she talked, the more some of them came around.

How could Mahalia ever forget the joy in cooking Christmas dinner? It was not a day or two-day or even a three-day affair. Very often, it was a weeklong preparation and cooking that led up to Christmas dinner.

Mothers, grandmothers, aunts, sisters all took great pride in creating something special for their families on Christmas Day. The meals they prepared were enough to make you ache they were so good. Mahalia remembered dinners with red beans and rice and French bread, toasted and buttered, with great big oysters from the Gulf of Mexico to drop on top. There was seafood—red snapper baked with tomato sauce and Louisiana seasoning; big platters of boiled crabs; and sea turtle cooked like smothered chicken. Big platters were piled with a vegetable called peppergrass that you eat like turnip greens after it's been cooked with ham, smoked ribs, or salt pork.

Mahalia told her family she hadn't eaten so good in 20 years. Though she often cooked one or two New Orleans and Cajun dishes for herself or friends, it was nothing like the full meals they cooked back home.

Her childhood friends, one by one, agreed to come to the church and sing for Garroway's Christmas show. Mahalia had shown them that she was, after all, the same Halie who used to love baseball and fight the boys and sing at church on Sunday. They were all excited but still a little nervous about coming to the church and singing on camera. Mahalia convinced them it would all be fun.

Mahalia wasn't just trying to convince them. This was important to her, to her memory of their childhood together. And, more importantly, each one of her friends had amazing voices, and any of them could be where she was if they'd believed and had the kind of faith that she had.

They were shy about it at first, but then they said they'd try. There was a rehearsal every day before the filming. Mahalia told them that all of the program wouldn't be shown on the show, but she hoped their singing "Time Again" would. They worked hard to get it just right. Mahalia's young cousin named Molly, a beautiful Black child with glossy hair and keen features, played Mahalia singing as a child.

As Mahalia watched her past coming to life, the memories of her childhood began showing up often. She remembered the days she skipped in and out of the church as a little girl. She was emotional as she sat in the church watching the child emulate her early life.

It was a warm Christmas in New Orleans. Mahalia walked up and down the streets of the neighborhood. She recalled the many days she'd watched the boats on the Mississippi River from China and South America.

How she'd lain awake at night listening to the Negro stevedores singing and whistling as they worked on the riverboats and the belt trains that ran alongside the river to pick up the ship cargoes.

She drove over to see the big changes on St. Charles Street, where they were converting some of the great, white pillared mansions into apartment houses and boardinghouses. She recalled they claimed there were 12 millionaires living right on that one avenue where she worked in the white folks' homes and where Aunt Duke cooked.

All the decent clothes she'd had as a child had come from the white people's homes, as did a lot of the food that helped feed their family. Now, though, there was a different spirit in the city. The Negro and whites were even further apart now than they were when segregation was legal, she felt. Aunt Duke said there was a meanness among some of the new white people she had never known. It seemed strange that New Orleans, a city of so much mixed and colored blood, should be carrying on that way. But the bitterness about the new rights the colored people were pressing for was causing it.

On Christmas Eve, Mahalia took all the children downtown and bought more horns and balloons. After supper, they went to Mt. Moriah Church for the Christmas Eve service. The new pastor was Reverend Robert Hack, who was just a young Sunday school teacher when Mahalia was a child attending the church. He had married one of Mahalia's friends before he was ordained as the pastor.

Johnny Jackson attended the program that night. So did her older brother Peter and her sisters Pearl and Yvonne. And, of course, Aunt Duke and Aunt Bessie, the two aunts who Mahalia credited with raising her, were there.

Bill Russell, an old friend and musicologist from Chicago, was now living in New Orleans, still studying Negro music. He came around with a surprise—a Christmas tree, which he set up for Mahalia. The friends stayed up late talking, and Mahalia jumped on the phone and called everyone she knew to wish them a Merry Christmas.

Mahalia slept late on Christmas morning, but woke up worried about the television program. She and Bill Russell went around to the church and found that the television crew was already there with their trucks setting up the special equipment. The neighborhood was very quiet. Mahalia knew most women were home finishing up Christmas dinner. She was nervous about what kind of crowd they'd have for the program and sent up a special prayer.

As if God received a direct dial from her, the people began to come. The streets outside began to fill up and the choir singers arrived right on time. Some were a little frightened, but they wouldn't let Mahalia or the church down. Everyone came in for a final practice and loosened up. The church was, after all, filled to the rafters. Mahalia couldn't hold back the tears as she looked out and saw the faces of the people she had sung with as a child. They were tears of happiness that she was truly back home.

When the red lights on the cameras blinked, Mahalia knew they were being filmed live. She had chosen two of her favorite songs, "Born in Bethlehem" and "Sweet Little Jesus Boy," which was slower but had a powerful moving feeling to it. Everything went just fine. To celebrate afterward, everyone headed over to Aunt Duke's home, turning it into a giant dining room.

Christmas dinner included: Louisiana gumbo, roast turkey with all the extra dishes, and blackberry pie, jelly roll cakes, and port wine for dessert. Throughout dinner, the telephone never stopped ringing, nor did the telegrams stop coming. Aunt Duke looked at her niece and smiled, finally admitting she had done good and how happy she was that Mahalia had stayed with the church.

Aunt Duke hesitated before sharing with Mahalia how hard it had been to see her go off to Chicago after she'd promised Charity she'd look after her. How could she look after her way up there in Chicago? The two women, the aunt and the adopted daughter, cried together as Aunt Duke shared just how much she worried and how often she prayed that Mahalia would be fine and stay with the Lord. "And you did. You did. And Charity is smiling down on both of us."

The day after Christmas, Mahalia's joy was dashed when she made a trip downtown to shop. Both whites and Blacks recognized her and came over to tell her how much they enjoyed her television special. The weather had turned even warmer, and it was so hot she could hardly breathe.

She searched for a place to sit and drink, but there was no restaurant nearby that served coloreds. That was when Mahalia realized that her success and fame only went so far. It didn't change hearts, and it didn't change racism that was as old as slavery.

Whites were calling her long-distance from all over the county and the world to tell her how much they loved her. But in her own hometown where she was born and bred, she couldn't get a cool drink of water, a place to sit and rest her feet, or a taxi ride back to Aunt Duke's. It would be a few more years before restaurants integrated, allowing Blacks to sit down in the same place as whites.

Mahalia vowed not to let this ugly truth about New Orleans and her country mar her homecoming. She would continue to visit New Orleans as long as she had family there, but she knew she could never live in a place that harbored such injustice in their laws and in their hearts. Chicago was home now, where she had become accustomed to freedom and equity.

Part 7

LOOKING FOR A HOME AND FINDING DESTINY
(1956)

"There comes a time when one must take a position that is neither safe, nor politic, nor popular, but he must take it because conscience tells him it is right."

—Martin Luther King Jr., "A Testament of Hope: The Essential Writings and Speeches"

LEFT: MAHALIA IN REPOSE AFTER MOVING INTO HER NEW HOME IN CHATHAM, CHICAGO (GETTY CREDIT). **RIGHT:** MAHALIA AND MARTIN AT CHICAGO'S SOLDIER FIELD, 1964 (TULANE CREDIT).

Finding a Home

Mahalia was 45 years old and feeling a lot older most days, often joking with her closest friends and family that she was just born a tired old
woman. Those who knew her realized there was some truth wrapped up
in her joking. Still, Halie sensed the new weariness might have something
to do with how fast her star had risen in the last 10 years—more fame and
fortune than she could have dreamed. Lord knows she'd worked for it, had
been working toward it since those early years at Mt. Moriah Church.

This exhaustion, though, was different from all those years ago when
she was washing clothes for the white families, taking care of white people's children, cooking and cleaning in the rich folks' homes, and in her
own home with Aunt Duke at the helm. Mahalia sometimes chuckled that
it seemed as if she'd always been taking care of white folks' houses, tending their children, or cleaning their dirty clothes. Back then, she had been
proud to say she could work like a mule all day, lay her body down at night,
and then wake up in the morning rested and ready to do it all over again.
Now, the weariness set with her, began in the muscles and inside her bones;
messed with her mind and spirit.

Still, she was Halie with the smile that lit up rooms and made friends
forget their woes and disbelieve she had any troubles of her own. Halie,
with the jolly laughter, witty comebacks, and pocketful of stories from old
New Orleans. Mahalia hid her exhaustion well, only letting it show itself at
night when she closed her doors to the world, or during those days when
those in her closest circle were there to soothe her anxieties.

Mahalia Jackson didn't know any better than to bring every ounce of
who she was with her when she left New Orleans in 1927. She didn't know
that the Southern immigrants wouldn't like being reminded of their harsh
back home experiences. Even the joys that were special in those old days
were tainted with the past.

She learned to choose carefully who she shared memories with, even
the ones laced with joy. The painful memories she pushed way down inside
her. The memories found a place to settle, in her joints, her heart, along her

shoulders, deep inside her spine. They sometimes slowed her down, made her doubt her right to be where she was in life.

Aunt Duke had told her you couldn't run away from who you are. In time, Halie's new pressures and old pains would contrive to fill her with unexplainable fears, force her to begin to question this thing the world called success. *I'm doing God's work, even if I'm dog tired. I'll continue to sing his songs, raise him up in praise.* Satchmo, Duke Ellington, Harry Belafonte…they'd all tried to convince Mahalia Jackson to "explore other avenues," but she'd never leave her gospel behind.

Not even her golden voice could protect Mahalia Jackson from America's racial troubles. A middle-aged Black woman making her way in Chicago during America's darkest era since slavery. Newly wealthy, globally famous, Mahalia was excited in 1955 about searching for and finally finding a home, something she'd dreamed about all her life.

With her natural sense for numbers and investing, Mahalia had started buying properties, land and buildings, as soon as she started making money. But this would be her largest investment yet—her own home.

It was Chicago in 1955, however, and there was a boulder that stood in Mahalia's way as she began the process of purchasing her home. It hadn't taken her long to realize that white owners changed their tunes quickly after they learned she was a Negro seeking to purchase her home in a predominantly white neighborhood.

Most people didn't know to call the racial boundaries that were so much a part of Chicago's real estate culture, "redlining." And, though segregation was deep in the DNA of New Orleans at the time, it was seen by both Blacks and whites as "just the way things are." There were mixed communities in New Orleans made up of poor Blacks and poor white immigrants who found themselves all scrambling for dirt cheap housing and manual labor.

Mahalia had spent most of her 46 years in Chicago, where the legal name for the racist real estate business was, indeed, redlining. Legal and hardly ever discussed, the housing policy continued for decades past Reconstruction, past the groundswell called Black migration into the city, and maybe was even bolstered by it. Redlining continued to restrict Black families from purchasing homes in white communities and twisted the real estate laws to ensure already impoverished Blacks almost always paid more for less in Chicago's housing community.

In 1956, redlining was alive and well in Chicago, predating the iconic docudrama "A Raisin in the Sun." First a play, then a movie, "A Raisin in the Sun" showcased the experiences of one Black Chicago family's fight to move into the community of their choice, a community which happened to be all white. Redlining, Mahalia would soon learn, was just one more of her new home's racial and cultural ills.

After months of disappointments, Mahalia received a call one day from her attorney. A white surgeon and his family were moving and were selling their home in Chicago's Chatham community, one of the neighborhoods Mahalia had fallen in love with. What's more, the doctor said, he adored Mahalia Jackson and her music. His family would be delighted to sell their home to the gospel singer.

Mahalia called the doctor's offer a godsend. While she and her lawyer had agreed that a lawsuit might be their next step, she was more than happy to find an option to that route. Shrewd and practical, she fully understood that taking on a legal battle would bring undesired media coverage, and in spite of her notoriety, the coverage would likely not be in her favor. She imagined her name appearing in newspapers and being broadcast on radio shows and even television shows around the country. She was certain that many of her white fans who loved her music wouldn't love her stand on integrating a white neighborhood. Such a move could very well prove harmful to her career.

Mahalia's attorney explained to her that redlining in the North was a more sophisticated separation of the races than the ones practiced in the South where Jim Crow was just as effective. She'd fast realized that the entrenched housing policy was alive and well in other Northern cities like New York, Detroit, Boston, and Washington, D.C., where more and more Blacks were becoming middle class and seeking better housing. Redlining was deeply entrenched in the American way and hard to fight. For decades, Black families had been prevented from pursuing the American dream of owning their own homes because of real estate laws that ensure that no matter how Blacks pulled themselves up by their own bootstraps, they wouldn't be moving next door to whites.

Just weeks before Christmas in 1956, Mahalia Jackson became a home-owner in Chatham, a beautiful neighborhood on Chicago's South Side. The predominantly white neighborhood reminded her of the New Orleans' homes she'd worked in for wealthy white families. The seven-room bunga-low home would in time become a tourist site for whites and Blacks alike once they learned who lived there.

Mahalia chuckled at the word "redlining," wondering why it wasn't called "blacklining" or "black balling." She didn't recall any real attention being put on segregating the community she grew up in, the place they once called "Nigger Town." Blacks, whites, Italians, French, Creoles, all lived together in the community. They all had one thing in common. They were poor as church mice, all scrambling for work to keep a roof over their heads and to feed their families.

New Orleans was such a mixed-up place, anyway. Who could ever figure out exactly what race anybody was? If you were poor, you looked for the place other poor people lived. The white immigrants coming off boats and Blacks coming off plantations were looking for the same thing—the dirt-cheap shacks to cover their heads. No one gave something like redlining a thought because nobody with money was dying to move into "Nigger Town," anyway.

Mahalia couldn't help but remember the stories her aunts told her of how the Clark family began moving into New Orleans around 1908. Their first home was a three-room shotgun house where 11 family members lived. It had a leaky roof, dirt yards, and aerated walls that rattled from the trains that ran just feet away, and the home was located close to the faulty levee that was there to protect the homes from the Mississippi River.

Mahalia's own childhood was surrounded by poverty. It was part of everything she knew and experienced. The trains and train tracks, she realized, followed poor people to whatever community they called home. Sometimes, to move forward, she had to push the harshest memories to the back of her mind. She was never able to completely shut them out, but she could forget them for a while. When they tumbled out, even as she sat inside her beautiful seven-room home, they brought with them a sadness and a weariness to Mahalia's beautiful face.

Mahalia's attorney drew up the papers and purchased the doctor's home for $40,000. Mahalia called and shared the news with Aunt Duke and begged her to come up and spend the Christmas holiday with her. The home on Indiana Avenue could have been plucked right out of her childhood dreams—seven rooms, a garage, a big beautiful lawn, and a fireplace—something she'd sworn she'd have one day as she cleaned the homes of the rich white folks in New Orleans.

Finally, Mahalia had a home of her own. Space to breathe, privacy, a place to bring her family and friends. And she had a kitchen where she could try all of Aunt Duke's old recipes, and a few new ones she'd picked up from Aunt Hannah and Aunt Alice. She could host holiday dinners. Oh, how she loved to cook and entertain family and friends.

All of this was twirling around in Mahalia's mind when she moved into her new home and realized just how ingrained the community's racism was. It wasn't the kind of welcome that a celebrity or anyone would take for granted. No welcome wagons. No care packages left at her door. No neighbors waving hello from the sidewalks as they passed.

No Welcome Wagons for Halie

Mahalia Jackson's welcome to her new home included weeks of racial bullying, slurs shouted outside her home; white men revving their cars waking her from her fitful sleep at night. The boldest shot through her front windows and threatened to bomb her house if she didn't leave. It was the shooting and bomb threats that forced Mahalia to employ her own protection team—mostly friends and relatives who agreed to keep watch of her home through the nights. Finally, the vigilantes' efforts ended.

Grateful and relieved that the nights and days now passed without threats or shots, Mahalia sealed the truce with an ice cream party for the children in the community. Some white parents hesitantly allowed their children to walk over to the large yard and meet the Black woman in the house. A few escorted their children there, made tentative small talk. Mahalia's smile, the home-made cake and ice cream melted the lingering reservations the children and their parents may have had about this new resident within their community.

Mahalia later learned there had been one Negro family who had moved into the neighborhood two years earlier. They'd moved away shortly before Mahalia moved in. She wished they had stayed. At least she'd have neighbors to visit with and to share some of her daily sorrows with. She certainly understood their decision to leave. She imagined all they must have endured. Still, she would have loved having them as friends and allies.

While she may have been only the second Black homeowner in the Chatham community, Mahalia was for certain the most famous—Black or white. Not only in Chatham, but in Chicago and the country. The tall, statuesque Mahalia with the warm embrace and the big smile that went straight to her small, dark eyes. And that laughter that everyone swore came from the deepest part of her soul and traveled out touching everyone in its wake.

But Mahalia was more than that. Those who knew her, knew she was neither soft, nor bendable like most who met her or heard her sing and perceived her to be. Mahalia was a force of nature—a woman who knew what she wanted and would fight to the very end to get it. No one knew exactly what fueled her unyielding drive. Was it the poverty she'd left behind in New Orleans or the will to make good to spite the many naysayers she'd met up North?

Some in her circle believed it was her childhood as an orphan, the harsh growing up in Aunt Duke's household. Others believed it was to spite the naysayers who doubted she could make it, including the prominent Black churches that pretty much told her she wasn't right for their church. But, more than anything, Mahalia wanted to make Aunt Duke proud of her, show her that she had kept her word to sing for the Lord and not for the world.

In 10 years, Mahalia had attracted hordes of white fans to her concerts and performances, but few of them would understand that her success was as much an emotional victory as a monetary one. She never mentioned how she'd grown up in a three-room shotgun house for the first 16 years of her life, in the poor and ignored New Orleans neighborhood with the interchangeable and derogatory names "Nigger Town" and "Pinchers Town."

Then, after moving to Chicago, she had, like so many other Southern Blacks, been faced with the realization that living could be just as hard, up North. For her first 10 years in Chicago, Mahalia had lived and slept in a cramped closed-in sunporch at Aunt Hannah's apartment, helped pay Hannah's rent by cleaning hotels and taking on a washerwoman job in West Chicago and by working briefly at a canning plant. Mahalia was fired from the plant because of car troubles that prevented her from returning home in time for work after a weekend singing job in another state.

Her aunts weren't quick to complain about Halie's husband—Ike Hockenhull. Halie and her new husband had moved in with Hannah and Alice for two long years—suffering through the aunts' complaints and an even more cramped arrangement than when she'd first arrived. Though Halie would later divorce Ike Hockenhull, he remained an important part of her life, forever defended as a good man but bad husband material.

Young Halie had arrived in the cold, dark city of Chicago filled with hope, confidence, and wonder. It wouldn't always be cold or dark, but even in the spring, her hopes were dashed more often than she could count. Her wonder dulled and her confidence dampened, it took all she had to revive herself over and over. But she did, always picking herself up, plastering on her "Halie smile," foraging deep within herself for good memories from her life back in New Orleans. She didn't come all this way to fail, Halie repeatedly told herself. She had always considered herself a good person and just couldn't understand the suspicion and nonacceptance she was so often confronted with from the Blacks in her community, and in the churches—the place she'd always felt most at home.

While she had been pushed to excel back in New Orleans, she had few expectations for her future in Chicago. Maybe her biggest disappointment was with her favorite aunt, the one who had encouraged her to follow her dreams, come to Chicago and work until her singing got noticed.

Why had Aunt Hannah given up on her so easily? Why hadn't she pushed Halie's dream to go to nursing school? That had been the one clear goal Mahalia had when she'd left New Orleans. The other dream was her singing. She'd always been certain God would direct her path in that direction. The nursing was something she imagined she would be so good at. Who would understand her pain and feeling that she'd somehow lost out?

Thankfully, Mahalia had brought God with her on this journey. He was the only one who kept her going after so many of Chicago's most prominent churches shunned her and laughed at her singing behind her back. She couldn't believe it, when most of the church families were made up of Southerners who had migrated to the city in the last decades. They called her singing country and old-timey. Even bluesy. Unacceptable for their city style of praising. There was no way around it; Mahalia found herself an outsider in the Black churches of Chicago.

They even snickered behind their hands at her country way of talking and when they learned she was now singing at tent revivals, and even down South. They made fun of her performing weekend concerts at the small storefront churches on Chicago's West Side. Yes, they knew they'd made the right decision about her.

Mahalia Meets Destiny—His Name is Martin

Not long after settling into her new home, Mahalia was back at her breakneck travel and touring schedule. She had spent enough money at McCormick Place; Sears, Roebuck; and Ace Hardware stores. She wouldn't need any more furniture or kitchenware for a decade. She'd worn the newness off the furniture rearranging it 10 times a day. Her need to move, to stand before a crowd, was back.

For several years, Mahalia had accepted the Black ministers' invitation to serve as music director for the National Baptist Convention. The group, made up of the country's most prominent Black ministers, had taken its own sweet time inviting her into the fold. Finally, they'd warmed up to Mahalia Jackson, after the rest of the world gave her a nod. Oh, she knew, alright. Nothing missed her tiny eyes. In spite of that, she showed up dressed to the T, with that 100-watt smile of hers. And when she opened her mouth to sing, she knew she'd be reminding the ministers of what they'd been missing all those years.

Still, Mahalia would never forget the many years she would have given her eyeteeth for an invitation to the convention. The group let her know, without actually saying it, that she and her strange gospel music didn't fit with their congregations. They were right, she wasn't educated, never took a music lesson, and couldn't stand straight as a board while she belted out a song.

It was only after her star began to rise with white and mainstream America that the Black ministers accepted her country wailing and sensuous moves. *"Dear Mrs. Jackson, we would be honored..."* the letter had begun, in her invitation to participate in their annual convention.

After that, the letter came every year. She quickly rose from a mere participant to the director of their music program. Mahalia didn't gloat. She knew this was just one more thing along with all the other blessings she had to be grateful for. One more blessing that came long after she wanted it to, but just in time like God said he would.

The year 1956 marked the 76th annual National Baptist Convention. It was held in Denver, Colorado, that year—the year Mahalia would later describe as when "I met young Martin." In truth, she met Martin Luther King Jr., his wife, and his alter ego Ralph Abernathy all around that same time, but what stuck in her mind was meeting Martin.

The convention was packed. Beyond young Martin, Mahalia would remember meeting another charismatic minister, the tall, handsome Reverend C.T. Vivian of Alabama, a mentor of young Martin's who introduced him to the convention audience.

And didn't young Martin preach! A rousing and memorable sermon on "Paul's Letter to American Christians." His beautiful young wife Coretta Scott King sitting stoic and prim in the front row wearing that smile that would become iconic in time. After her husband's message, she'd risen with all the poise of a queen and made her way to the piano. The young woman was an accomplished classical musician who had studied music at Antioch College in Ohio and the New England Conservatory of Music in Boston, Massachusetts. Her dreams had been to become a classical musician. But that was before she met young Martin Luther King who would take them both on a journey to change the world. Coretta would sing as Martin's mother Alberta Williams King accompanied her on the organ.

It was another good-looking and charismatic young preacher who'd formally introduced Mahalia to young Martin that day. Reverend Russell Roberts was someone she'd met the year before, and someone with whom she'd begun something of a love affair—a not-so-secret love affair.

Mahalia had been greatly moved by Martin's sermon, and when she met him, she found herself even more drawn to his quiet, but confident manner. While she took to his friend and colleague Ralph Abernathy immediately, it was the young Martin that made her think there was something more to this meeting.

Mahalia, with her piercing stare, must have ruffled Martin, but not enough to deter him from his mission. The slight young man with the shy, but captivating smile and hypnotic voice was following God's directions. And their meeting that day would change the trajectory of his and Mahalia Jackson's lives and realign her destiny.

Martin's timid smile hid the questions he had about the amazing Mahalia Jackson he'd heard so much about, especially from Reverend Russell. Martin could see why the young man smiled so when he mentioned her—tall, statuesque Mahalia had a regal beauty and a presence that overshadowed almost anyone around her. Was she aware of this natural power she had over others? No one believed she had an oversized ego, but those around her always felt that irresistible force, just like Martin Luther King Jr. and Ralph Abernathy did that day.

Russell Roberts of Atlantic City, New Jersey, was tall, dark and movie-star handsome. Those who knew Mahalia best would always believe Russell was the one true love of her life. She would never dispute that fact—even after marrying and divorcing twice, including husband number two who some whispered was just a lighter version of Russell. Mahalia kept a photo of Russell Roberts by her beside and openly mourned his early death throughout her life.

Mahalia and Martin and Ralph

That fateful day in December 1956, Reverend Roberts was excited about introducing three people he so admired. Martin was a 27-year-old minister and an up-and-coming civil rights activist. His close friend who was almost always at his side was the young Reverend Ralph Abernathy, just three years older. Mahalia would learn a great deal about the young Martin and his friend during this first meeting, but much more over the months and years as their friendships grew.

Both Martin and Ralph, she'd learn, were educated men. Martin was one of the esteemed "Morehouse Men." He'd graduated from the historically Black all-male college in Atlanta in 1948, before enrolling at Crozer Theological Seminary in Upland, Pennsylvania, where he received a Bachelor of Divinity degree. He had gone on to gain his doctorate in systematic theology from Boston University. After getting to know Martin better, Mahalia would jokingly tell him she'd always had a real weakness for good-looking, educated men.

Young Martin's very first pastorate had begun two years earlier at the historic Dexter Avenue Baptist Church in Montgomery, Alabama. The church was founded in 1877 as Second Colored Baptist Church and would later thrive under the leadership of civil rights activist Vernon Johns, whose philosophy mirrored that of his young *protégé*. Civil rights and equal justice were integral foundations of the church that was founded in a slave trader's pen. When the church was moved to Dexter Street in 1885, it was renamed Dexter Avenue Baptist Church. Sixty years later, young Martin Luther King became president of the Montgomery Improvement Association (MIA), formed on December 5, 1955, by the Black ministers and community leaders in Montgomery, Alabama.

Mahalia and Martin—they must have been a sight: the tall, buxom Mahalia and little Martin Luther King Jr. as handsome and debonair as they come, but inches shorter than Mahalia. How he must have laughed at her homey tales, sometimes a lot raunchier than what the young preacher ought to be listening to.

Mahalia, truthfully, wasn't the type of demure, educated, and sophisticated woman Martin and Ralph usually attracted into their circles. She wasn't a Coretta Scott King, the highly educated, classic musician; or a Juanita Abernathy, the Tennessee State University graduate with a business degree and whose family in Uniontown were considered the most successful Black farmers in the "Black Belt" South at that time. The Black Belt region referred to some 200 counties from Virginia to Texas with majority Black populations and majority cotton production.

But Mahalia was…Mahalia Jackson, exactly what the men needed at this moment in their struggle. She had a huge following. She was as rich as any Black person they knew, and she could draw a crowd with that voice. And, Lord, that voice. Mahalia's voice often woke Martin and his circle in the early mornings as she rose to cook them a hot breakfast before they resumed their journey. Oftentimes, when she cooked her famous jambalaya or bread pudding, the men would find themselves nodding off only to be awakened by Mahalia's singing.

Mahalia had brought all of her with her from New Orleans, including Aunt Duke's favorite recipes she'd eaten during her childhood—and others she'd created herself. The rest she'd copied from her Chicago aunts during her almost decade as a roomer at their home.

Oh, the times Mahalia and Martin had on Indiana Avenue in that big, beautiful home that Mahalia had made her own. The preachers who'd gone through there, the singers and actors. If walls could talk, Mahalia sometimes thought, laughing to herself. Martin was the "goodest" man she knew, but even he wasn't no saint.

And, then there was the sturdy third wheel in this unusual friendship, the serious and thoughtful Ralph Abernathy. The friend who would follow Martin to hell and back, but only after he'd spent hours trying to talk him out of it. Where in the world would Martin be without this friend whose practicality perfectly balanced Martin's dreams? Maybe he didn't have the charm, charisma, or voice that moved mountains. But Ralph was exactly what Martin and the movement needed in 1956—the exact grounding that would prevent Martin Jr. from floundering with his pretty words and lofty dreams.

Martin was 26 years old, and Ralph Abernathy was 29 when they organized and led the Montgomery bus boycott. Only God knew what the outcome of the boycott would be. Martin and Ralph were moved by their gut instincts and by what they knew should be. What they felt in their hearts was that they had to try. They were both as surprised as the Black and white communities of Montgomery when the boycott turned out to be the most successful civil rights campaign in the nation at that time. The boycott brought national attention to Montgomery and the South's segregation policies. Most importantly, it shined a light on the young, courageous, and charismatic Montgomery minister—the Reverend Martin Luther King Jr.

As Martin Luther King's star continued to rise throughout the country and even the world, his friendship and dependence on the Reverend Ralph Abernathy continued to grow. The two men had met as fellow pastors in Montgomery in 1954. While their journeys were similar in some ways—both were Southerners, highly educated, and ambitious for change—Abernathy often said it was his service in the U.S. military that truly opened his eyes to America's most overt racism.

While King hailed from a prominent Atlanta family and a long line of ministers, Abernathy came from a family of farmers, large farmers in Linden, Alabama. Young Abernathy attended college at Alabama State University, graduating in 1948 with a bachelor's degree in mathematics. Unlike Martin who never served in the military, Ralph served two years in the military before enrolling and graduating from Atlanta University with a master's degree in sociology. In 1951, Abernathy was ordained as pastor of First Baptist Church in Montgomery while working as dean of men at Alabama State University.

The King family was a ministerial hierarchy in Atlanta. Everyone seemed to know the Reverend Martin Luther King Sr., pastor of Ebenezer Baptist Church, one of the most prominent Black churches in Atlanta. The Reverend King Sr., known as "Daddy King," had once served as an assistant pastor to his wife Alberta's father, A.D. Williams. According to King legend, the Reverend A.D. Williams grew the struggling church from a basement congregation with 17 congregants to several hundred. It is said to have grown so rapidly that the congregation eventually moved in 1914 to Atlanta's historic Sweet Auburn community.

It was A.D. Williams, Martin Luther King Jr.'s grandfather, whose journey the young Martin would emulate. Williams, a self-made man, born to slaves in Greenwood, Georgia, claimed January 2, 1863, the day after President Lincoln issued the Emancipation Proclamation, as his birthdate. It is believed that he was actually born in 1861. Williams, along with a handful of other ministers, created a uniquely African American version of the social gospel—a combination of Booker T. Washington's Black business philosophy and W. E. B. Du Bois' call for civil rights activism.

One of the cofounders of the Atlanta chapter of the NAACP, A.D. Williams' years with Ebenezer Baptist Church were marked by moving gospel and pragmatic social activism. He promoted Black businesses, urged his congregation to become homeowners, and pushed for adequate public accommodations for Blacks, despite Jim Crow segregation laws.

Mahalia Jackson had known the affable "Daddy King" and his wife Alberta for years. At least, since the National Baptist Convention had invited her to serve as music director. She was well aware that "Daddy King" had pastored Ebenezer Baptist Church since 1931 following the death of A.D. Williams, but she was surprised that it wasn't until 1956 that she met his son.

It just so happened that 1956 was important in Mahalia and Martin's lives for more than just their first meeting. It was also the beginning of the deep and ongoing dissension between the National Baptist Convention and the birth of Martin Luther King Jr.'s civil rights movement, which pushed for increased public activism, demonstrations, and protests. The Convention's middle-ground stance on civil and racial issues was contradictory to Martin Luther King Jr.'s highly controversial civil rights stance. Most of its membership churches made salvation, rather than political activism, their focal point.

While the Convention president, Joseph Jackson, had supported the Montgomery bus boycott of 1956, shortly afterward, he began to urge the Convention to disengage from civil rights activism. Jackson was a staunch ally of Chicago Mayor Richard Daley and the Chicago Democrats who would eventually mark Martin Luther King Jr. as too pushy and asking for too much too soon. Chicago's young Jesse Jackson Jr. (no relation to Joseph Jackson) was an aide to Martin Luther King Jr. and was also placed on that list of pushy young civil rights activists.

Part 8

STANDING FOR JUSTICE AND SINGING FOR HOLLYWOOD

"… listening to those colored leaders talk in my home, right there in my own living room in Chicago, I learned a great deal. I realized I had lived to see a new day dawn for the American Negro, and history was being made. I rejoiced that I had a chance to be a small part of it and join in it as a Negro and as a church-going Christian."

—Mahalia Jackson

MARTIN, MAHALIA, SIDNEY POITIER, HARRY BELAFONTE
AT CHICAGO RALLY (TULANE CREDIT).

Rosa and Mahalia—Sojourners for Truth and Freedom

"I don't know nothing about politics," Mahalia told friends after meeting the young Martin Luther King. The last thing she would ever consider herself was a politician. Yet, by all accounts, her meeting with Martin Luther King and Ralph Abernathy was a huge success. Beyond their wildest dreams. The two civil rights activists had shared as many details of their work and their dreams as necessary to convince Mahalia of their serious commitment to changing America.

They were even successful at convincing Mahalia that politics was simply about using one's power—be it one's voice, stories, poetry, athleticism—to help persuade people to change for the better. Right now, they reminded her that she, indeed, had the power of her voice, and the world would listen.

Mahalia would think on all that the two men had told her. As she thought back on her life journey, Mahalia hummed and closed her eyes. She seldom dwelled on the harshest days, the hungry days. She fell on her knees each night to thank God for all her blessings. Not counting her earliest years in Chicago, it had taken her roughly 20 years to rise from the little-known gospel singer who washed white people's clothes and cleaned hotel bathrooms to the most commercially relevant and wealthiest African American in the country. All thanks to the voice God had blessed her with, the songs he inspired, and her ability to deliver them to audiences around the world—from the elite white folks' halls, the commercial arenas, the churches, and even still, the Southern revival tents.

The two young men had not expected to be drawn so effortlessly into the orbit of this Queen of Gospel. They hadn't known she would speak with such clarity and understanding of the racial and social troubles in the world. They were humored by her self-deflection. *"Everything I know I read between these two covers,"* she'd say, as she held her age-worn Bible in the air.

It was a blessing, they thought, that Mahalia, in spite of her new wealth and notoriety, related to their mission and shared their beliefs about the world's troubles. Who would have thought it to be true? Certainly not her white followers who were drawn in by Mahalia's wide smile and warm hugs. Yet, any Black woman from anywhere in the South—even the self-described exotic New Orleans—would have experienced the racial atrocities at some point.

While much of their 1956 visit with Mahalia had been introductory, getting to know each other, what they made abundantly clear was that they were on a mission. They needed an army of young people with fervor, excitement, energy, and time. But, most importantly, they needed patrons—a faithful few with talents, money, and connections to help continue their sojourn for justice and freedom.

The Montgomery bus boycott was, in fact, the impetus for the young Southern ministers seeking Mahalia Jackson out at the Denver National Baptist Convention. At a second meeting at Mahalia's Chicago home, Reverend King and Reverend Abernathy shared more details of their work and more details about how, on December 1, 1955, one woman had taken a simple action to spark the most significant date of the civil rights struggle. Four days later, the Montgomery bus boycott was launched. No one would have guessed the boycott would last 382 days—from December 5, 1955, to December 20, 1956, and would in time be recognized as the most significant civil rights effort in history.

Mahalia's name and connections would be invaluable to the cause. Her financial assistance would help ensure the campaign was successful. Yet, no one could be more practical about her career than Mahalia. Her participation in Martin's cause wouldn't be looked on kindly by many of her most ardent followers—the white fans who loved her voice and how she made them feel with her good church woman persona.

They wouldn't understand her taking on a role in the civil rights struggle. She'd have to go slowly. She didn't need to tarnish her public image and, in the end, the cause by having her name front and center of this campaign. There was no question she believed in the cause, and she believed in the two young preachers…but for her sake, and their sake, she would need to work from behind the scenes as much as possible given who she was.

While Mahalia's help was critical to the cause, the woman whose name would be forever tied to the campaign would be Rosa Parks, a quiet and unassuming young woman who had spent her early life during the Jim Crow era in the state of Alabama and part of her adult life in the city of Montgomery.

On that fateful December day in Montgomery, Rosa Parks had, just as she'd done hundreds of days before, caught the Cleveland Avenue city bus after her workday. On this day, rather than pass the many empty seats designated as "whites only," she sat and simply would not be moved. No one—Black or white—was surprised when Parks' action resulted in her arrest and trial in the Montgomery police court.

The beautiful Black woman's arrest was the spark that set the fire of civil rights protests in the South. Of the 50,000 Black residents in Montgomery, 25,000 refused to ride the city buses on the day Mrs. Parks was brought to trial. The next day, about 90 percent of the Negroes joined the bus boycott.

Between the Montgomery Improvement Association led by its president Ralph Abernathy and the Black ministers and their churches led by Martin Luther King Jr., they raised the money needed to get carpools organized to ensure workers could get to their jobs—without the use of the city bus.

Mahalia often retold the story of that day in December 1955, when she'd said "yes" to young Martin and traveled to Montgomery to sing to the people working and marching toward justice.

She recalled how that day in Denver, Reverend Abernathy and Reverend King had talked to her about the Montgomery Improvement Association. Out of the association came the most important Negro movement since the NAACP—King's nonviolent protests campaign, the idea of meeting the white man with nonviolence and passive resistance. It was the same successful campaign that Mahatma Gandhi had led for India's independence from British rule, and which Reverend King now preached.

What Mahalia saw in Reverend Abernathy was a brave young preacher who wasn't afraid of any man no matter what his color. As for Reverend King, she said he was not a big man in size, but a giant in spirit. She recalled how quietly he spoke, with such calm. Yet, the power of his words and his strength were overwhelming.

King and Abernathy had asked Mahalia, point blank, if she might be able to come down to Montgomery and sing at a rally to raise money. Without hesitation, she told the two men that she would be pleased to travel to Montgomery.

Mahalia and her pianist Mildred Falls were "put up" at Reverend Abernathy's little white frame house. The preacher and his pretty wife gave up their own bed to her and Mildred. Mahalia would never forget that godly gesture. It would be what defined Reverend Abernathy for all the time she knew him.

Mrs. Abernathy cooked dinner with her own hands—greens, cornbread, and ham hocks, and they all prayed together and went off to the Methodist church in Montgomery where the rally was being held because it was the largest church in the city.

Mahalia's performance was scheduled for 8 p.m., but she recalled the Negroes had been coming since early afternoon, and the loudspeakers had been set up in the street for the overflow crowd.

Mahalia also remembered that there was the ominous presence of police throughout the town and cars filled with white men driving fast and loud, back and forth around the church. There was no question everyone knew that these men were out to make trouble. But the Blacks didn't stop their rally.

Mahalia remembered with joy how the service was filled with the spirit, how they sang and the ministers spoke. It was a great success, and the white people of the town knew it. So, because they couldn't shut down the rally, the white men began to start fights with the Negroes, knowing the police were on their side.

When she returned home to Chicago, Mahalia heard about the bomb that blew out the living room and bedroom of the Abernathys' home. Then they began dynamiting the churches and homes of other Negro ministers and some whites who sympathized with the cause. Colored women with little children to support were fired from their jobs, and the men were told to get out of town.

What continued to sustain Mahalia was the fact that Reverend King and Reverend Abernathy kept right on fighting, working from their churches and their homes. They never stopped marching and leading the bus boycott in Montgomery through the winter and into the next summer. The bus boycott, in some ways, stirred the Negroes even more than the Supreme Court decision to integrate the schools. It gave Blacks confidence and hope that their actions could make a difference. There was to be no turning back.

The bus boycott continued for 382 days. Thousands of Blacks refused to ride the buses, traveling in carpools or Black-operated cabs, or walking to their destinations. In time, the city's bus lines became desperate for money because of the boycott. They were forced to charge white passengers twice as much fare to ensure they were able to keep operating the buses.

They tried running the buses over different routes, but they went deeper into debt.

The boycott was a huge success. Blacks had won the battle. The next year, the U.S. Supreme Court handed down a verdict that declared segregated seating in buses in Montgomery was unconstitutional.

Mahalia was moved by the words of a newspaperman who said, "Montgomery is a legend that was written by cooks, janitors, and country people."

There was little noticeable parallel between 42-year-old Rosa McCauley Parks' life journey and that of the 46-year-old Mahalia Jackson, except both women were Southerners with similar racial histories. Both would become friends of the young Martin Luther King Jr. and, in their disparate ways, help further his life goal of racial equality and justice. Both women had married men a decade older than themselves. Yet, while Mahalia and Isaac Hockenhull's marriage had ended after a few years, Rosa and her husband Raymond Parks were celebrating their 12th wedding anniversary in 1956.

Rosa Parks was not a name recognized around the country or the world before she sparked the Montgomery bus boycott. And, though Mahalia had not sat down at the front of a bus during the height of America's Jim Crow era, her name was one of the most recognized in the land. She rubbed elbows with the rich and famous. She had eaten and sung at the White House. The president of the United States had sent her a personal letter. She had traveled across the ocean and sung before crowds of hundreds of thousands of people who called her name though it was the only English they could speak. The differences between Rosa Parks and Mahalia Jackson couldn't have been starker. Yet, their commitment to changing the wrongs of the world were equal.

Rosa Parks became an active member of the Montgomery NAACP in 1943, 10 years after marrying Raymond Parks and 12 years before her name became synonymous with the civil rights struggle. The day she refused to give up her bus seat in 1955 was not her first interaction with the bus driver, James Blake. She'd stepped onto the crowded Cleveland Avenue city bus 12 years earlier and resisted the bus driver's rule that Blacks disembark and reenter through the back door. When the bus driver became enraged and grabbed her sleeve, Rosa left the bus, refusing to ride.

Most ironically, Rosa Parks was also a sexual assault investigator for the NAACP before she sparked the Montgomery bus boycott. In her first years in the organization, she worked specifically on criminal justice and its application in Alabama communities. One part of this was protecting Black men from false accusations and lynchings; the other was ensuring that Black women being sexually assaulted by white men would get their day in court. This particular issue was close to Parks' heart, as in 1931 a white male neighbor had attempted to assault her.

Mahalia's home on Indiana Avenue became a regular meeting place for the young reverends, King and Abernathy. During and after Mahalia's trip to Montgomery, she got to know Martin Luther King Jr. much better. Martin, Ralph, and their advisers and supporters would often meet at Mahalia's home during their trips to Chicago to make speeches for protest rallies and raise money among the prominent Blacks in Chicago to continue the fight down South. They would be reminded often throughout their friendships that sitting and eating together was the best bonding glue there was.

The more Mahalia saw of Reverend King, the more she was convinced the Lord had indeed anointed the young man with the education, the faith, and the courage to fight for civil rights. After the victorious Montgomery fight Mahalia had participated in, Martin moved to Atlanta to the Ebenezer Baptist Church. It became his headquarters for his newly found Southern Christian Leadership Conference, which was dedicated to spreading the gospel while fighting nonviolently for civil rights. Mahalia would spend time with the Kings during Martin's trips to Chicago.

Mahalia remembered that the white folks in the South had formed the White Citizens Council to fight against integration, and they worked on the Negroes to make them feel their cause was helpless. "They tried to oppress them and defeat their spirit," she said. "They kept telling them, *'You ain't nothing, and you didn't come from nothing.'* And, young people were hurt by it."

An Interlude in Love

Reverend Russell Roberts was a true Yankee. Though he resided in Atlantic City, New Jersey, his home state was Massachusetts—a long way from New Orleans. Mahalia met the tall, good-looking minister in Chicago in 1954 where they worked together on two fundraisers for youths.

Russell was smooth and educated but was also down to earth. He loved to joke with Mahalia and have a good time. All those were traits that Mahalia liked, but more than anything, she couldn't resist a good-looking, educated man, one who looked as if he could have stepped right out of *Ebony* magazine. And, Russell was about the best-looking man Mahalia thought she'd ever seen—except for her father Johnny Jackson.

Russell had smooth, tan skin and wore a thin mustache that he kept neatly trimmed. His hair was naturally curly, but he may have done a little bit to set the waves just right. The fact that he was a great preacher, Mahalia thought, was just icing on the cake.

There were whispers about Mahalia and Russell at the National Baptist Convention. He came to New York City to listen in while she made a recording. She stopped in Atlantic City to visit him when she was up that way. By 1956, things had become serious. But Mahalia was wary, cautious. She'd married Ike and learned her lessons about jumping into a relationship too soon. She didn't want to make another mistake. She confided in her friend Celeste Scott, "The thing is, I'm wondering if he loves me or Mahalia Jackson?"

"Mahalia, you're the only one who can answer that. That, and how do you feel about him?" asked Celeste.

Mildred Falls, Mahalia's pianist, thought Mahalia and Russell made a beautiful team in the pulpit in Atlantic City. Mahalia seemed to know just the right songs to prepare the way for Russell's preaching. But he was too high-minded for down-to-earth Mahalia, Mildred thought. "I just don't think he's for you," she told Mahalia. Mahalia exploded, and Mildred bit her tongue forever after that on the subject.

By the following spring, Mahalia seemed ready for marriage. But she was anxious and having trouble breathing again. She went to see her doctor, Dr. William Barclay, who said the problem was sarcoid disease in her lungs and being overweight. He prescribed the drug prednisone, which increased her appetite, and at the same time, he told her to lose a lot of weight. She told him, "If I lose all you want me to lose, people won't think I'm Mahalia Jackson—and I won't think I'm Mahalia Jackson."

There was a time that being a bit overweight was a sign that you were eating well, that you were successful. The days of State Street chicken were over. She could have ribs any time she wanted, or heaps of fried chicken. Or steak.

Besides, Russell didn't think she was too heavy. If he did, why would he ask her to marry him? Mahalia said had yes to Russell. They talked about a wedding and a honeymoon in Europe. Then Russell got sick. Cancer. He took treatments, and she prayed, alone in the night, *"Take his hand, precious Lord."*

But Russell got worse, not better. Mahalia, desperate, sandwiched a quick trip to Atlantic City into her schedule. She pulled $10,000 from her purse and gave it to Russell. "What can I do? Besides giving you this for the best treatment in the country. What can I do?" She went home with a record he had made of his preaching, and a heavy heart.

Early one February morning in 1959, she got a telephone call. Russell had slipped away. That night she performed a big concert in Chicago's Orchestra Hall. But at two o'clock in the morning, she called her friend Nettie, sobbing, asking her to come and stay with her. She lit candles next to Russell's framed photograph in the pink bedroom next to her bedroom. She paced, prayed, and played the record he gave her. "I feel his presence so close," she told Nettie. "Russell is here, and I don't know what he's trying to tell me."

Mahalia continued to feel lonely and distraught for months, especially at night. She'd phone Nettie: "I can't sleep. I wish you'd come down here." And her warm-hearted friend always came. Night after night, Mahalia lit the candles and played the record until at last she knew what Russell was trying to tell her. He loved her, truly. She kept his photograph on her dresser for the rest of her life.

Mahalia Takes Gospel to Hollywood

In between her work to help Martin Luther King Jr. and the struggle, Mahalia never considered slowing down her music career. She felt she could do both. She rubbed elbows with the Hollywood stars, the gospel greats, the blues and jazz heroes of the day, as well as the greatest actors of that time.

Her heart, however, belonged to the struggle led by her friend and confidante, young Martin. His work eased her conscious and her soul, but it didn't put money in her bank account, or pay her bills.

The singer and television personality Dinah Shore probably had as much to do with Mahalia's successful, but not so smooth, debut into Hollywood as anyone. Shore was not powerful enough to prevent white sponsors from pulling their support from Mahalia's show over time, or to expand Mahalia's coverage beyond the Chicago area. But, for years, she remained a huge supporter of Mahalia and, over time, a real friend.

Other iconic moments of Mahalia's Hollywood years were her and Nat King Cole singing "Steal Away" on Nat's TV show in 1957. There was also her role in the 1959 movie classic *Imitation of Life,* starring Lana Turner, John Gavin, and Sandra Dee. Mahalia singing "Trouble of the World" in the film would be one of the most memorable performances in television history.

On the heels of Mahalia's television show, a telegram came from Las Vegas offering her the opportunity to sing her own material for $25,000 a week. It was a startling sum. Five years earlier, Danny Thomas had made entertainment history at $10,000. Now, this Black woman from "Nigger Town" in New Orleans was being offered $25,000 to sing the gospel in a night club!

Mahalia stared at the telegram. The telephone rang. Someone was calling from Las Vegas. If Miss Jackson had objections to the whiskey being served while she sang, there would be none served, or any orders taken. Not since "The Hot Mikado" had Mahalia been so tempted to go against her promise to God. She wrestled with the idea through a long night. Was it the Lord, or was it Satan making this offer to her? The next morning, she awoke with her answer already on her lips. "The Devil don't ever sleep, honey," she'd say of that night. "He'll keep prodding and pinching and twisting you—he figures to catch you one day, some way."

Turning down the Las Vegas night club offer had opened up the movie role in 1959 for Mahalia, a role that would stick to her for the rest of her life.

Mahalia was getting used to sold-out crowds, but she was still always grateful to God for greasing the wheels for her. One such event was the sold-out concert at Constitution Hall, the largest concert hall in Washington, D.C., on March 24, 1960. It was the same hall where Marian Anderson, the critically acclaimed African American classical singer, was prevented from performing some 20 years earlier.

Mahalia's concert was sponsored by the 3,000-member Interdenominational Church Ushers Association (ICUA). Tickets to the concert had sold out well ahead of the actual event date. The association's press release announced, however, that a second booking had already been secured with "the world's greatest gospel singer" for another concert in Constitution Hall on November 26, 1960, in response to the overwhelming demand to see Mahalia Jackson.

The ICUA reserved rooms for Mahalia and her entourage at the Statler Hotel, just blocks from the White House. While in the city, she would help the National Council of Negro Women with a fundraiser to help children who "had been left school-less since 1959 when Prince Edward County closed schools to circumvent court-ordered integration." Mahalia would join volunteers in knocking on doors to solicit funds to help educate the children.

According to the press release: Mahalia's *records have sold over 8 million copies, and she has won great acclaim from critics and audience all over the world. Taking her religion seriously, she has refused fabulous offers to sing in night clubs or to sing the blues.*

The press release quoted Mahalia in a *Saturday Evening Post* article as saying: *'I'll never give up my gospel songs for the blues. Blues are the songs of despair, but gospel songs are the songs of hope. When you sing gospel, you have a feeling there is a cure for what's wrong. But when you're through with the blues, you've got nothing to rest on.'*

"Mahalia Jackson," the press release continued, *"has appeared on all leading television programs and in concert halls throughout the world, staging performances which have revolutionized the field of gospel singing."*

The recording "Move on Up a Little Higher" would catapult Mahalia Jackson to international fame, selling over 2 million copies and revolutionizing the gospel singing field.

While in Washington, Mahalia was also scheduled to attend a reception by her good friends Congressman Chester Bowles and his wife in their Georgetown home. The Bowles were great admirers of Mahalia.

Her last stop would be a reception sponsored by the ICUA at Howard University. Some 500 guests were expected, including Robert McLaughlin, president of the Board of Commissioners for the District of Columbia, who would present her with the key to the city.

Finally, Mahalia would stop by Voice of America and tape a broadcast.

Weaving Gospel into Presidential Politics

When the U.S. presidential campaign got rolling in 1960, Martin Luther King was taking part in the sit-ins that had spread down into Georgia. In the middle of October, he was arrested in Atlanta and sentenced to serve four months hard labor at the Georgia State Penitentiary. Negroes all over the country were aroused, and the long-distance telephones were buzzing.

"I was in New York when I got the news," recalled Mahalia, "and I managed to get through to Mrs. King, who was going to have another child. She was terribly upset and fearful about what might happen to her husband in that state prison and hoping that they might do something up in D.C. But President Eisenhower did nothing, and Vice President Nixon kept his mouth shut.

"Then we got the news that out in Chicago presidential candidate John F. Kennedy had picked up a telephone and called up Dr. King's wife, himself. He had told her how concerned he was and promised he would do something. That afternoon his brother Robert Kennedy telephoned down in Georgia and spoke to the judge who had sentenced Martin Luther King to jail. The next day Dr. King was set free."

In the Negro world, word of what the Kennedys had done spread like a brushfire. There was much bitterness about President Eisenhower and Richard Nixon keeping silent, and Negroes began jumping on the Kennedy election bandwagon.

Martin's father was an old-fashioned Baptist who just naturally was wary of the Catholic church. Like many other Negroes, Martin Luther King Sr. had been cold toward Kennedy and intended to vote for Nixon. But now King Sr., called "Daddy King," had switched over, saying: "This man was willing to wipe the tears from my daughter-in-law's eyes. I've got a suitcase full of votes, and I'm going to take them to Mr. Kennedy and dump them in his lap."

On Sundays, Negroes in churches across the nation heard the story of what the Kennedys had done while the Republicans did nothing. From then on, the colored votes began going for Democrats.

"I've been told that across the country, 7 out of 10 Negroes are believed to have voted for Kennedy," noted Mahalia.

In Chicago, the colored people went for Kennedy by about 4 to1, and in Detroit, it was about 6 to 1. The Democrats carried Illinois by only 9,800 votes. And about 250,000 Negroes in the state voted for Kennedy. Michigan was carried by only 70,000 votes and again 250,000 of the colored people chose Kennedy. The telephone calls the Kennedys made for Martin Luther King Jr. turned out to be one of the most important events of the presidential campaign, and the politicians in both parties found out that the Negro was a force to reckon with.

"Voting for the Democratic ticket was nothing for me," Mahalia recalled. "I've been a Democrat since the days of the New Deal. For 20 years, I've been singing and hollering around the 2nd and 3rd wards on the South Side of Chicago for people like Congressman William Dawson. That man has opened so many doors for Negroes in Illinois. He has chosen to stay in Chicago and help his people there. Dawson has not so much the gift of gab as the gift of getting things done."

Mahalia recalled that once when she was having a hard time making enough money to get by, Dawson "told me that I was so big and strong that he'd like to recommend me for work as a policewoman. I told him that I was afraid those delinquents would be too much for me. I felt I might curb delinquency better with a song such as 'Let Us Walk Together, Children,' rather than with a badge. Many of those that were young and wayward had gotten to know me, and I was able to walk down many a dark alley around Chicago without anybody ever laying a hand on me."

When Mahalia got a call from Hollywood actor Peter Lawford, the presidential campaign was just settling down. He explained that they were planning a big inauguration gala for President Kennedy in D.C. Frank Sinatra would be producing it, and they both wanted her to be there and to sing "The Star-Spangled Banner."

While Mahalia said she'd be happy to be there, she had never sung the national anthem in public before. She'd have to practice, mostly in her Chicago kitchen.

On the week of the inauguration, Mildred Falls, Mahalia's longtime piano accompanist, rode with her on the train to Washington, D.C. They were joined by Mahalia's friend and mentor Congressman Dawson; her other mentor Mayor Richard J. Daley; and her friend John H. Johnson, the publisher of Ebony and Jet magazines.

By the time Mahalia and Mildred arrived at the D.C. armory, things were already jumping. Dozens of entertainers were there rehearsing their songs or dances or other skits. Stagehands were hammering and sawing and stringing up flags and banners.

Mahalia couldn't believe her eyes. Frank Sinatra and Peter Lawford had persuaded American stars to come home for the inauguration from all over the world. Big names like Milton Berle, Jimmy Durante, and Joey Bishop. And some of the greatest singers in the country like Nat King Cole, Harry Belafonte, and Ella Fitzgerald who had flown in from Australia; and Hollywood greats like Bette Davis and Frederic March.

They'd closed down two hit shows in New York so that Sir Laurence Olivier, Anthony Quinn, and Ethel Merman could have the night off to participate in the gala. Leonard Bernstein was conducting the orchestra. Tony Curtis and Janet Leigh had flown in from Hollywood. Sidney Poitier had crossed the ocean from Paris, and Gene Kelly had come from Switzerland. They were expecting an audience of 12,000 people.

It was a wonderful madhouse, with everybody rushing around the armory trying to find Peter Lawford and calling out, "Hey Frank!" to Frank Sinatra. In the midst of all the confusion sat Frank as cool as a cucumber.

Everyone knew that Frank Sinatra had a bad rep for being mean. Mahalia wasn't privy to that hot temper and harsh words. He greeted her with a warm hug and a kiss. She described him "as nice as anybody I ever met in the theater or television."

It was a hard two days, but everybody worked hard at rehearsals, learning their songs and routines. And, in the end, it paid off. Everything would have gone off perfectly, except for the Washington, D.C., winter weather.

The gala was to begin at 9 p.m. on inauguration eve. In the middle of the afternoon, it began to snow. By suppertime, the flakes were coming down so thick no one could see across the street.

Washington traffic began to pile up, and the automobiles and buses and streetcars were skidding around and getting stuck all over the city. Mahalia and her accompanist barely made it to the armory. They had worried about being late, but when they arrived, they found everything at a dead standstill.

The entertainers were sitting in snowdrifts all over the town. Leonard Bernstein finally got there in a police car, wearing Harry Belafonte's shirt which he said was two sizes too big for him. Some of the actors and actresses had to go onstage in their street clothes because they couldn't get back to their hotels and change.

It was long past 9 p.m. before the audience began to trickle in, glittering with jewels and covered in furs. At 10 p.m., President Kennedy arrived to take his place in the center balcony box. When he found that the gala was still delayed because of the weather, he opted to wait in a backstage room.

Finally, at 10:30 p.m., Leonard Bernstein led the 75-piece orchestra in "The Stars and Stripes Forever." Then, as President Kennedy entered his balcony box with his whole family, the orchestra broke into "Anchors Aweigh."

Everybody was standing up cheering and applauding. Bugles blew, spotlights hit the side entrances and in marched all the famous actors, actresses, singers, and dancers as the orchestra played "Walking down to Washington," which had been specially written for the occasion.

For Mahalia, it was as thrilling as a big nominating convention. She loved the excitement. And, though she long contended she was not a politician at heart, she loved the intrigue and power of politics. She also believed that good politicians could make the world better.

When the theater lights dimmed, it was time for Mahalia to sing "The Star-Spangled Banner." Since she always sang with her eyes shut, she couldn't see how the audience liked it, but she was told afterward that people thought it was wonderful.

The big show with skits and dances and singing lasted until almost 2 a.m. Then guests and performers were ushered to a big supper that Frank Sinatra had arranged for the entire cast. Mahalia met Vice President Lyndon Johnson's family and President Kennedy's father and mother.

At 3 a.m., a tall, thin young man in a blue suit walked up to Mahalia's table. It was President Kennedy, and he'd come over to say "Thank You" to Mahalia for opening the gala. He said that he had known about her singing for a long time and truly enjoyed it.

Mahalia would say later that "the president looked into my eyes as if he was looking right into my soul, and I suddenly knew how he was able to draw people to him in a magnetic way. He made me feel as if I was a part of his life and time."

The next morning, Mahalia was invited to sit on the front row of the bleachers to watch the inauguration where Kennedy took his oath and delivered his inaugural address. While it was bitter cold even with the sun shining, everyone in the audience seemed transfixed by the young president's words. Everyone, she believed, felt they were part of a great moment in history.

Mahalia would later write: "I thought to myself, *'I feel that I'm a part of this man's hopes. He lifts my spirit and makes me feel a part of the land I live in.'*

"Suddenly, I felt that we Negroes who were fortunate enough to travel abroad to other countries could answer foreign newspaper reporters' questions about segregation and integration because now we had a president who really believed in equal rights and had it in his heart to do something about it."

All that day, the day of the inauguration, while the bands played and the parade marched by, there seemed to be a new spirit in Washington—a spirit of jubilee.

"Everybody felt excited and proud about being there, and it was a great moment for Americans," Mahalia wrote. *"I haven't changed my mind about President Kennedy since then, and I never will."*

Part 9

MAHALIA AND MARTIN'S DREAM

(1963)

MAHALIA WHISPERS TO MARTIN LUTHER KING, JR., AT ILLINOIS RALLY
FOR CIVIL RIGHTS, 6/21/1964 (TULANE CREDIT).

Mahalia's Awakening—The March on Washington

Given all the work she'd been doing with Dr. King, part of America was beginning to see Mahalia as a spokesperson for her friend, the civil rights leader. Just a few weeks before the big trip to Washington, D.C., for the March on Washington for Jobs and Freedom., Mahalia was invited to Carnegie Hall to perform on behalf of a voter education drive. Someone had asked her about a *Jet* magazine story where a white girl from Oregon said she'd been saved by listing to Mahalia's record "In the Upper Room."

In Dayton, Ohio, where she performed for the Congress of Racial Equality (CORE), Mahalia told a local newspaper: "I don't support every so-called freedom organization. I'm not about to help any cause that would destroy our country."

Then, in Carbondale, Illinois, she said in an interview: "There must be some way to settle these problems as families settle problems—by compromise, conciliation, talk, understanding. Congress is treating us as though we are provoked children. Understanding—that is the key. So many white people talk at colored people, not to them."

August 28, 1963, was just around the corner, and as passionate as Mahalia had become about civil rights, she was still in love with pretty things, and nothing more than a beautiful hat. Ida Beal created a hat especially for Mahalia's trip to Washington, D.C., where she'd be singing for Dr. King at the March on Washington. It was brown chiffon with leaves and berries in the petals. "If they have any kind of breeze at all," Ida had said, "those berries will show. Just be sure you pin it good. You know how you are."

Mahalia could hardly contain herself as she held the hat, turning it around and around. "Washington gone know what I mean when I say I got a friend in New Orleans who can beat all those hats in New York. Why don't you stay on, Ida, come go with me?"

August 28, 1963, had finally come. It could not have been a more perfect summer day; though before it was over, the sweat would be dribbling down the back of women's dresses and men's shirts. Mahalia found herself standing beside Dr. King on the steps of the Lincoln Memorial. They were both quiet as they looked out at the tens of thousands of Americans, Blacks and whites, there to take part in history for the March on Washington for Jobs and Freedom.

Powerful labor union leader A. Philip Randolph was already there. One of the preeminent civil rights leaders in the country, Randolph was the person who first proposed the march more than a year before to protest job discrimination. Almost 25 years earlier, in 1941, Mr. Randolph had played a crucial role in President Franklin D. Roosevelt's creation of the Fair Employment Practices Committee, but only after the powerful unionist threatened that 100,000 Negroes would alight in Washington to protest job discrimination. This time, Randolph saw the need for Blacks to come together to speak out in one mighty voice for equal rights for all Blacks, the poor and others.

Mr. Randolph had worked for nearly a year on the plans for the 1963 March on Washington and would later say that no one was excited about the plans early on. Both Black and white leaders spoke against the march, saying people from all over the country wouldn't take off from their jobs and go to Washington to be a part of a march in the middle of August. Besides, they said, Congress wouldn't listen.

And, that was Black Americans talking. Most whites were against the march, seeing it as a pun by Blacks to stir up trouble. A. Philip Randolph heard all his naysayers but refused to call off the march. He went to work recruiting young Negro men like Bayard Rustin, an influential young civil rights activist, to help him with the organizing. Mr. Randolph also traveled across the country getting church groups and union groups and young Negro student groups to promise they would join in.

Randolph was swimming up tide all the way. White newspapers and political leaders continuously talked against the march, which seemed to make Black Americans more determined to see it come to fruition. When whites realized that the march was actually going to take place, there was an aura of fear that overtook the communities, fear there would be violence and rioting. Some locked themselves inside their homes. Others left town for the weekend.

No wonder they feared Blacks coming into town. Just weeks ago, during a peaceful springtime demonstration for civil rights, Black men, women, and children had been beaten, bombed, blackjacked, and sent to jail by the thousands.

The night before the 1963 march, D.C. had the aura of a city about to be captured by an enemy army. Houses were dark, and the streets were deserted. There were hundreds of police and soldiers patrolling the streets.

One hotel worker excitedly predicted that there would be people rolling into Washington all night long by bus, by train, and by the carloads. Five hundred busloads were expected from New York, and 18 special trains were coming from the South and from the Midwest. There would be plane-loads of Blacks flying in from New Orleans and California.

Young CORE members were walking all the way from New York City. One man had come in from Chicago on roller skates, and an old man—80 years old—rode in from Ohio on his bicycle.

Mahalia was beside herself with excitement throughout the day. She hadn't known what to expect, but this surpassed any of her expectations.

On August 28, the morning of the March on Washington, Mahalia awoke to a bright, sunny day, with a breeze that softened the sunshine. She found that an army of people had come to Washington during the night, spreading out on the grassy slopes and under the big elms and oaks in the big park between the Washington Monument and the White House.

Families were getting comfortable, spreading out picnics. Mothers were feeding tiny babies, while fathers were taking their children up to the top of the Washington Monument, then over to watch the fountain on the White House lawn.

It all reminded Mahalia of a big picnic back home, or a church rally. And, just like church, everybody was dressed up in white shirts and dark suits, and Sunday's best dresses and hats. The park had hundreds of ministers from all over the country.

Mahalia would recall how the police and young soldiers there to protect the city and the people from the rioters were puzzled by the peaceful crowd. There was nobody to arrest—just peaceful Black people and white people united by a spirit of good will. Mahalia would later say the day had filled her with pride and so uplifted her that she was near tears.

Mahalia took out her own camera and started taking pictures of the other celebrities who had come be part of history, like Josephine Baker and Sidney Poitier who had both flown in from Paris. Jackie Robinson, Harry Belafonte, and Lena Horne had come in from New York. Whole planeloads of actors had come from California. Before the day was over, Mahalia had snapped pictures of Marlon Brando, Sammy Davis Jr., Burt Lancaster, Paul Newman, Charlton Heston, and Dick Gregory.

Besides the celebrities, there were thousands of Blacks who had fought so hard for civil rights in the Deep South, such as Mrs. Medgar Evers—whose husband had been killed in cold blood by a shot in the back fired by a white man in Mississippi—and Daisy Bates who led the first colored children into a white school in Little Rock, Arkansas.

There were the Sunday school classmates of the little girls who had been killed by a white man's bomb in a colored church in Birmingham, Alabama, and brave preachers like the Reverend Fred Shuttlesworth, who had shown the courage of a lion in helping his people stand up to the white racists in Alabama. There were all the young students—many of them fresh from Southern jails—who had marched against snarling police dogs and tear gas, guns, and billy clubs in Alabama and Mississippi.

For many Black Southerners, it was the first time many of them had been outside their communities. Most had never dreamed of traveling to Washington, D.C., especially for a freedom march. For the oldest marchers, it would be a final memory of their moment in history.

As the charter buses and special trains rolled into town, the crowds grew larger and larger. The reported number was more than 250,000 Americans—the largest protest crowd that had ever descended on the nation's capital.

Old spirituals, church hymns, and new "freedom" songs wafted throughout the park. Tens of thousands of voices sang "We Shall Overcome," "We Shall Not be Moved," "Blowing in the Wind," and "Oh Freedom!" which included the line *"Before I'll be a slave, I'll be buried in my grave, and go home to my Lord and be free. Oh, Freedom!"*

Thousands of marchers moved toward the Lincoln Memorial shortly after noon, still singing hymns and songs and waving American flags and banners and signs about the civil rights bill. There were old folks in wheelchairs and men and women on crutches.

After she arrived at the Lincoln Memorial, Mahalia climbed the marble steps where the great statue of Abraham Lincoln sat looking out over Washington. She took her seat in a wooden chair to listen to the speakers introduced by A. Philip Randolph and awaited her turn to sing for the marchers.

Mahalia would later write: *"The summer sun was beating down on us, but I never gave it a thought as I sat looking out at the great sea of people and*

banners, spread out as far as I could see. I couldn't look hard enough or long enough. The beautiful day and the great multitude gathered there had such a special meaning for me that I felt as if I were hypnotized. I was living and breathing history."

"I, myself, was the granddaughter of Negro slaves who had labored on a Louisiana plantation. All around me were the great Negro leaders of my own generation—men like A. Philip Randolph and Roy C. Wilkins—and the new young leaders like Martin Luther King and Whitney Young and John Lewis, who with the help of the young Negroes were bringing about another revolution in American history. Sitting and standing side by side with us were white people—Catholic, Jewish, and Protestant clergymen and powerful union men like Walter Reuther [president of the United Automobile Workers].

"Near me sat Dr. Ralph Bunche, who had raised the American Negro to a new eminence in the United Nations, and Thurgood Marshall, now a federal judge, who as an NAACP lawyer, had waged the case against segregated schools until he won the famous Supreme Court decision in 1954 [Brown v. Board of Education].

"Here on these same marble steps, Marian Anderson had sung in 1939 after being rebuked and barred from Constitution Hall by the white members of the Daughters of the American Revolution.

"I thought back on how in the 50 years since I was a child on the Mississippi levee, I had seen my people and my country move forward in so many ways until now we were at the threshold of salvation.

"It seemed to me that despite the hatred and fears Negroes still had to face, the American people were beginning to fall into step with us, and the hopes for days to come seemed as bright as the sunshine that sparkled over the Potomac River and shone on the tall Washington Monument.

"With a truly exalted feeling, I rose to sing. I'd thought long and hard about what was the right song for me to sing that day. It had been Martin who gave me the answer. When he heard me talking about it, he had said, 'Mahalia, why don't you sing "I been Buked and I been Scorned" for us?' There're probably only a few white people who ever heard that song, but it's an old spiritual that is known to colored people up and down the land. It was exactly the right choice for the day because its words reflected the depth of feeling of all the colored people who had come to Washington, and it would reach out to all the millions who might be watching and listening to us on radio and on TV. At first, I sang the words softly…

'I been buked and I been scorned.

I'm gonna tell my Lord

When I get home

Just how long you've been treating me wrong….'

"As I sang the words, I heard a great murmur come rolling back to me from the multitude below, and I sensed I had reached out and touched a chord. All day long I'd been going back and forth between tears and laughter. Now I wanted to let the joy that was inside me about this day come pouring out. I was moved to shout for joy. I lifted up the beat of the rhythm to a gospel beat. I found myself clapping my hands and swaying, and the great crowd joined in with me with a great wave of singing and clapping.

"I had my new hat pinned tight on my head so I could let myself go. I could sway and bounce as much as I wanted, and Mildred Falls at the piano went right along with me. People were joining in to sing with me. All through the great crowd I could see their hands clapping, and people who had been dipping their tired feet in the long reflection pool began to splash and rock to the rhythm. The flags were waving, and people shouting. It looked as if we had the whole city rocking. I hadn't planned to start a revival meeting, but for the moment the joy overflowed throughout the great rally.

"They said later that my singing seemed to bounce off the golden dome of the Capitol far down the mall, and I've always hoped it reached inside to where some of these congressmen were sitting!

"I had scarcely sat down and caught my breath when Martin was on his feet delivering a speech that was to make him famous. In his speeches and sermons, Martin never lets himself go in the shouting and stamping style of an old-fashioned Baptist minister. It's just not in his nature to reach the people that way.

"Although he has become the most beloved and respected and powerful Negro leader in America, he is still a quiet-spoken man who can preach a whole sermon without getting his collar wet.

"But, on this wonderful afternoon, the pride and joy he felt about the great march and the spectacle of that multitude of people with all the hopes they cherished for their children carried him away, too. It was the greatest speech of the day, and when it was over, everybody was all used up.

" 'Go home,' A. Philip Randolph told us. 'Go home and continue the fight in every nook and cranny of the land.'

"As quietly as they had come, the great crowds began to steal away. The last songs died away. By evening, the last of the special trains and chartered buses were pulling out of town. Some of the people that had come from the Deep South had 20 hours of bus riding ahead of them, but as one old woman said, 'We've had the biggest day of our lives. When I get home, I'll be ready. I don't care whether it's picketing or marching or a sit-in, I'll be ready to do it.'

"Over at the White House, President Kennedy congratulated Philip Randolph and all the other march leaders on the way the day had gone.

"We had shown the white man that the American Negro has as much dignity and thinks as deeply as he does. We had let Washington feel the weight of our determination. We left in triumph, but we left as we had come—with peace and good will to all. I may not live to see the complete freedom that Negroes seek come to America, but I got the vision of it that great day."

1963—Martin's March on Chicago

After the March on Washington, Mahalia was suddenly flooded with memories of when Martin Luther King had brought his nonviolence campaign to Chicago just a few months earlier.

For the first time in her life, Mahalia, the gospel singer, would defy the president of the National Baptist Convention and most other big church ministers in Chicago. It was a serious decision. She knew it would cost her relationships, friendships, and some singing gigs. But she was doing what God wanted her to do—present Martin Luther King to Chicago.

Martin, in his quiet but coercive way, had a way of convincing Mahalia that she walked on water. He had told her that she was the only person who could successfully bring him into Chicago. Mahalia laughed and shook her head, saying the most wonderful thing about God is that he gives people the intelligence and ingenuity to depend on themselves.

Look at me…these old songs I brought up from the South—they're like throwing bread on the waters. It comes back buttered on both sides. I am not a great artist. I am just Mahalia Jackson.

After weeks of back and forth to make sure that her busy schedule was clear, Mahalia and Martin settled on May 27, 1963. She wasn't looking forward to facing Chicago Mayor Richard J. Daley and the local politicians with her plans.

During her travels leading up to May, Mahalia sought talent for "the cause" in Chicago just a few weeks away. She was upset by the "stars" who kept telling her they had already given one benefit.

Mahalia reflected on the situation: *Well, they have to keep on giving them, cause the people keep going to jail and the money gets used up as fast as we give it. Me, I'm ready to join a picket line or anything else. Not for Dr. King—for me. Because I have walked all over this world, and I'm not free enough to have a decent TV show.*

Mahalia was deploying the troops and warning her soldiers they were working for justice and for right, not to get an extra paycheck.

In this world, you got to have a made-up mind. No straddling the fence. Lean on the word of God. I'm working two months for Martin without a dime, and you all can just do the same. And I don't mean sitting on your behinds and saying you helping Mahalia Jackson. I got no use for dry shells. I want the meat. This thing's going across the country.

Though she might never admit it, Mahalia Jackson had crossed over into politics. All day and every night, 8358 Indiana Avenue looked like an election headquarters. They spent most of the day planning for Martin's Chicago debut, running down sponsors and stars. On April 5, they closed things down long enough to go out to vote. Once again, Mahalia would make sure her friend Mayor Richard Daley knew that the Black wards spelled the difference for his reelection—82 percent. Chicago's lone Black congressman, William L. Dawson, was a shoo-in as well.

Mahalia received the news that Martin was down in Birmingham, where his squad kicked off their protest—and where they were met by fire hoses and police dogs. Two thousand young and old were arrested. Two thousand bails had to be paid for.

Mahalia coaxed, cajoled, prodded, and pushed everybody she could into donating services and/or wares for a benefit concert for Martin Luther King's cause down South. Her first stop was the mayor's office. She walked out with the nearly 5,000-seat Arie Crown Theater in Chicago's McCormick Place, contributed by the city—operating costs thrown in. The musicians' local waived rules, and Mahalia got 28 men free—stage-hands, ushers—all free.

Mahalia announced her steering committee for the benefit concert during a dinner at her house with the goal of raising $50,000. She was proud that a member of her old group the Johnson Singers, Robert Johnson, was joining her for this important event; along with Reverend Abernathy; Mayor Daley; John H. Johnson, publisher of *Ebony* and *Jet*; and S.B. Fuller, publisher of the Courier newspapers. They represented all the publicity she'd need. The radio community threw in free advertising as well—if Mahalia personally made the announcements. Thanks to her wrangling skills, tickets for the benefit concert were just $170.

In spite of her working day in and day out on Martin Luther King's benefit concert, Mahalia had to make herself available for three events that month. She helped Jack Paar narrate films of his trip through the Holy Land and sang spirituals during a guest appearance on his talk show on Good Friday. On Easter Sunday, Mahalia sang at an engagement in Louisville, Kentucky, though she was fighting a cold—sipping hot lemonade backstage. And she talked actress Jane Russell and singers Connie Haines and Beryl Davis into headlining a benefit for the Mahalia Jackson Foundation.

That was all in addition to her trip back to the White House, where she sang at the First Lady's Tea with the wives of the American Society of Newspaper Editors. Mrs. Kennedy knew the editors were accustomed to having the president speak at one of their convention luncheons, and their wives were invited along for the White House reception.

President Kennedy was delighted to see Mahalia again, proudly introducing her to George Healy Jr., editor of New Orleans' The Times-Picayune newspaper, then offering her a personal "presidential tour of the White House." Too smitten by the young President Kennedy and too kind to tell him that both former President Truman and Mrs. Eisenhower had already done the honors, Mahalia walked and listened as Kennedy shared history in his beautiful New England accent. She would later say that his tour got the highest marks because it was the first time she'd been asked to sit in the president's chair, a moment the New Orleans washerwoman would never forget.

Mahalia took an evening off to help Mayor Daley welcome the Grand Duchess Charlotte of Luxembourg, who arrived on the arm of William Rivkin, the U.S. ambassador to Luxembourg. The duchess invited Mahalia to visit her in her country. Mahalia said she would be honored to, then hurried home before the typewriters had been covered for the night.

In early May, Mahalia made an impassioned plea for the benefit concert at a local church. She promised the congregation they'd witness the greatest collection of stars that had ever performed in one night in Chicago.

I'm hot, and I'm hurt. Don't think you're doing Mahalia a favor by coming—you're doing yourself a favor, and you're helping your brothers and sisters down South to help you have the dignity of your identity.

Still on a mission, Mahalia talked the telephone company into contributing a special phone line so Dr. King could address her pep meetings of the workers. And a week before the benefit, Dr. King took to the pulpit of the First Methodist Church in Evanston, Illinois, for two sermons. Afterward, King told the congregation: *"We seek to obtain justice for Negroes, not to reverse the social order. We must not substitute Black supremacy for white supremacy—for one is as bad as the other."*

Martin, Meet the Mayor

Hollywood came to Chicago. Some were there for Mahalia, some for Martin, and most for both. The star-studded event was one of the most important in Mahalia's career. It wasn't just another "bringing stars to Chicago and raising money" kind of occasion. This was important to Martin Luther King and Mahalia, and to the future of the country. Mahalia was committed wholeheartedly to Dr. King's civil rights struggle. His cause was her cause.

Dr. King arrived in the city with his right-hand man Ralph Abernathy and regular traveling aides Wyatt Walker and Fred Shuttlesworth. It was important to Mahalia that they were welcomed with as much fanfare as the city could spare. Arrangements were made for gleaming black limousines and an open car to transport Dr. King and his colleagues to City Hall. And Mayor Daley sent an escort of six police motorcycles and squad cars.

Mayor Daley promised Mahalia he'd remain in his office past quitting time to greet Dr. King and his entourage. He waited while Mahalia stopped by the Chicago Defender newspaper for a brief interview and photo op, then by Johnson Publishing Company, where the ever-professional publisher John Johnson coordinated a press conference with the city's Black and white press.

Finally, they were off to meet Chicago's most popular and longest serving mayor. As promised, Mayor Daley, the wise and consummate politician, put aside his personal feelings about Martin Luther King's visit to his city and welcomed the young minister with a smile.

Mahalia's benefit concert sold out. They could have filled another 1,000 seats with just those who were turned away, but the city demanded that not another soul could enter the event.

Popular radio personality Studs Terkel, the emcee for the night and one of Mahalia's dearest friends, called on the ushers to take their baskets down the aisles to raise money for the march in Birmingham. Several thousand dollars were raised. To help move attendees to give, Mahalia lent her voice to the event.

Martin Luther King Jr. walked to the podium near midnight. His speech was as fiery as if it was noon—warning of what could be the outcome if change didn't come. Dr. King challenged President Kennedy to sign an executive order outlawing segregation. He reminded the audience of how Alabama's segregationist governor, George Wallace, had stood at the entrance of the University of Alabama to block Black students from entering. King suggested that Kennedy fly to Alabama and walk with the Negro students through the university's doors.

The Chicago audience were shocked when Dr. King described Chicago as equally segregated as Birmingham, Alabama. It took young Aretha Franklin to warm the audience up again, singing one of Dr. King's favorite songs, "Take My Hand, Precious Lord."

It was 2:30 a.m. when Martin was whisked away to a private reception in his honor. Mahalia stayed back to oversee the money. Only her most-trusted friends were allowed to help with counting, tallying, proving, then bundling the night's account. Mahalia wiped sweat from her forehead and nose as they counted the collection to the penny. With all the pledges in, she had reached her goal, and then some—more than $50,000. She would sleep well that night.

The first thing Mahalia did when she woke the next morning was to get breakfast started. She wanted everything ready when Martin and his friends arrived. The second thing she did was to remove the bundle of money from the hiding place. One last time before Martin arrived, she would count it again, "proving" it with fresh eyes. It didn't take long. The first count was off, so she slowly recounted. No mistake this time, $5,000 were missing. She counted once more, as a sense of panic rose in her throat. There were $5,000 less than was there just hours ago.

Martin and company piled into Mahalia's home in time for one of her amazing New Orleans-tinged breakfasts. They rehashed the night as they ate, including endless words of gratitude to their host for the previous night's successful event and for the breakfast. Martin joked that everyone should be careful because Mahalia was known to put New Orleans magic in her food—the spicy omelets, pan fried potatoes, Sunday-fried chicken, and cheese grits.

Mahalia basked in the gratitude, noting that her dear friend looked tired and needed to rest. By now, though, she knew there was no rest in sight. There was no time for rest, no matter how exhausted. Who would stand in for him, do the necessary work? She would say an extra prayer that night. And, then there came that boyish grin infusing her with hope, convincing her that all would be right with the world because Martin was leading the struggle.

After breakfast, the men grew quieter, almost in whispers as they discussed their next stops. Mahalia excused herself, went into her bedroom, and came back with a box just large enough to hold all the bills inside. She beckoned Martin over, and they sat for a moment at the kitchen table. She set the box on the table and told him how much was inside. There was that young boy's glint of love and awe for this woman called Mahalia, as a grateful Martin thanked her and hugged her to him.

Martin didn't need to know that she'd somehow come up short since last night. That she'd called her banker to meet her at the bank to withdraw $5,000 to make up for what was now missing. After all, she'd promised Martin she would raise $50,000.

A long, deep sigh escaped Mahalia as she collapsed into a chair at the kitchen table after Dr. King left. She couldn't pinpoint exactly why she was weeping, whether it was sadness or exhaustion. She searched her memory, prayed, then put the strong suspicion about the missing money deep in the back of her mind. She would not attach a scandal to Martin's event.

Part 10

LOVE COMES AGAIN

MAHALIA AND SIGMOND "MINTERS" GALLOWAY,
HER NEW LOVE, CIRCA 1964 (GETTY CREDIT).

1963—Summer Love, Fall Sorrow

Aside from the historic March on Washington that August, there were two occurrences in 1963 that touched Mahalia Jackson to the core. Separately, they represented one of the highest points in her life, and one of the lowest. The high point was that summer when Mahalia was introduced to Sigmond "Minters" Galloway, a California musician and one of the most handsome and charismatic men she'd ever met. That meeting would impact the rest of Mahalia Jackson's life.

And, then, in the fall, November 22 to be exact, the date would mark one of the saddest days in Mahalia's life—the day that President John F. Kennedy was taken from the world by an assassin's hate-filled bullet. This untimely death of a young president who Mahalia also considered a friend was traumatic. She found it hard to sing for a time, and it was Sigmond Galloway who comforted her through her season of grief.

In a radio interview shortly after Kennedy was assassinated, Mahalia said that Kennedy had done more than any other American president to make the American Negro feel that Washington and the U.S. Capitol belonged to Black people as well.

"It had often seemed to me when I traveled around Europe and talked with people from so many different countries that Americans back home didn't really understand how much the rest of the world loved and respected our president. His greatness didn't really dawn on them until that terrible day in Dallas, Texas," Mahalia told the interviewer.

She would often relive the moment when she learned of his death that warm fall morning in California. Mildred, her pianist and traveling aide, was with her, and they were preparing to leave their hotel room enroute to Columbia Records' recording studios. Just as Mahalia prepared to walk out the door, Mildred ran into the room with the news—a reporter had just announced that President Kennedy had been assassinated.

Mahalia, in shock, found herself too weak to walk. She sat and asked Mildred to tell her exactly what she'd heard. Even then, she just wouldn't allow herself to believe it. How could that be? The young president—so full of life, with a face made for big smiles and deep sadness—was gone. All of that promise. All the possibilities. This president, she remembered, had even given Dr. King hope, even when King had goaded him to do more.

Sigmond Galloway was a widower, living with his 5-year-old daughter Sigma in California when Mahalia met him during one of her business trips there. Was it providence, then, that she met a man who she could lean on at a time like this? Sometime later, she'd joke that meeting a good-looking, educated man like Sigmond Galloway was almost as unlikely as a washerwoman from New Orleans' "Nigger Town" befriending the young, handsome president of the United States. The famous singer looked up into the heavens and whispered, *"Man, you got to be kidding me."*

It had been 22 years since Mahalia's marriage to Ike Hockenhull had ended in a slow fizzle. She was still a naive 30-year-old at the time, and for most of the years since then—except the one-year love affair with Russell Roberts—her life was wrapped up in her singing, traveling, and performing. She was half-joking when she sometimes told her church audience that out of all the good-looking Negro men she saw in her audiences, she ought to be able to find herself a husband. Sigmond was never in those church audiences.

She never saw it coming—falling in love again, daring to consider sharing her life again with a man. There were more than a little misgivings about the situation. Could this finally be a man who understood her and accepted her as she was?

She was rehearsing at Columbia's recording studio when an old acquaintance, Ruth, stopped by with a man she wanted Mahalia to meet. It was Ruth's brother Sigmond, a local jazz musician. The good-looking man with the soft voice had lost his wife six months earlier to breast cancer. Mahalia jokingly asked Ruth if her brother could talk, as Ruth seemed to

227

be doing all the talking while her brother stood in the background with a shy smile.

Sigmond could talk, and took over from there. He was a studio musician and had his own combo band. The combo had just finished a job in a Rock Hudson movie. It wasn't long after that that Mahalia was telling friends that Sigmond Galloway was someone she enjoyed being around, was easy to talk to…and very easy to look at.

Had Sigmond expected the introduction to result in a first date? Had Mahalia been prepared for the way she didn't want to just leave it at "nice meeting you?" Mahalia said she'd had a draining day at Columbia producing a new album when Ruth asked her to join them for dinner. Instead, Mahalia offered that she'd pick up some Texas greens at one of the local grocery stores, and they could come over to cook them. She made the offer to both, but Mahalia's eyes settled on Sigmond.

Mahalia hadn't grown up with her half-siblings, the Jackson children, but by now she'd met them all. She grew close over time to her half-brother Johnny Jackson Jr., who everyone declared was the spitting image of their father. She hired him to manage the apartment complex she owned and lived in when she traveled to Los Angeles. In time, Sigmond learned that a good meal was a way to Mahalia's heart—especially when the man was the one who cooked the good meal. Sigmond was a fast learner and began inviting her frequently to his home for meals whenever she was in town.

His kindness was reciprocated. When the legendary singer and jazz pianist Nat King Cole, one of Mahalia's dear friends, was honored at a dinner during one of her California visits, she invited Sigmond to join her. If Sigmond hadn't been sure before, he would soon learn just who this woman was. Of the 3,500 friends and friends of friends at the dinner, Mahalia and Nat Cole were the only celebrities to receive standing ovations. Nat insisted that Mahalia sing "Elijah Rock."

Mahalia had met members of the Galloway family of Indiana from her earliest days of traveling the gospel Chitlin' Circuit through the Northern, Eastern, and Midwestern churches. The family resided in Gary, Indiana, one of the cities Mahalia frequented. They were good church people. Sigmond was already married to his wife, Celeste, and was living in California at that time. Jazz music had always been important to Sigmond. He sometimes played in the Los Angeles orchestra and had even been invited to do some music arrangements.

During the winter of 1963, Mahalia spent a lot more time in California than in previous years. She was as busy as ever, though, performing concerts and gospel gigs in Hollywood and recording at Columbia Records. Sigmond was performing with the Los Angeles orchestra, but always found time to visit Mahalia, either at her recordings or at her concerts. He was one of her biggest fans and supporters. In time, the two of them even worked on rearranging a few of her gospel songs.

Mahalia admitted to friends that from the very beginning she was taken by Sigmond's soft-spoken and kind demeanor. She didn't believe him when he told her he wasn't already in a relationship. Why? She wondered. He was one of the most handsome men she'd ever met. Why wouldn't he have already been swooped up? What red-blooded woman wouldn't want to spend their days and nights with him?

Mahalia Jackson was falling in love. She found herself looking forward to their time together and missing him when they weren't together. She loved their dinner dates and the increasingly intimate times they spent after dinner. She was proud to have him escort her to Hollywood parties and dinners that she had for years attended alone or with girlfriends, or male relatives.

In less than a year, their relationship blossomed into a full-fledged love affair. When she realized she had another European tour on the horizon, she thought seriously about asking him to join her. Something told her, though, it was too early. She needed to pray about this new man in her life.

No one loved children more than Mahalia. She'd wanted a child of her own for as long as she could remember. Whenever she'd imagined being married, having her own child was as much a part of that marriage as a husband was.

During her time in California in 1963, Mahalia was invited to visit a children's center where most of the children had physical disabilities. It took all of Mahalia's strength to hold herself together as she remembered her early years of being looked at as a "cripple," as they called children with physical disabilities back in New Orleans. She told the children: "*My legs were crooked and bent when I was a child. I was terribly deformed. And now my legs are as straight as anybody's. I am walking evidence of what God can do.*"

Before leaving town, Mahalia stopped by Columbia Records for the public announcement of her new contract with Columbia. By now, Mahalia had won two Grammy awards, the most prestigious award given in the music industry—her first in 1961 for "Every Time I Feel the Spirit" and her second in 1962 for "Great Songs of Love and Faith."

Sigmond Minters Galloway

Ever-inquisitive, or "nosy," as Aunt Duke always called her, Mahalia learned as much as she could about Sigmond "Minters" Galloway and his family. Each time they spent time together, she plied him with questions. Some of what he shared she already knew. He had grown up in Gary and had worked for his uncle's construction company before moving to California to follow his dream of becoming a musician. He was a sax man, but also loved the flute. His combo had worked for 10 years at Hermosa, California.

Was there anything this man could tell her that would put an end to her falling deeper in love with him every time she saw him? Probably not, if she was honest with herself. How could she not be drawn in by his soothing voice and his sweet pampering, which surprised her, especially coming from a man who probably had been pampered most of his life. A man who insisted on cooking her meals after her long days performing or taping music. It would be a while before she realized the truth—that his godmother, who lived nearby, had smuggled most of those delicious dishes into his home just minutes before Mahalia arrived for dinner.

By fall 1963, Mahalia was in the middle of an emotional whirlwind. Except for the monthslong interlude with Russel Roberts, she'd forgotten what it felt like to be in love. Now, 22 years later, she wondered if this wasn't a different level of love from what she'd known before. She felt her life changing. She was waking up expecting something good to happen in her day. And Sigmond Galloway was the cause of this emotional upheaval. She'd never felt it exactly like this before, not with Ike, and not with Russell, who had left too soon to really test their love.

In February 1964, Mahalia was back in California for a rash of studio sessions and rehearsals, including for her role, appearing as herself, in the movie *The Best Man*, with Henry Fonda, Edie Adams, Cliff Robertson, Lee Tracy, and Margaret Leighton.

Mahalia's manager Lou Mindling wasn't thrilled about her growing infatuation with the handsome Minters Galloway. He frowned when she left after rehearsal and after a Hollywood event to be with Galloway. He didn't trust this quick romance that had Mahalia acting so differently.

Minters would often join her at the studios. Sometimes he brought his young daughter Sigma around to spend time with Mahalia. Mahalia adored the pretty little girl who reminded her of herself when she was young—tall and gangly, a foot taller than most of her friends. There was, however, a big difference—Sigma's legs were perfectly straight, and she wore the prettiest little outfits.

Mahalia sometimes awoke from a beautiful dream and realized it was her reality. She had long realized she wasn't the Hollywood version of beautiful, even though there were men who, from time to time, told her she was. When Sigmond said it, she believed him. She looked into his eyes and saw the reflection of the beauty he saw.

Mahalia's close circle of friends and family sensed the dramatic change in her. There was something softer, less hard and pushing. Who was this California musician, anyway? Protective and concerned that she wasn't heading for heartbreak, no one was brave enough to voice their concerns unless Mahalia asked. And, even then, the storm in Mahalia's eyes made them know she didn't want to hear their truths, or their questions.

Her bravest friends, the ones with whom Mahalia would share her darkest secrets, asked: *"What are you going to do with a new husband, Halie, when you're the most famous woman in the land? What's the need?"* It hurt Mahalia when friends wouldn't be happy for her, for her last chance at happiness with a man that most women would give anything to share their bed with.

Mahalia was more and more reluctant to leave when she visited California. But this time she had an important commitment, the monthlong European tour. Commitments were common for Mahalia, and Minters never complained. In fact, he was always as excited about her fame, as she was.

Mahalia was back home in Chicago, and alone. Minters was a thousand miles away. The heaviness of what she didn't have pressed down on her. She chided herself. Why couldn't she be excited about this European tour? She had a month to travel to some of the most beautiful cities in the world and to meet interesting fans who loved her and her music. In time, Mahalia would admit her love-hate relationship with performing. Only for the last few years had she begun to question if it had all been worth it. The hard trudge up that mountain to become somebody, to realize in time what she had to give up to hold on to that role.

Yes, this European tour would be a month of running herself ragged, singing till she just about made herself sick, meeting so many people—people clamoring to say hello, just so they could say they'd met Mahalia Jackson.

Mahalia was already thinking about her return home a month from now—returning to this empty house; no one here to welcome her back, or tell her how much they missed her. No one to relive the ups and downs of her monthlong tour, or the people she'd met.

She lay clutching her worn Bible in her hands, staring up at the ceiling. "Fame and fortune, my foot!" she spat out the words, her face clouding over. It wasn't all people thought it was. But, Lord, there was the money… more money than she could have imagined in her head down in New Orleans.

But the price of fame cost so much, it demanded so much. The exhaustion sometimes was like a liquid that soaked down into her bones—sometimes it weighed her down so, making her too tired to lay down, or get up. And the loneliness, the thing she feared all her life. She was sure it was because of Charity—losing her mother so early in her life. Something was always missing. She needed people. She needed love.

The deep emptiness pressed down on Mahalia, making the house that much larger and quieter. The next morning, she lay in bed a little longer. Exhausted from…life? She looked over at Russell Roberts' photograph in the very spot she'd sat it the night he died. Her tears were about what she'd missed and the strangling fear that loneliness would be her only companion throughout the rest of her life.

Mildred, They Love Me!

In 1964, Mahalia flew off to her third European tour—one month, this time. Her manager, Mr. Mindling, had all their airfares, plus hotel and food, written into the contracts.

In London, Mahalia's audience was downright emotional, and she appreciated the way they responded to her songs, whether they were fast and beating, or slow and fervent.

In Brussels, Mahalia gave a command performance to an audience of 5,000, which included members of Belgium's royal family, though King Baudouin and Queen Fabiola were not in attendance.

In Amsterdam, she was moved to tears when she was taken to the John F. Kennedy flower planting in early May. She felt the pain of his death all over again. She knelt and prayed for his peace.

Mahalia was overwhelmed by the large youthful crowds in Europe. The young people's interest in her and her music was a lovely surprise. There were 28,000 young people representing the Youth Christian Society in Utrecht, in central Netherlands. In all her years, she'd never seen this many blond children. It took a squad of police to hold back the crowd of youth pushing to get near her.

That night, Mahalia sang again, for an audience of 5,000 adults whose adulation very much matched that of the youth earlier in the day. She'd joke later, "I thought I was the Beatles!"

Only in Sweden was there a hiccup during her European tour. Mahalia would share later: "This sweet, young Swedish girl was making over me backstage, and she put a pair of eyelashes on me. I don't wear such a thing, but I let her go on and please herself. So, I had these false teeth—this bridge—that I had put in just before I left Chicago. And I had those on, and now false eyelashes, too!

"Well, I'm singing away. So, what I first realized was my teeth are gone! There's a huge crowd of these pretty young people on stage right up around me—there were so many people. So, I said to one of them, *'come close... I believe I lost my teeth. Has anybody seen my teeth?'*

"They answered, just as polite, *'Yes, Miss Jackson, they're right over here.'* Oh, I was so embarrassed, but I didn't let on, I just said real sweet and polite, *'Oh? Is that right?'* and looked down around on the stage and picked them up.

"Then one of the children said, *'Miss Jackson, your eyelashes are coming off, too.'* Sure enough, I'd been so wrapped up in my singing, and so embarrassed about the teeth, I hadn't noticed. They were both coming off—one was hanging by the tip end."

Mahalia was busy at every stop. During her concerts in Holland, she found that the people were just as religious as they were back home. She was swept off her feet by the numbers who came out, and the excitement. Everyone seemed to know her songs and all her records, especially the young people who crowded into the concert halls in Brussels and Amsterdam to hear American gospel hymns and spirituals.

Finally, Mahalia was on her way home, satisfied that everyone graded the tour a resounding success. She sailed on the big ocean liner the S.S. *United States.* As she crossed the Atlantic Ocean, she was thinking of her future and Minters Galloway. Though she still had a deep fear of flying, this time it was a comfort to fly from New York to Chicago, rather than drive all that way across the country in her big car.

Mahalia was happy to be back home, tired, but not the same kind of tired. The depression that swooped down on her before she left for Europe had disappeared. She was excited about what her future might hold. Was she fated to become Mrs. Sigmond Minters Galloway? She still didn't know. She knew she loved the man and loved spending every minute she could with him. But, did that mean she should change her life, maybe her career? She had worked so hard, sacrificed so much to be where she was now. Was she willing to risk it all for love?

235

Mahalia tried to turn off her aunts' hard questions about her new romance. She stifled the anger it brought up in her. "This prestige mess isn't everything," she'd shot back to her aunts, anger and hurt roiling in her eyes. Why didn't they want her to be happy? Even Adam was given a companion when the Lord saw that he was lonely. Mahalia wanted and needed companionship.

The more she thought about it, the more she remembered the good times she had with Minters. She wouldn't ask him, but if he got brave enough to start visiting her in Chicago, she couldn't make any promises.

Mahalia Pays Homage to America's New President

On May 26, 1964, Mahalia was scheduled to perform at a salute to President Lyndon Baines Johnson, a late inaugural ball for the unelected president. The Democrats were raising funds with this inauguration, the same as they did with President Kennedy's successful inauguration—two inaugural balls, in both Washington, D.C., and New York. The tickets were certainly for "those who could." Mahalia shook her head, $100 a ticket for the show, and $1,000 for dinner beforehand!

Mahalia had fallen ill after her European tour. Her friends said she always gave more of herself than she had to give. Ailing or not, she couldn't say no to the new president and his wife. She flew to Washington to perform at President Johnson's dinner, but told him that she wouldn't be able to make it to New York.

The National Baptist Convention was coming up, and she had to get herself well enough to travel to the convention. Mahalia never missed the convention. It had been too hard to get invited in the first place. The Baptist ministers had vetted her for more than a decade before she was finally accepted. She'd never miss as long as she was healthy.

Mahalia was receiving her third Grammy Award nomination. This one was for "Make a Joyful Noise." She was too tired and sick to be happy, though she imagined Columbia Records was head over hills about the nomination. She sometimes wondered if the white people just couldn't find another Black person to give all their awards to. The League of Labor and Education was also giving her an award for "Outstanding Contributions in the Fields of Labor and Education."

Now people were calling about the big Illinois Rally for Civil Rights planned for June in Chicago's Soldier Field stadium. Mayor Daley and a lot of the colored Democrats weren't a bit happy about Dr. King coming to Chicago again and revealing all of the city's dirty laundry.

Much as she loved Martin, Mahalia didn't want to get sideways with Mayor Daley. He had been too good to her over the years, and she still needed his support. She made it clear she was not sponsoring the rally, that she was Martin's friend and a singer at the event. It was mostly a union business, she said. But after repeated calls, Mahalia agreed to arrange a motorcade and help drum up the crowd. Besides, she couldn't let Martin down. She called New York promoter Joe Costic and told him he'd need to reschedule her Carnegie Hall date. Martin needed her. Joe understood.

For years, she'd learned to balance her crazy schedule with just a pencil and a writing pad. But as her career grew, she needed help. She brought in friends or friends of friends to serve as secretaries, assistants, or personal assistants. It didn't take long for them to see that Mahalia would always be in control. None of her assistants quite lived up to her expectations. And, no one understood how she kept all her business in her head, just scribbling down the barest of information on those writing pads. For most of her life, she'd tended her business inside her head, giving out information on an as-needed basis.

Right now, Mahalia's mind was in a jumble. Her mind kept drifting back to Minters Galloway. He'd arrived in Chicago that week, and without much ado, he'd proposed. Minters had asked her to marry him! Oh, my God. She was not ready for this…yet, it was what she wanted more than anything in the world. If she didn't say yes, would he ask again? Would she regret not grabbing the chance when it presented itself?

Trying to make up her mind wasn't helping Mahalia's health. Dr. Barclay, who had been her internal doctor for more than a decade, was a lot more than just her medical adviser. She took her problems to him, wanting his feedback. Not that she always followed his suggestions, but it was always good to hear what he thought. Over the years, she had brought him into many parts of her life, and he'd counseled her sometimes for hours at a time. She had told him about Minters and wasn't pleased with his response.

It was obvious, the doctor told her, that she had some misgivings, or she wouldn't be bringing it up. "And, he's a jazz musician?" Dr. Barclay had asked. "Now, how are you accepting that after all these years lambasting the devil's music?"

"What would you say if I told you I was getting married again, Doc?" she'd responded, lying on her back as he examined her heart and pulse.

Dr. Barclay frowned and shook his head. "I'm against it, Mahalia. When did all this happen? I didn't even know you were seeing anyone."

He reminded her that she'd just told him she was too ill to attend the presidential salute in Madison Square Garden, as much as she'd wanted to be there. The woman constantly pushed herself above her physical condition, which meant that her canceling the trip was a sign that she was not feeling well.

Mahalia was taken aback by Dr. Barclay's honest thoughts, but he wasn't finished yet.

"Mahalia, I think you feel like there's such a thing as a perfect marriage, that it'll take care of everything you're missing right now. Have you talked to your friends about this? What do they say?"

"I know there's no such thing as a perfect marriage, Dr. Barclay. I just want me somebody to call my own. Someone who respects me as a woman and respects my career. I want to share my home with someone…."

Dr. Barclay was convinced she was putting her hopes on something that would, in the end, exacerbate her illness, not help it. But he knew Mahalia. She would do what she wanted to, in the end. It angered Mahalia that most of her family and friends—including her trusted pianist and her aunts—were against the marriage.

Mahalia would have doubts one day, be positive the next, and then have doubts again. She felt like a grandfather clock. She didn't have a heap of time before Minters would walk away.

Mahalia brought Minters in to introduce him to Dr. Barclay. Though he would never tell her, Dr. Barclay was even more apprehensive after meeting the man and seeing the two of them together. Here was a sick woman who would need a tremendous amount of tender loving care and support. Would a man like Galloway, who looked like he was used to being the center of attention most of his life, give Mahalia the kind of care and attention she would need?

Right in the middle of her indecisions that were causing her blood pressure to rise, Martin dropped in for an overnight stay for a meeting before the big June rally. Neither Martin, nor Mahalia was able to sleep that night. Martin was uptight about the rally, and Mahalia worried about making the right decision about marriage. They both sat up and talked most of the night.

By the next day, Mahalia had a houseful of visitors. She was her old self, at least on the surface, making everyone feel at home, and cooking up a storm.

On June 21, 1964, Mahalia led a 5,000-voice choir at the Illinois Rally for Civil Rights at Soldier Field in Chicago. Dr. King was one of the principal speakers at the rally, which drew a crowd estimated at between 57,000-75,000, and included people from all walks of life, races, and religions. At the time, it was the second-largest civil rights demonstration, after the March on Washington nearly a year earlier. Less than two weeks later, President Johnson would sign the 1964 Civil Rights Bill into law.

The Soldier Field rally was a huge success. And Mahalia was happy to do her part, singing and making sure there were other gospel groups there to back up Martin's program. It was a wonderful diversion from thinking about marriage. She paid for it afterward, though; her body pretty much giving out.

Part 11

A NEW BEGINNING

MAHALIA WITH AUNT DUKE
(JACKSON FAMILY ARCHIVES).

Becoming Mrs. Galloway

Young Halie had been a tall and skinny girl, with beautiful smooth, dark skin—so dark that her friends often joked they could see themselves in it. She was a tomboy with boundless energy, camping out with her community crew who roasted acorns and black birds in the park, played baseball like she was born to do it, and fought the boys like a boy. She ran New Orleans' streets when Aunt Duke wasn't looking and fell in love with the city sounds, especially the hard-singing jazz and blues songs Aunt Duke hated so much.

But there was that other side of Halie Jackson of Pinchers Town. She was always, always, hypnotized by the pretty things that sparkled and twinkled. She couldn't resist gold and silver, things seldom found around Aunt Duke's shotgun home.

Mahalia, the Gospel Queen, would never link the way she was drawn to Minters Galloway to her childhood fascinations. The dilation of her pupils when he walked through the door was one in the same in how she'd stared at those pretty objects she just had to have.

So, there it was. There he was. A beautiful man by even his archest enemies' estimation. Smooth, suave, charming, and—dare Mahalia say it— sexy, unbelievably sexy, with that delicious voice and just the right way to use it.

Yet, Minters Galloway was not a mere boy toy. There was substance to him. He was a fine jazz man and performer. His music was known around Los Angeles. He had ambitions. And, while Mahalia didn't see all of what Minters was, she was focused on the shiny parts that kept her awake at night, turning and fretting.

Minters, the shiny bauble lying in the road along Mahalia's journey. She couldn't resist stopping, wouldn't dare just leave it where it lay. Yet, call it insight, intuition, or that third eye like Aunt Bessie was born with, Mahalia worried that the shine wouldn't last. It never did. Never mind that, she had to have him, take him home, and know that he would be there waiting anytime she left and returned.

On a hot Thursday in July 1964, Mahalia planned a dinner party, inviting a select group of her friends to meet Minters Galloway, including her friend and fellow gospel singer Albertina Walker.

She had a conversation with her pastor, the Reverend Leon Jenkins of Greater Salem Baptist Church. He didn't say much, but Mahalia had a lot to say. She called her manager Lou Mindling, telling him she was ready for him to give a bride away. Lou was not surprised. He'd known how the story would play out, maybe before Mahalia did.

Mahalia was still tired from her recent European tour. Wore out, but too much in love to pay her exhaustion much attention. She wanted to share her love and this man with her friends and family. Her close circle, not the reporters or photographers. Not yet.

Lou Mindling had been Mahalia's manager for a long time. Some in her circle mumbled about Mindling's sense of propriety when it came to Mahalia. Mindling had all but told Mahalia he wasn't sure about her relationship with Minters Galloway, but what did that matter? Mahalia had fallen head over heels in love with Minters, and her marriage certainly would prove she was still her own person.

Even with his misgivings, Mindling had dropped everything to fly from Los Angeles to Chicago when Mahalia called. Keeping his enemy close would be how Aunt Duke would put it. Mahalia was really going to marry this man, he thought. She had already sent her secretary Polly Fletcher for the marriage license, sent for the minister, and asked Mindling to give her away.

Mindling smiled through the evening, watching both Sigmond and Mahalia. But seeing something in Mahalia's eyes gave him an opening. He told Mahalia he didn't think the marriage was a good idea, that it wouldn't work, and he offered to hold the license up if she gave him the word.

Mahalia, not angry or surprised, merely said it wouldn't be right.

Everyone was there that needed to be there. Her pastor, the Reverend Jenkins of Greater Salem Baptist, Mahalia's church since moving to Chicago; Reverend Elijah Thurston, her spiritual adviser; and Brother John Sellers, her godson. Then, of course, there was Polly who had the license and Mindling who would give Mahalia away. And Minters, the groom, stood off to himself with a strange little smile on his face. Brother John was surprised he'd walked into a wedding, but not surprised Mahalia was marrying Sigmond. Hadn't she said she would? And hadn't he told her to go for it?

Mahalia had whispered to Polly that she was having second thoughts, as Polly was helping her to get dressed in her wedding attire. But Polly knew she'd go through with it. There'd be no ring. What did Mahalia need with another ring?

Reverend Jenkins performed the ceremony in Mahalia's living room. The bride wore her favorite blue dress and a corsage of white orchids. The groom wore a black suit that fit him perfectly. Mahalia became Mrs. Sigmond Minters Galloway on that hot July evening. Mindling had set up a press reception immediately after the wedding. Mahalia declared that beginning that day, her home would be a happy home.

The wedding party went to the Top of the Rock restaurant on the roof of the Prudential Building in downtown Chicago. As the waiters poured champagne, Mahalia held Sigmond's hand and gazed out on the lights of the city that had watched her grow up and become the Mahalia Jackson she was. Chicago was such an important part of her life. But no more so than the life she'd left behind in New Orleans. On this day, one of the happiest days in her life, she was remembering Charity, the mother she could hardly remember but missed with all her heart. She was also remembering Aunt Duke, the one who raised her, a hard raising, but one that stuck to Mahalia's bones no matter how high or low she'd go in life.

When the party toasted Mrs. Galloway, it took a while for Mahalia to realize that was her new name. At the top of the Prudential Building, one of Chicago's first downtown skyscrapers, Mahalia introduced her husband to the press. She proudly described him as working "in the building contracting business in Gary."

World, Meet Minters

Mahalia had been prepared for the critics. In her gut, she knew what most people were thinking. Sigmond was a good-looking man, and she was the famous Mahalia Jackson. Was this a marriage of convenience and opportunity? What she was not prepared for were the hundreds of letters from fans who spewed anger and vitriol that she would dare marry. Most were fearful that her marriage would rob her attention from the church, or her charities. Some felt offended, even betrayed by Mahalia's marriage. One writer asked if her husband was white.

Sigmond Galloway knew how to spoil a woman. He cooked Mahalia's breakfast and brought it to her in the mornings, even fed it to her; drew her baths and pampered her to Mahalia's delight. When he made himself a drink, he made her hot tea. He enjoyed talking music with her, so much so that he began screening her calls, saying she shouldn't be disturbed at night. Even the calls from her closest friends and family.

Before long, Sigmond convinced Mahalia that their house should be expanded, for entertaining and for making room for his daughter Sigma as she grew older. Mahalia wanted her stepdaughter to be happy. She wanted her to go to the best schools and have everything she needed.

In time, like all marriages, the newness began to wear off. Mahalia was ready to resume the life she'd put on hold so she could settle into marriage. She checked her schedule and decided there were events she could do. She called Mindling and told him she was ready to get busy again.

Mahalia hadn't met Minters' mother, Mrs. Mary Lou Jenkins, before their marriage. She told Minters they should plan a dinner party in his mother's honor. She'd invite his mother and his sister Ruth. Mahalia wouldn't admit to Sigmond just how nervous she was about meeting his people. Unlike herself, Sigmond's people were high yellow, sophisticated, and educated. She wasn't sure how they'd feel about her. It turned out she had worried needlessly. Sigmond's mother was immediately drawn to Mahalia, and Sigmond's uncle spent the evening sharing stories about the South.

Mahalia had invited many in her close circle, the ones Sigmond was trying his very best to weed out. He was not pleased with the way they all simply showed up invited or not, demanding Mahalia's attention in spite of her new marital status.

Mahalia was taken aback when she first learned that Sigmond drank alcohol. They argued about his taking drinks too early in the day and during dinners when pastors dined with them. It just wasn't proper, Mahalia said. When Mahalia suggested that ministers should be offered only coffee, Minters laughed, and said that most of her minister friends took more than a little drink in their own houses.

In spite of the newness fading in her marriage, Mahalia was in love. For the first time since the tragic loss of Russell Roberts, the love of her life, she now had a man in her life who made her happy. She felt complete and especially blessed to not only get an attentive husband, but a daughter as well. Sigma was a little introverted, but Mahalia would help bring her out of it. And she'd try to be home more often and find things she and the girl could do together. She really did want to be able to spend more time at home with her new family.

Sigmond let her know that he didn't want or need a stay-at-home wife. He'd married a star and wanted her to remain a star. He would join her as she traveled, rather than her changing her schedule to stay home. What would her fans think if she suddenly chose her family over the people who mattered—those who paid to come to her concerts and buy her albums and records.

Sigmond was bothered by other parts of Mahalia's lifestyle, too, including the ever-present parade of friends and relatives in their home. Some were there for days and even weeks. Why did she need all these people in her life, he wondered. When Mahalia was told about a story in *Jet* magazine alluding to Sigmond's disdain for her circle of family and friends, she was hurt that he would say such a thing in public. But she let it lie, wanting to keep the peace and remain happy in her marriage.

Mahalia thought Sigmond's irreverent complaints about her preacher friends crossed the line. They were there to offer spiritual guidance and prayers, she told him. Besides, Mahalia liked people; she needed people. Where would she be without them? Sigmond questioned whether she actually needed a husband.

Mahalia heard rumors that her husband hadn't portrayed himself exactly in a true light, that he was in fact a big partygoer who loved women and drink—and not women who looked like Mahalia.

Mahalia put her mind on life's serious troubles, like the news of the terrible killings taking place down South, in her part of the world. Bob Miller, her friend who was executive secretary and editor for the National Funeral Directors Association, had just returned from Jackson, Mississippi, where three civil rights workers were missing and presumed murdered.

Miller told Mahalia that he already saw benefits of President Johnson's Civil Rights Act of 1964. For the first time, he was able to stay in a downtown hotel. Dr. King, who was staying at a friends' home, called Miller and asked him to join him at a meeting. On his way to the meeting, Miller reported, he'd been stopped three times by the local police. About halfway to his destination, a civil rights lookout escorted him the rest of the way.

Miller told Mahalia there was still reason to fear the unexpected. He was shocked to see shotguns leaning against the wall of the meeting room where Dr. King met with local ministers and community leaders. He also complained about the bright lights behind his hotel. His fear was that whites were planning to take aim at Blacks in the hotel.

Martin laughed and told his friend that the people out back of the hotels were Negroes. The hotel backed up into their neighborhood.

Miller wasn't much relieved. As he talked, Mahalia kept seeing those shotguns, and Martin laughing and laughing, but clearly ever in danger. That night she prayed for him, and for President Johnson. She'd promised to work for the president during the whole election campaign. She told her manager Lou Mindling to open up her schedule so she would have time to do some campaign events. Johnson had to win, she thought. There was so much important freedom work that depended on him.

Halie's Ailing

It was a composite of so many things in Mahalia Jackson's life that saw her health take a dramatic turn in 1964. Only those who saw Halie the woman, not Mahalia the performer, would see the sometimes slow, and sometimes rapid, devolvement of the spirited, courageous, charming Mahalia. Her "ailing period" began with light complaints and would, in time, evolve into serious, chronic illnesses.

Over the years, Mahalia had dealt with the simple, nonthreatening feelings of exhaustion and weight gain or weight loss. But Halie being Halie, she hadn't made the life changes needed to nip some of the illnesses in the bud, before they got too out of hand. She couldn't slow down or bother with her doctor's warnings that came too often with a smile and deferral to Mahalia's wishes. After all, she was "The" Mahalia Jackson.

For the next several years, she would experience a long string of illnesses. Some of her ailments were in deed physical and health related, but some for certain may have been partially psychosomatic—as would be the diagnosis of some of her doctors, and certainly Minters. At the apex of her fame and fortune, her body and spirit were in conflict, and Mahalia would suffer the consequences.

For a time, the University of Chicago's Billings Hospital became Mahalia's home away from home. She was visiting Dr. Barclay's office there so frequently, he considered setting her up an office space there, too. He was the person Mahalia called on for every foreign hurt or pain. Who knows what secrets the doctor must have known about the international star. What he knew without a doubt was that Mahalia was not a healthy woman, and her hectic touring schedule was not helping her condition. The more he tried to warn her to take care of herself the more she complained that he was trying to put her in the poor house.

"If I don't work, I don't eat," she would respond. "If you put me on all these pills, I won't be able to work."

Sigmond joined Mahalia on a few of her doctor's visits and always found his way to cornering Dr. Barclay and asking him about his wife's condition. Dr. Barclay was the man whose advice Mahalia had sought when she had qualms about marrying Minters, then promptly married him in spite of the doctor's advice.

Sigmond wanted the doctor to tell him what Mahalia's "real" health problems were, making clear he wasn't sure his wife was as sick as she claimed. Dr. Barclay, suddenly protective of his patient, gave Sigmond an education in Mahalia's health history, including about the problems of her progressive sarcoid illness. The two men left it at a standoff. Barclay was convinced Mahalia's new husband wouldn't be good for her health, and Sigmond was convinced Mahalia had fooled the doctor, just like she had fooled her circle of friends, about the seriousness of her ailments.

Mahalia returned to her work, being the public Mahalia that her fans and family loved. Her next stop was St. Louis, Missouri, where she was performing at Kiel Auditorium. Married just a few weeks, Mahalia had asked her new husband to come with her, but Sigmond had other plans.

During the St. Louis concert, Mahalia was singing "I Don't Know About You," when she lost her breath and stopped singing for a while. She'd nodded to Mildred to keep playing and soon finished her performance. As always following her exhausting performances, Mahalia greeted the fans, autographed pictures, then went up to her room and entertained a few guests before going off to bed.

The next morning, she headed home to Chicago. On the way, she had a coughing spell and began sipping tea, hoping the hot liquid would tamp it down. For seven hours, Mahalia coughed. She and Mildred and the driver kept stopping along the way so they could find a restaurant and order hot tea. But nothing helped Mahalia's coughing.

If only she could make it home to her own bed and sleep, she'd visit Billings Hospital in the morning, Mahalia thought. The doctors at Billings already knew of her heart troubles. Now, though, Mahalia was having deep dry heaves and found it even harder to breathe. Mildred and the driver took her directly to the emergency room in a little hospital they saw on the way home.

Little Company of Mary Hospital was in Evergreen Park, a south sub-urb of Chicago. Mahalia told the registering nurse there that she thought she had indigestion. They listened but directed her to a room for more tests. Mildred, frightened, gave out the admitting information and called Sigmond to let him know that Mahalia was at Little Company of Mary.

During the weeks that Mahalia remained hospitalized, press from around the world clamored for news of her condition. She had visitors from all over the state and the country. Photographers tried to get into her room. Friends demanded to see her. A special public relations desk was created, and media bulletins went out several times daily regarding Mahalia's health. Mahalia received thousands of letters and cards from all over the world. Her assistant plastered the cards to the wall so Mahalia could enjoy them.

Mahalia refused the hundreds of flowers sent to her, saying they reminded her of embalming fluid. She asked that they be donated to St. Jude Children's Hospital or shared with the other patients at Little Company.

Mahalia loved the nuns there, thinking of them as angels of God. They reminded her of something she hadn't thought of in many years—how, when she was just 12 years old, she had gone up the steps to the Dominican Convent of New Orleans on her knees, asking God for a steady job.

Mahalia also received personal notes from some of her celebrity friends. The notes she treasured most were from friends like Dinah Shore, Arthur Godfrey, Duke Ellington, Harry Belafonte, Vice President Hubert Humphrey, Martin and his wife Coretta Scott King, Mayor Daley, and of course from President Johnson and the first lady, Lady Bird Johnson. This created quite a buzz inside the little hospital.

"Lady Bird and I were most sorry to learn of your recent illness, and we hope that this note will find you well on the road to recovery. You have always given generously of your talent and energy to our country and your voice has gladdened and uplifted many a heart. All America

joins me in warm wishes for your renewed good health and for your happiness in the years ahead."

The next day, there was another message from President Johnson:

"I was distressed to learn of your illness and want you to have this brief note to wish you a speedy recovery. Mrs. Johnson joins with me in hoping that you will soon return to your fine career. Our thoughts and prayers are with you."

Mahalia was tended by Dr. Earl Vondrasek. His records showed Mahalia was suffering from hypertensive heart disease manifested by acute coronary insufficiency. Her symptoms included shortness of breath, marked fatigue, and outbreaks of profuse perspiration. Mahalia's exhaustion had been going on for several days. And she was increasingly experiencing severe chest pains and some choking sensation in her throat. Her blood pressure was also somewhat elevated, and her electrocardiograms (EKG) were abnormal, suggesting damage possibly from a heart attack. The public was not made aware of Mahalia's true condition.

According to press reports, Mahalia was ordered to remain in bed four to six more weeks due to exhaustion and heart strain. Sigmond and Mildred were at the hospital daily, and at night. Mahalia's driver had picked up Aunt Hannah and Aunt Bell. Ike Hockenhull, Mahalia's first husband, was also allowed hospital visits. He had stayed away since her marriage to Sigmond, but thought Mahalia's condition was too serious to not see her now.

Mahalia sent for Mother Gay, a charismatic singer whose ministering had been helpful in 1952 before Mahalia's trip to Europe. Sigmond looked on, straight-faced, as the two women prayed together. The next day, Mahalia awoke with a song in her heart. The Lord had given her a song to pass on to President Johnson. Sigmond wrote the music. Two days later, a beautiful blue velvet folder was mailed to President Johnson with the imprint: "Onward President Johnson—A Song Written by Mahalia Jackson, Music Arrangements by Sig Galloway."

Mahalia was discharged from the hospital on October 13, 1964, and learned that same day of her new five-year Colombia contract, with better terms.

A Hard Leaving—Losing Aunt Duke

On New Year's Day in 1965, there was a houseful of visitors at Duke's. She was now living on New Orleans' Delachaise Street. The sickly Duke was quiet, but happy to have company. Isabell "Bell" stuck close by, realizing that her sister was much sicker than she let on and was also showing signs of senility over the last months.

Because she was sick as well, nobody wanted to be the one to tell Mahalia about Duke's illness. Now, it was too late. Duke passed away at midnight that New Year's night. Someone would have to tell Mahalia, and soon. It fell on Isabell.

Mahalia had tried to talk Sigmond into traveling with her to New Orleans, saying Aunt Duke had been like her mother. He insisted he couldn't. Mahalia knew her family was overwhelming for a man like Sigmond. Still. She would have felt a lot better if he was there with her at a time like this.

Mahalia chose to ride the train to New Orleans, and it brought back memories of her first train ride from New Orleans to Chicago almost 38 years ago. A small smile appeared on her face as she listened now to the quiet whoosh of the wheels on the tracks and flashed back to that day. She remembered the sad, scared, but awe-struck girl. She remembered how she had missed Aunt Duke for her first months in Chicago, always sad that Aunt Duke hadn't given her blessings as Halie left New Orleans. Hard, but good, Aunt Duke.

Thirty-eight years—many of them hard years. But she had survived because that's what Clark women do, find a way to survive in spite of what the world throws at them. Mahalia admitted she was content having this time alone, away from her house, even away from her husband who she loved with all her heart, but who oftentimes proved to be unreliable. How could you love someone so much, but find solace in being away from him?

Duke was gone. It hardly seemed possible. Mahalia's whole life had been centered around that woman, her substitute mother, who had taken her and her brother Peter in, had raised them the only way she knew how. It was a hard raising. Her love wasn't the soft love of their mother Charity's.

Mahalia arrived on Delachaise Street with no fanfare. There were tears all around. She wouldn't hold it against them for not letting her know earlier. She didn't really want to see the Duke that Bell described. It wasn't her Duke.

As she sat and caught her breath, Mahalia felt her family's eyes sweep over her. They were surprised to see their Halie—always the strongest of them all, second to Duke—looking so frail. Mahalia tried to comfort her Aunt Hannah, who was taking Duke's passing harder than anyone. Was Hannah remembering how she'd taken Halie away from Duke all those years ago? How it had been years before they'd made up and put the disagreement behind them?

Halie was numb with sadness, pushing away the most painful thoughts as much as she could. Yet, she did wonder. She was the last one to ever question God's wisdom, but…why would it have to happen on New Year's Day? What did it mean for the rest of the year?

The aunts insisted Mahalia take the guest bedroom. Mahalia couldn't sleep. She kept dreaming that Duke was there, and she dreamed about her childhood inside Duke's home. Duke had been everything worth anything to Halie after Charity's death. It was Duke, not her good-looking father who lived just blocks away, who fed her and kept her and taught her the hard lessons of life. Lessons she hadn't wanted to learn, at least not in the hard way she had.

But how could she argue that Duke's lessons had worked? Look at what God had done. Halie had brought those very same lessons with her to Chicago. They were part of her daily bread…like never sit around waiting for folks to give you gifts with a smile…or the best gifts were given unknowingly. It was Duke who told her that hard work was the lot of the colored woman, and if it didn't kill them, it made them stronger.

If Mahalia lived a hundred years, she could never with a straight face call Aunt Duke a loving woman—good, yes—loving, no. As a child, Halie didn't believe there was a soft bone in Duke's body. It wasn't until she was good and grown that she'd see softness in the woman.

Lord knows she hadn't cuddled Halie as a child or made her believe she was anything special. But then Aunt Duke had never shirked her responsibility to Halie or Peter. She'd kept her promise to their mother and did the best she knew how. Duke and Emanuel had been their rock when God took Charity away.

And, Halie had made Duke proud. Duke had finally said as much. Mahalia's name was known all around the world; she had friends in high places; and she had all the comforts anyone could need, including a husband to keep her company at night. Pretty good for a woman turning 54 in six months. Still, losing Duke, was like losing the steadiest part of herself.

On Wednesday, January 6, the newspapers reported that Mahalia had been nominated by the 1964 Gallop Poll as one of the "Most Admired Women in the World." Mahalia smiled weakly. Right now, she wasn't feeling like anybody that the world admired.

The service for Duke went as well as could be expected for a funeral service. Crowds of people filled the churchyard and lined up down the street. People from all over New Orleans were there. Many of them didn't know Aunt Duke. Most of them were there to see Mahalia Jackson, not to pay respects to her adopted mother.

Never mind. People are people, Mahalia knew. She kept her mind on Jesus and Duke. Hannah took it hard. Back at the house, they were relieved the service was over, and spent the rest of the evening reliving old times.

Mahalia lay in bed, bewildered. What did all this ailing mean? Ever since she was knee-high to a grasshopper, she had worked. Worked like a grown woman since she was 8 years old. Nobody who knew her then could believe that Halie would be so sickly now. Where did it all come from?

Mahalia thought back, trying to pinpoint when her body had started betraying her. Not in her 30s. Those were the peak years for her, when she started coming into her own. After the failure of her marriage to Ike, she'd realized it was all up to her. She couldn't depend on anyone else to hang that star for her. She'd cut her teeth on the years she sang with the Johnson Singers at Greater Salem Baptist. Then she had spent a few years on the road, touring off and on with Thomas Dorsey in the 1940s as a "fish and bread" singer, as she liked to call herself.

After that, for the next almost 20 years, God had been carrying her higher and higher, like he'd strapped her on roller skates and sent her off to lead the gospel world like nobody's business. Mahalia had taken every opportunity that came her way, saying yes when she probably should have said no. Working until she was dog tired. She would take a nap, then get back up to work some more.

And that had been right smack in the middle of the Jim Crow years. Lord, she'd had to deal with racism in Chicago—the place they'd called the promised land. During the trips she took back down South, she would get stopped by mean white men because she was a colored woman in a big old shiny car. They didn't see a person, just a colored woman. Then there were the mean Black men who didn't have much more respect for her, not because she was colored, but because she was just a woman.

Those years convinced Halie that she'd learned more from Aunt Duke than she ever knew. She'd learned how to be hard when life called for it. She surprised herself at how hard and mean she could be, in the name of survival. But she always knew God was on her side.

She and Mildred could write a book, she joked. Many days and nights they had to sleep in that big old car because no white hotel, no matter how small or dirty, would let colored people sleep there overnight. They also had to cook their own meals before leaving on long trips because no white restaurant would serve them.

Many nights, after they locked the car doors, Mahalia stuffed her night's pay in her bra, or in her panties, and sometimes in Mildred's too. Music promoters thought they had it easy with the big, Black gospel singer from down South, thinking they would pay her what they thought she was worth and she'd be happy with that. It didn't take long for the word to get around: *Don't mess with that gospel woman, Mahalia Jackson. Don't short her pay. Don't ask for a few days to get her money to her. Don't pay her with nobody's checks. Don't think you can outthink her…'cause you can't.*

When Mahalia failed to scare them with her hard, cold stare, the curse words she didn't even know she knew would come bursting through her thin lips. And finally…when nothing else worked, she'd introduce them to Mr. Colt .45.

Mahalia had been faster, stronger, smarter than all the rest put together. That's what had brought her so far. She wouldn't buckle under a little headache or back pain or any of that emotional stuff that stifled others and sometimes truly made her feel so low. She just wouldn't give in to it.

Now, it seemed to Mahalia that God waited until she was an old woman to bring her down. Had she flown too high, Lord? This chapter of her life, when she should be enjoying the fruits of her labor, found her suffering some days, but most nights wracked with pain and filled with exhaustion down into her bones. *"Hadn't I been a faithful soldier, God?"* she asked.

No matter what the doctors said, Minters refused to "baby" Mahalia or pamper her with love and attention, saying he couldn't believe that one week she was strong as an ox, and the next she was so low she couldn't get out of bed. Hadn't she had two months of nothing but rest? He understood that the doctor said Mahalia had heart strain, but surely she was doing fine, now.

Sigmond was flustered; beside himself. There was a table full of invitations for Mahalia, including the invitation to President Johnson's inauguration on January 20, 1965, and Mahalia was telling him that she just wasn't up to going. Halie cringed at her husband's hard stare and harsher words. He had rifled through her mail, especially the invitations, as if they were thousand-dollar bills. He declared that if she was too sick to go, he would go and represent her well.

Mahalia shook her head, remembering how his godmother had told her Minters had a thing about glamour since he was a child. He wanted to get to the White House and rub elbows with the rich and famous.

Mahalia checked into Billings Hospital. Her cousin Emma Bell believed Halie had put herself in the hospital to keep from going to the inauguration with Minters.

At the same time, Dr. Barclay continued to try to convince Minters that his wife was indeed sick and that it wasn't a normal kind of sickness. There were several things going on, most of them had started years ago, but didn't really show themselves and knock her down until now.

Dr. Barclay was convinced, no matter what other doctors told Mahalia, that her illness was due to sarcoid disease. He'd obtained the EKGs from Little Company of Mary Hospital. The doctors there thought she'd had a coronary occlusion. Barclay consulted other cardiologists who went over Mahalia's history. All agreed that Mahalia had both sarcoidosis of the heart and lung, very rare at the time. This, Barclay, told Minters, was the root cause of Mahalia's strange ailments.

Mahalia was not an easy patient. In spite of Minters' declaration that she loved being babied, she loved nothing more than standing before a crowd and singing praises to God. She complained that the doctor was keeping her from her work.

"You'll be singing soon enough, Mahalia" the doctor had promised his patient, and he hoped to God he was right. Dr. Barclay increased the dosage of her medication, telling her she would need to stay in the hospital another few days until they could get her illness under control and make sure the dosage was right.

Eight days later, Mahalia left the hospital feeling better. The doctor reminded her that the increased dosage of the medicine would also increase her appetite and that any weight gain was not good for her. His report showed Mahalia suffering from tremendous malaise, great pain, a dragging fatigue along with a range of other sarcoid manifestations.

By the time Mahalia arrived back home, Minters was in Washington, D.C. He was gone almost a week and returned strutting like a peacock. He was babbling on about all the people he met, and about a little difficulty he had with the hotel suite that was reserved in her name only. He'd straightened that out, ensuring them he was her husband. However, Minters couldn't hide his disappointment in returning home to find Mahalia still in bed.

"Mahalia, I believe if you had a toe ache, Dr. Barclay would say it was sarcoid—whatever that is; nobody ever heard of it."

"He said I had heart trouble."

"Well, they say the worst thing in the world for people with heart trouble is to baby themselves. Get out of the bed and go out somewhere with me. People are going to forget you exist."

"They wouldn't if you let 'em up here to see me," she'd responded.

"Now you can't have it both ways," argued Minters. "You complain I'm never here; and if I'm never here, then who's keeping the people out?"

Halie's Health Woes—Prayers of Intercession

Still ailing, Mahalia sent for Mother Gay, the woman she believed was blessed with special prayer powers. Mrs. Gay was matron of one of Chicago's most prominent female gospel groups, the Gay Sisters. She and her husband had cofounded Chicago's Prayer Center years before and brought up five children through the Word, and God's music. Evelyn, Mother Gay's daughter and one of the Gay singers, accompanied Mother Gay "to see after Halie."

The evening before, the family had discussed Mahalia's request. They were certain that Minters Galloway wouldn't allow them in the house. He'd barred them before. Thankfully, an old friend Luberta Lindsey was there and ushered the mother and daughter into the house. Mahalia lay prone on one of the beds downstairs, surrounded by her Aunt Alice and another friend, Willa Jones, who were there to watch Mahalia and keep her company.

Mahalia smiled weakly as Mother Gay and Evelyn walked in. "Thank you, Mama," Mahalia said earnestly.

Mother Gay prayed. Her soft voice seemed to infiltrate the aching parts in Mahalia. No one would ever convince her that God wasn't working in direct partnership with the praying woman. "When I pray," explained Mother Gay, "I begin just to pray, and then if the Lord direct me to lay hands, then I lay hands on that place, wherever he directs me to, and I ask him to take away the pain, aches, and the throbs, those annoying throbs, and heal whatever the condition is."

Finally, Mother Gay, still in almost hypnotic prayer, lay her hands softly atop the areas Mahalia told her needed healing. Her prayers were fervent and melodic. When she stopped, Mother Gay looked deeply, directly into Mahalia's eyes. "Mahalia, the Lord is going to heal you," she said with finality.

Mahalia looked steadily at Mother Gay, then closed her eyes to sleep. It a short slumber, no more than 10 minutes, and Mahalia was opening her eyes, seemingly transformed. Her guests smiled in awe as Mahalia's old smile lit up her face. There was a new surge of energy and joy as she stood and moved. She rejoiced, throwing her arms around Mother Gay, thanking her and God for this rejuvenation in her body and spirit. Her hands went up, and she had a private conversation with God.

Then, she pulled Mother Gay into a corner and whispered about her dreams for her temple, where there would be divine healers like Mother Gay to help rid the world of earthly troubles, pains, and illnesses. Mother Gay smiled and nodded. "I know about your plans, Mahalia," she said, even though Mahalia had never revealed them to her. "But the Lord revealed it to me, Mahalia. He told me you were to have such a temple."

Mahalia asked Mother Gay if she would join her upstairs, and continue to pray for her as she fell asleep. Mother Gay followed her upstairs, and as they turned into the bedroom, she saw that Minters was laying half-asleep and half dressed. As he walked past her and into his own room, Mother Gay made no comment. That was outside her province. She began to pray. Gradually Mahalia went off to sleep. Mother Gay went downstairs, and she and Evelyn left Mahalia with new, unspoken prayers for her and her home.

Part 12

THE RETURN OF THE GOSPEL QUEEN

MAHALIA WITH SINGER AND TALK SHOW HOST
DINAH SHORE (GETTY CREDIT).

Mahalia's Singing Again…

In early February 1965, Mahalia called her agent Lou Mindling and told him he could begin booking dates again. She could resume her television performances, but she didn't think she was up to doing concerts yet. Mindling told her that March might be the earliest they could book her.

Hours later, Mahalia summoned the press. The headlines reported that after five months' recuperation, Mahalia Jackson was getting back to work with a series of upcoming television appearances in the next month. A photo released to the press showed Mahalia and her husband smiling as they stood at her piano.

So buoyed was she at the prospect of singing again, that five days later Mahalia could take it in stride when she was jolted by the death of Nat King Cole from cancer. She smoothed her hand over the warm brown cabinet of the color TV set he'd given her. *As beautiful as that boy was inside,* she mused, *his soul ought to have no trouble at all getting over.* The New York Post called for reminiscences of Nat King Cole's early days, and Mahalia remembered him to the press.

Just days away from her first performance following months of recuperation, Mahalia's heart palpitations were back. She was as weak as a newborn kitten. How would she be ready for her television appearance? She went to see Dr. Vondrasek, who had treated her at Little Company of Mary Hospital. He listened to his most famous patient. He noticed that Mahalia was looking somewhat better, but she was missing that sparkle and glow he always saw in her.

In his report, the doctor noted that *'MJ's biggest symptoms were that she was weak, tired, and developed heart palpitations.'* Mahalia had complained throughout her visit that she had public engagements, mostly television performances, and she needed him to do something to make sure she could make those performances.

Dr. Vondrasek studied the summary submitted by the University of Chicago after Mahalia's last hospitalization there. The findings included pulmonary sarcoidosis, and something else, a hysterectomy in 1952. In light of the changes in her electrocardiogram, he had considered sarcoid. Though it was a disease he had not treated, he was aware of its manifestations. Because of Mahalia's history of hypertension and overweight status, he felt coronary disease was far more likely.

Now, however, he diagnosed a mild, but very real, case of depression. He imagined this was brought on by the pressure on Mahalia to keep her performance contracts and her manager Lou Mindling's push for her to fulfill her engagements. The manager had had the nerve to allude to Mahalia's mental health being the culprit, not her physical health.

Dr. Vondrasek shared Mindling's assessments with Mahalia and noticed the flair of her nostrils as she listened. The doctor was worried about Mahalia's general health, especially how her blood pressure dropped dramatically when she stood or moved. She had lived with hypertension for several years, he knew. Now, her blood pressure was low, which explained why she felt weak when she stood up to sing for any length of time. Dr. Vondrasek sent Mahalia home with a long "to do" list, including wrapping her legs and using an abdominal corset. She had accepted the instructions with a questioning look.

Mahalia fretted as the dates for her performances drew closer. How could she possibly stand long enough to sing? She imagined herself keeling over before millions of people watching her on television. She fretted, and slept on it, and prayed. The next day, with tears in her eyes, she called Lou Mindling and directed him to cancel her performances.

Mindling couldn't hide his disappointment and mild anger—never mind that Mahalia was suffering and was at least as devastated as he was. She promised her manager she'd get better and let him know when she felt well enough to perform again. Her depression wasn't just from being sick and unable to perform, but also from inactivity, which was foreign to her.

It was March, already, and the winds blew cold as Mahalia headed back to Dr. Vondrasek. Her blood pressure was still quite low. She told the doctor she felt a little better, off and on, but still had the palpitations.

Dr. Vondrasek examined her. The EKG showed significant changes. He wondered if Nitroglycerin would work for his patient. Mahalia balked, clearly afraid to take it. She'd heard of people who ended up with worse blood pressure and "killing headaches." The doctor opted to give her a stimulant to keep her blood pressure up.

During Mahalia's next visit with Dr. Vondrasek, again he noted that the old impish grin and the light that always emanated from her eyes weren't there. Minters happened to be with her during the visit.

On Sunday, March 7, 1965, Mahalia turned on the television in time to catch the news report of the voting rights march from Selma, Alabama, to the state capital of Montgomery. She sadly shook her head as she saw the peaceful marchers stopped by dozens of Alabama state troopers and sheriff deputies wielding nightsticks, bullwhips, and tear gas. The violent confrontation at the end of the Edmund Pettus Bridge became known as "Bloody Sunday." Mahalia's heart dropped as she listened to Martin announce that he himself would lead a second nonviolent march from Selma to Montgomery two days later.

On Monday morning, Mahalia dictated a telegram to President Johnson:

Dear President Johnson:

"In the name of the Lord, please send protection to Dr. Martin Luther King and the civil rights marchers in Selma, AL. Don't let him get killed. God has given you the power to free us and all people. I ask you this in the name of the Lord to send protection to the civil rights

workers tomorrow, Tuesday, March 9th, Selma, AL. Thanking you for the consideration you might give this message,

Yours in Christ,
Mahalia Jackson

On Tuesday, the day of King's Selma to Montgomery march, Mahalia waited for news, and relaxed only when the newscast showed no interruption. She knew a pact had been worked out by presidential go-between LeRoy Collins. The march had gone only so far, short of Martin defying an injunction.

President Johnson went before a joint session of Congress, which agreed to pass his federal guarantee of voting rights. On Wednesday, March 10, Martin called Mahalia from Selma, with a weary chuckle in his voice. "God is real, my sister." She believed that, but truly wished God would tell her what he had in mind for her. She felt as if her future was blowing in the cold March wind.

Mahalia awoke from a dream that showed her lying in her coffin. Her heart was pounding. She saw every detail, including the lid closing down on her. Now, awake, she turned the dream over in her head. She prayed the strange dream had nothing to do with reality, or was it God's vision for her?

Feeling God's Promised Favor

In October 1965, Mahalia had checked in with her regular doctor, Dr. Barclay, to get her sendoff. That wasn't nearly enough for a praying woman, though. She corralled her prayer warriors, told them she was venturing out after a year, on her first concert, in Port Huron, Michigan. Minters was excited about Mahalia getting back on the road and in front of audiences. He was her biggest encourager, now helping all he could to prepare for the trip.

As she always did, Mahalia said one last prayer as she stared into the mirror, then gave her pianists Mildred Falls and Edward "Eddie" Robinson the nod. After they'd walked onstage, sat, and begun the prelude, Mahalia walked out, looked around, and bowed her head. Anyone who could see the sparkle in her eyes and the set of her mouth, knew this would be a good night. Mahalia felt God's promised favor.

Port Huron was her first concert after a long, dark year, and she repaid God's blessings with two hours of singing and praising. The cheers and applause were deafening. The audience rose to their feet again and again. Mahalia felt the need to say something: "It took God to heal me. If you people are really Christians, you will take inventory on yourselves every day, and ask the Lord for his mercy. Faith and prayer are the vitamins of the soul; man cannot live in good health without them."

The next morning, Mahalia arrived in Washington, D.C., for President Johnson's gala. She was remembering President Kennedy's inauguration back in 1961, as she and Minters checked into the prestigious The Hay-Adams luxury hotel near the White House. They would then travel on to the State Department auditorium for rehearsal for the new president's gala. Minters was back to his old self, the way he was before they got married. After lunch, she checked in on Dr. King's civil rights meeting being held there in the nation's capital, but left in time for the 8 p.m. cast call.

It was midnight before Mahalia got back to the hotel. She was so exhausted she agreed to Minters going out to "look around a little." She had been up all day and was really feeling it now. She was down 50 pounds from her singing weight.

The next day, Mahalia's dressing room was like a train stop, with the Washington press in and out, getting as many photos as they could for their papers.

"Politics," Mahalia chuckled, as she waited for the program to begin. President Johnson had come up with "A Salute to Congress" gala as a thank you to the members of both houses of Congress for passing his civil rights and voting rights legislation. Mahalia knew the president was like her, putting his hand into every little thing, making sure it was to his liking. His guests were greeted with flowers and military music as they arrived at the East Gate around 7:30 p.m., and military aides escorted them to the building.

The starting time for the gala had come and gone as the guests of honor, the members of Congress, were still in session, debating the first lady's highway beautification bill. But the congressmen could come to the gala directly from Capitol Hill as no ties and tails were necessary.

First lady Lady Bird Johnson had hoped this evening would go well, given her other big worry—President Johnson's impending gall bladder surgery at the Bethesda Naval Hospital. Though he refused to cancel the gala, he promised Lady Bird and his aides he would go straight to the hospital after the program and wouldn't allow anyone to corner him with chatter as they walked out the door.

Mahalia, like the rest of the night's performers, was getting antsy. She read her Bible and meditated. She was feeling weak and hoped the program would begin soon. Where was Minters, she wondered, though she wasn't worried, seriously. He'd find his way back here before long.

Finally, the band struck up "Hail to the Chief." The president was walking in, and actor Fredric March was speaking. Then, the president was thanking Congress for their support and their tireless work. Mahalia nodded in agreement. Yes, they had done good; given Black folks some hope for the future in this country. When she walked onstage, she felt a pride she rarely felt even in places like the White House.

Mrs. Johnson had great respect for Mahalia's faith, saying, "Mahalia's deep and abiding belief in the Almighty give a special dimension to her personality and her performances—a light from within…how could one ever forget being enfolded in that voice? And because Lyndon was scheduled to have surgery the very next morning, I know the faith and love she radiated was deeply meaningful to him."

As he was known to do, President Johnson backtracked on his promise to head straight for the hospital after the gala. Mahalia found herself standing there with the president and first lady going on and on about the Holy Spirit and how the Lord would take care of the president's ailments. Mahalia had a special liking for Lady Bird Johnson. She admired how the first lady hovered over her husband and tried to take care of him even when he didn't want to be taken care of. Mahalia was convinced that her feeling of closeness to the Johnsons had something to do with the fact that they were both from the South

Mahalia hadn't been home a week before the picture from the White House arrived. Sigmond drooled over it. There he was, standing there with Mahalia, the president and the first lady. The president had also sent Mahalia a letter from his hospital bed, expressing his deep gratitude. And, something almost as special arrived that day: Hugues Panassié sent his review of her "Greatest Hits" album from 1963. It had just been released in Europe. Mahalia couldn't read the French words, but the French critic had written at the bottom in English, "Wonderful." She smiled to know she had not been forgotten.

Hollywood, though, was a tougher crowd. What would they think of her after her long absence from performing?

Martin's Chicago Campaign— Fighting the Devil with the Lord

On July 10, 1966, Mahalia was shaky, standing in front of the huge crowd in Chicago's Soldier Field. Some 40,000 people had gathered in near 100-degree heat for the Freedom Sunday Rally, kicking off Dr. Martin Luther King's summerlong nonviolence campaign in the deeply segregated city.

Dr. King delivered his three-point rally cry: 1) for fair and open housing; 2) for equal justice—scarce in many precincts if your skin was Black and your pocket empty; and 3) for jobs—a prickly, dangerous corridor in Chicago. Blacks were barred from Chicago's trade unions, and most were ill-trained for the "better" jobs even if they had been open to Negroes. Dr. King was rallying and marching to try and bring about change.

Two days later, Tuesday, July 12, 1966, marked the first civil rights march for open housing in Chicago. Mahalia wanted to go to the march, and the march organizers wanted her to go. They got her to go on WBEE radio to urge Black women, especially, to join in the march. "Clean your kitchen, clean your house, and then go march for something better!" urged Mahalia.

"Look what I get for paying attention to Martin!" Mahalia panted proudly but shaken. March organizers had expected hateful outcries along the march route, but they hadn't expected rocks and bricks would be thrown at them, or to see some angry whites waving Nazi Swastikas.

Mahalia was worried to death because Martin's wife Coretta had come up with their four little children, and they were staying in a Chicago slum that Martin had rented to raise awareness of poor living conditions during his Chicago campaign. Mahalia sensed something mean, bad in the air.

Black people marched in the sun, and they marched in the rain, but they would not let Mahalia go again. "We need you here when we get back."

Mahalia wrote Mayor Daley. *"In the name of the Lord, let them march, but give them protection. We don't have a toothpick to fight with."*

Mayor Daley wrote back thanking her for her letter, and saying it was nice to hear she was improving in health.

On August 5, Dr. King led a march in Marquette Park in Chicago's Gage Park community on the city's Southwest Side. Everyone had been warned that Gage Park was a tough, segregated white community. But to the Reverend Ralph Abernathy this was like a heat wave, the sound and the feel of heat on both sides and ahead as they marched—through the pelting of rocks, bottles, bricks, spit, curses, jeers, debris. Police kept the white mob from the line of marchers, but some still managed to duck in to get their licks in or to spit on and curse the marchers up close.

Suddenly, Martin had stumbled, fallen, bleeding. A stone had been lobbed directly at him, and knocked him to one knee. His aides rushed to shield him from the angry white crowd. The next day, front-page photos showed the pain in Dr. King's face, the blood trickling down his forehead.

At Mahalia's dinner party the night after the march, it was as if they'd spent the day just like any other day. Martin was the center of everyone's attention as he talked about the day. A bandage on his forehead was the only reminder of the danger he had faced. There was laughter, joking, food... and even drinks. They looked at the newspaper, the photo, and laughed as if it was a lifetime behind them.

Martin, with a serious face, said, "I have never before seen violence on this scale—hate like this. Nowhere. Not anywhere in the south. Not even in Mississippi have I seen mobs as hostile or hate-filled as I've seen in Chicago."

His friend Reverend Abernathy agreed. "This was 'Bad Sunday,'" he said. Martin caught Mahalia's brooding, worried look, and returned to his jovial banter. Minters played the perfect host, and Mahalia tried to make sure everybody had everything they wanted. Before they left, she whispered to Martin to get Coretta and the children out of that slum apartment.

When the Black West Side exploded a day or two later, Mahalia's first thought was to thank God that Martin's children were all staying at Reverend Leon Jenkins' home and that Martin and Coretta were staying with her. The slum apartment they had been renting was almost unbearable in the heat. Martin had made his point. The riot was in response to the city's decision to turn off the fire hydrants at the apartments.

Mahalia was angry. This was just mean. They always let the hydrants run for the kids in the summertime. Dr. King decided he'd ride to the West Side, see if he could help calm the people down. Mahalia agreed to go with him. There was nobody in Chicago held in more esteem than the gospel singer. Sigmond accompanied his wife to the scene of the unrest.

On the West Side, Martin spoke from the car. Mahalia spoke and sang, too, fighting the devil with the Lord. But what was happening was beyond words.

Late that night, while meditating, Mahalia thought of Aunt Bell—the sweetest person who ever walked the earth. "If there's a person," Aunt Bell had told Halie and her cousin Celie, "…if there's a person who will give you a stone, you give them bread and leave them in the hands of God, for God can right all wrong. And God can turn hate into love." The two cousins had been sitting under the hackberry tree after Halie jumped those Italian boys meddling her from the neighborhood, Mahalia recalled. Blessed Aunt Bell—what would you have found to say tonight? Mahalia wondered.

The Divorce—Jackson v. Galloway

Mahalia Jackson's divorce had been a field day for the media. Now Minters went to his portable typewriter. He first tried to work out what he wanted to say on some yellow sheets of paper. Finally, he came up with what he wanted to put in print:

"After reading this week's Jet, I couldn't help but spend many hours reflecting on the two years I spent with Mahalia. My wife has gone to great lengths to discredit me as a man. In spite of Mahalia's fame and fortune, she was a lonely, unhappy woman. I, too, while not sharing her fame and fortune, was a lonely, unhappy man….

"Our mutual need seemed our main attraction. My happiness in finding a good mother for my daughter, and a wife whom I thought wanted and needed me, made me willingly commit myself to most of Mahalia's wishes.

273

"*Giving up my personal pursuits in life and becoming my wife's employee was possibly the greatest mistake of our marriage. With this control, my wife made me the puppet on the string: in many instances being more an employee than a husband….*

"*I would have been happy to have been the bread winner in my home. Mahalia knew of my financial limitation….*

"*Being overwhelmed by the love of the great Mahalia Jackson, I gave up all of my personal pursuits to be worthy of her love.*

"*I was gainfully employed before my marriage as a jazz musician. Since this pursuit would not add to Mahalia Jackson's public image, I willingly gave up this employment at her request….*

"*I became devoted to her way of life, spending many hours, night and day, helping her in her gospel arrangements.*

"*I became content just to walk in her shadow. She paid me a salary of $500 per month, even though ordinary musicians are paid twice this amount. I was willing to make this monetary sacrifice just to be a devoted husband and companion to Mahalia Jackson.*"

Minters watched Mahalia's face in court and thought he saw something there.

Mahalia walked out of the courtroom and told her lawyer, "I'm moving on…."

At 8358 Indiana Avenue, the first thing Mahalia did was change all the locks. Minters might be mad enough to come over and cause trouble. Aunt Alice came to be by Mahalia's side, and Ike Hockenhull showed up, saying quietly that he was going to stand guard—Mahalia needed a man who could handle that fellow.

Coming to Mahalia's home after he left the racetrack, Ike sat up in a chair at night just inside the downstairs bedroom assigned to him, the door kept open. Mahalia told him to go on to bed, he'd hear if anything was wrong. Aunt Alice was upstairs with her; but Ike said no, he'd rather be up.

Mahalia's Uncle Porter came for a month. He and Ike could talk about the old times. But, if Mahalia so much as grunted out loud, Ike was up the stairs in seconds to check on her. Her cousin Allen Clark decided he'd come back to stay. Mahalia said he could work for her; she'd pay for moving his things back. He lined up an apartment in a relative's building.

Old friends who'd kept away during Mahalia's marriage to Minters made a point now of spending time with her. When young singers came asking for her advice, Mahalia told them, "I am famous through being disappointed. Accept your disappointments, let them make you wise and help you work. There is plenty of room at the top. New singers come up like fine grass. But you must study your music. There are no more Mahalias. I am the last, and my success is the work of the Lord."

For a time, until the pain of losing Minters healed some, Mahalia sang little more than twice in a month. She performed at a concert in Albany, New York; then there was no singing for two weeks or more except for at a Sunday church service, before she rose to sing at an Israel Bond Rally at Chicago's Opera House.

In June 1967, Mahalia was still struggling to make it through each day. Subdued. Diminished. Mahalia prayed. She had to make it to Europe. After the divorce went through, her manager Lou Mindling said he was going to work up a concert tour for the fall. Mahalia hadn't said no—but fall seemed a long way off. Then, Frank Calamita and the people at Columbia/CBS Records came up with a big TV show in Berlin on August 26—a gala to celebrate the opening of the color television network in Germany.

Europe was getting close, but right now, Mahalia had a big date in Denver, Colorado, on July 23. She went a day early to help with the promotions.

Then, she was off to Toledo, Ohio, on July 28. It was going to be a tight squeeze for Milwaukee, Wisconsin, and Oakland, California, and what she wanted to do first, in Los Angeles—but the way opened up.

Mahalia's heart was pounding again, and she was experiencing fatigue. And Europe was so close. Dr. Barclay examined her thoroughly. There was a new sarcoid lesion in the left eye. He'd been hoping that the sarcoid would burn itself out; it often did. He knew more about the disease now than he had 15 years ago. Of course, there was still some severe damage. He put Mahalia back on prednisone and cautioned her. Actually, Dr. Barclay thought Mahalia had sought him out as much as anything to mourn her marriage.

Part 13

MAHALIA'S ENCORE IN EUROPE (1967)

MAHALIA MEETS THE POPE, 1968 (TULANE CREDIT).

Giving Her All

The Europe tour was just around the corner. Mahalia's friend Ida Beal stayed to see her off, and her assistant Polly Fletcher set about getting Mahalia ready to leave. There were so many things to attend to before departing, but Mahalia felt a quickening in her pulse when she suddenly remembered the audiences in Europe yelling her name, "Ma-HAYL-ya!" Those people loved her. But, Mildred, what was she going to do about Mildred? Mahalia had eyed her pianist steadily, with sorrow, hearing her out.

She thought a lot of the woman. She just wished it could be another way. When Mildred left, after being Mahalia's faithful accompanist for over 20 years, Mahalia called her agent, Lou Mindling. Within days, three tickets arrived for their flight to Frankfurt, Germany—one for Mahalia, one for pianist Edward "Eddie" Robinson, and one for organist Charles Clancy. Jim Mindling, her agent's son, was in Paris and would join them there as road manager for the flight to Berlin.

Shortly before she left, Mahalia felt her heart start beating faster. Dr. Barclay was out of town. She called Jean Childers, her secretary, and asked if she knew a doctor who'd come see her. Jean called Dr. Quentin Young, who gave Mahalia something to quiet her, and he suggested she rest before she left. Mahalia called Lou Mindling and told him about her heart. He told her the best doctors in the world were in Germany.

Mahalia looked up from checking over her clothes. "Ida," she said, "I need me a white velvet hat to go to Europe."

"Okay," said Ida, calmly. "I'll go down and get a frame and some velvet." Halie grinned, pleased. "And get me a brown hat," she said. "I want a brown one to go with any suit."

For Ida, the two hats were a full day's work, as Mahalia looked on with interest. And they put her on the plane in the white velvet hat.

On the flight to Europe, Mahalia tried to keep her mind off her main topic of concern—her divorce. She kept going over all the factors that led to the break. She was rejecting what many people knew was the prime cause—her husband's greed. She would prefer any combination of the dozen other reasons.

In Berlin, it seemed, everybody was delighted that Mahalia Jackson was there—the Germany sponsor Kurt Collien, the hotel staff, CBS-Germany, the press. After an interview upon arrival, Mahalia was supposed to have two days' rest before rehearsals began. But radio people came for separate talks, and people with the show, and people from CBS Records, and some soldiers who wanted to tell Mahalia Jackson "Hi" from home. More than any of that, though, there were three strange musicians—a bass player, a guitar player, and a drummer—to get together with before Mahalia Jackson walked into any rehearsal. They were all right, though; the people from CBS had picked some good men.

Rehearsal went well enough for the first of four rehearsals for the complicated show. Young Charles Clancy, a classical music student, was taking Mildred's place on the European tour, and bringing his wife along as well. Mahalia's segment would run just six minutes, plus the finale. But she was an old pro at this, and four days of rehearsals meant putting in four days full time. By that Friday, she figured it would've been easier to do a whole concert. She looked forward to her day off after the show. Then would come the Berlin concert for her sponsor Kurt Collien, and she'd be on her own.

Friday night, Mahalia's heart was pounding rapidly. She was frightened. A heart specialist was brought in to examine her. He gave her another prescription. A second check on Saturday showed that her electrocardiogram was all clear. That night's concert was sold out, and Mahalia gave them her all. The audience couldn't stay in their seats when she sang, "Go Tell It on the Mountains," especially the way Mahalia sang it…swaying, bouncing, swinging her hair until it looked like it would fly off her head.

She was, again, drenched when she made it back to the hotel and ate in her suite.

On Sunday morning, her traveling aides arrived at Mahalia's suite to find an ambulance had been called to take her to the hospital.

Mahalia wanted Dr. Barclay. At least they could call him about the pains in her chest. Jim Mindling reached him in Chicago. Dr. Schroeder, the highly respected cardiac specialist at West Berlin Westend Hospital, spoke to Mahalia's Chicago doctor, and listened carefully as Dr. Barclay explained her medical history and suggested medication.

On Monday morning, Dr. Schroeder issued a statement: Miss Jackson's European tour was postponed indefinitely, upon his advice. *"The burden of performing would have been a great strain on her heart and could have led to a heart attack,"* he said firmly. In her bed on the hotel's second floor, Mahalia cried. She'd tried her best.

Despite the many cards, flowers, telegrams, and telephone calls, there was no cheering up Mahalia. She was worried about business. What about all the contracts? This hospital was going to cost a fortune. And having all these people here, she ought to send them back. But, then, she'd be here all by herself.

Her heart leaped, as Paul Siegel of Radio-TV Berlin came in with a conspirator's smile. *"You got it!"* whispered Mahalia. He'd smuggled in a steak for her. She was tired of this hospital stuff. One of the other reporters had promised to bring her one the next day. Ah. This looked more like it. She wished she could have had some good old Texas greens with it!

Mahalia's Tour Collapses

On September 5, Kurt Collien saw Mahalia off as Pan Am took her to Frankfurt, and Lufthansa flew her to a welcome-home gathering in Chicago. An ambulance took Mahalia to her home on Indiana Avenue. *Thank you, Lord!* Her bed never felt better. Dr. Barclay came that same evening to check Mahalia over. He instructed her to be at Billings Hospital at

3 p.m. for an electrocardiogram. Dr. Barclay praised the care Mahalia had had in Berlin. He told her she needed a good long rest.

"Aren't you going to give me any medicine?" Mahalia asked.

"Oh, you've taken too much already," said Dr. Barclay.

"You know I'm afraid of dying," said Halie, making a joke of it.

Dr. Barclay smiled. "I want to wait about 10 days or two weeks and let you get over that plane ride. Then I'll bring you in for some tests."

The next day, Mahalia dictated a letter to Dr. Schroeder in Berlin. She told him she was thankful to God and to him. She told him of Dr. Barclay's praises, and asked: *"In your examinations, did you find any traces of sercois (sic)? I am a little worried, and I would like for you to write me immediately."*

Mahalia was deluged with flowers—from Mayor Daley, from Martin and Coretta King, from radio disc jockeys, friends, and fans. Get-well prayers poured in through the mail like a steady rain that was nourishment for her soul. She put her secretary Polly to work typing Thank You letters, while her assistant Allen took care of business.

Her sponsor Kurt Collien's appeal had been written while Mahalia was still in the Berlin hospital, but Jack Higgins of the Davison Agency in London had not forwarded it to Mahalia's agent Lou Mindling until Mahalia was discharged. Now Mindling sent both letters to Polly and asked her to please discuss the matter with Mahalia.

Collien said he was badly hurt financially, and Mahalia's doctors in Germany are convinced that she will be able to work fully again in about six weeks. She could start the concert tour in the middle of October. He also said that in all fairness for his loss, the fee should be reduced. Lou Mindling wrote Polly that he agreed on that and instructed her to pay off some London expenses.

Mahalia listened and pushed her lip up. She wasn't going back to Europe in six weeks or five months; she wasn't going back till Dr. Barclay and the Lord said go. She had Mindling to go ahead and pay the London man his money.

The closer it got to Christmas the better Mahalia's spirits got. Her cousins Allen "Son Baby" and Celie wanted her to come down to New Orleans. She had half a mind to, until she thought about how her house was so lonesome last Christmas with her out and Minters staying there temporarily. She put her giant Santa out on the back porch upstairs. They also put up Mary and Joseph and Baby Jesus statues and the Three Wise Men. Then all around, they strung the beautiful Christmas lights. By the time Russell Goode came, they were decorating the three Christmas trees—one inside the house, one on Indiana Avenue, and one on 84th Street.

On Christmas Day, the house was so full, there was hardly room to breathe, much less lift your elbows. Mahalia looked drawn and somewhat ill to her friends, but obviously she was determined to have a good Christmas and stuff every gut in sight, including her own.

Mahalia had never been anywhere in her life on New Year's Eve except in someone's church, and she didn't aim to miss out now. But this year, she made an exception for Martin. "You not going to have me out New Year's Eve! I'm going to be in somebody's church on my knees!" She let herself be persuaded on one condition, that she'd leave at 11 p.m. in plenty of time to get to a church.

So, at 9 p.m., Mahalia and a very pleased Martin Luther King, plus his traveling companions—Bernard Lee, Chauncey Eskridge, and Russell Goode—went around the corner on East 84th Street to the Maybells' home. It wasn't a big party—they'd be the party, their hostess said.

Martin was in a mood to sing. He sang for Mahalia some of the gospel songs she liked best. Then Mahalia sang his favorite, "Take My Hand,

Precious Lord," the song that was like a prayer to her. Then they sang together, Russell Goode falling easily into the gospel beat. "Russell, you watch the time!" Halie cautioned, and he nodded. They were having such a good time. So was Martin, Russell could tell; he didn't want it to end, either. Suddenly Mahalia broke off. "Russell! What time is it?"

"Five minutes to 12."

"Oh my God!" said Mahalia. She ran into the closest place, the bathroom, and got on her knees and said her prayers until midnight. Then she came out. She was just in time to hear Martin say something that was completely different from the atmosphere in the room. He lifted his head at midnight and said, "This is going to be a terrible year." Russell made a joke of it, and Martin shrugged it off and started another song. Mahalia came to join him, and they sang together.

1968—Mahalia's Second Chance

Mahalia felt like God was giving her a second chance. And if this chicken business worked, she could just see, hear, and taste her temple!

She would get healthy, too. Nobody believed she'd check herself into the hospital and have them separate those last two fused toes on each foot. Her toes had been that way since she was born with her legs curved. But they hadn't been a bother until she got up on those high heel shoes. Oh, the pain! But those heels were pretty, and necessary for her image, her friend Celeste had said.

The chicken business stayed on Mahalia's mind. It sounded fine, but…. Mahalia called Bob Miller at his funeral parlor and talked about her Mahalia Jackson Foundation. Then she asked what he thought of her chicken business proposition. He promised to give it some thought. She figured she'd better get Judge Ben Hooks up here, because Bob Miller was asking questions that she didn't have answers to.

Ben Hooks had started researching the chicken business as early as last year, and in a way much further back. Back in 1956, at the National

Baptist Convention, when he was a fledgling preacher and lawyer, Hooks had met Mahalia. Then, in 1959 when he was actively running the Volunteer Ticket for elections in Memphis, Tennessee, Dr. King had come to Memphis and somehow charmed Ben Hooks into serving on his SCLC board. From there, the two men became close friends, and Mahalia was in the mix. Hooks maintained his deep admiration for her through the years.

Though Judge Hooks was a successful financier, a minister, and active on television twice weekly, he was now ready to give up his judgeship and throw all his energy behind this chicken business—if he could convince this magnetic, dedicated, absolutely maddening woman to become a partner.

Hooks told Mahalia that he and his associates were prepared, with ample financing, to launch a nationwide chicken franchise business. All Mahalia had to do was to lend her name, and make periodic public appearances. They were ready to pay her well for her role.

Hooks had thought Mahalia would be immediately interested, but so far, she hadn't signed on the dotted line even though he'd met with her and received a warm response months earlier. When she summoned him, this time, he was sure she was ready to sit down with her own legal advisers and make a decision. That was not the case. The business was still a "maybe."

Mahalia was back in California, and worried. The cramp in her leg had come back, and the hoarseness in her voice hadn't broken like it always did. She'd see if she could get through one more song, and if it didn't clear up, she wanted to see a doctor.

Dr. Lincoln Best examined Mahalia carefully, listened to the long recital, and looked at the array of bottles she'd brought to his clinic. She certainly had more than her share of medication. But none covered the three immediate problems: a muscle relaxant should take care of the cramps, bed rest and care should clear up the respiratory infection, and the other would take more treatment.

Mahalia learned that she had diabetes, something she didn't recall her other doctors mentioning. Dr. Best wrote a prescription to control the chronic health condition. He explained that she would have to watch her diet very carefully—and revise any idea of 200 pounds being her "singing weight."

Mahalia's hair was coming out by the handfuls. She was convinced her worrying during the divorce was the cause. She should ask Dr. Best about that the next time she sees him. Mahalia was worrying herself sick about Minters, her friends said.

She realized that Aunt Bell had diabetes, and it likely ran in the family. Her cramps had eased at one point, but now were back with a vengeance. She wondered if she should call a different doctor. She decided it wouldn't hurt to call Dr. Robert Peck, ask him just to stop by. He had studied under her own Dr. Barclay.

Sick or well, Mahalia's hectic schedule was back to the old whirlwind of running to one television show after another. One day it was "The Tonight Show" with Johnny Carson, where she talked about her Mahalia Jackson Foundation. Three days later, she appeared on "The Steve Allen Show," and again, she talked about her foundation. *"Somewhere there must be another Pearl Bailey and another Marian Anderson who seeks to come forth. Somewhere there's another Mahalia—one better than me. Through my foundation, I will find them, and they will find their open door."*

That sounded fine, to her aide Richard "Dick" Yancey, but what he wanted to hear was her voice. She just hadn't been letting out. Afraid to, he figured—thought she didn't have a voice anymore.

After one of Mahalia's TV appearances, people were flocking around like they were worshipers! When things settled down, a man introduced himself as Elvis Presley's public relations man. He said Mr. Presley would like very much to meet Miss Jackson, but was filming and had sent a car. Would she come to the set?

Mahalia hated to leave right then. She'd done her airtime, but she wanted to get the stars' autographs. Still, she didn't like to be impolite. Climbing into the back seat of the limousine, Yancey was elated. Presley kept a closed set, and here he was going in to see Elvis Presley with the gospel queen.

"Mahalia!" Elvis Presley's face lit up as he rushed to greet her. He led her to meet Colonel Parker, his manager, and had his personal chair brought next to the camera. "Now, sit right here; I don't want you to move." Between each take, then, he would come over quickly, take her hand and stare intently at her, smiling. It made Mahalia a little nervous—him just staring, but he went on staring; and he's the greatest star. Finally, "Mahalia," he said softly, "you're just like my mama."

"Oh!" Mahalia said. "Was your m…," she broke off. He hadn't noticed, he was so set on what he was thinking. Later on, somebody told Mahalia that Elvis had sneaked into one of her church concerts in Mississippi when he was a child. And, he'd grown up Pentecostal. That explained a lot about that boy's singing.

Welcome to The Bahamas!

Mahalia arrived in Jacksonville, Florida, on March 23, 1968. When she was on the road, it was like contracting a whole building. There were just that many people to deal with. She'd sing in Jacksonville the next day, then immediately go to The Bahamas. Her schedule included performances in Mobile, Alabama, and Tampa, Florida. Maybe they could get some sun in that Mobile-Tampa gap. It was still so cold back home in Chicago. It was also hard to imagine just lying still around Mahalia. It was a pleasure to do for her, though. She was so appreciative of the least little thing.

As they stepped off the plane in The Bahamas, there was a giant sign flapping in the breeze, "Welcome Mahalia Jackson," and an eager crowd had amassed, waiting for a glimpse of the gospel queen. All of the islands' dignitaries greeted her formally and presented her with flowers. A band was playing island music. Mahalia spoke briefly on the air for a radio broadcast. Then, she and her organist Charles Clancy, her pianist Eddie Robinson, and her secretary Jean Childers rode in procession to the hotel for a reception. Everywhere, everyone seemed ecstatic, in awe of Mahalia's presence in their islands. Finally resting in the hotel, Mahalia was smiling, wondering why it had taken her so long to come to the beautiful Caribbean islands.

Mahalia's concert would be held at the Hangar Auditorium, outside Nassau. Mahalia was ready early. She wanted to check the microphones and instruments. The auditorium seemed a good long way from the city.

"People walk a lot on the roads, here," Mahalia murmured.

"They are walking in from all over the island to hear you, Miss Jackson," their escort assured her. At that point, they turned into the airport, which was puzzling until they discovered that "Hangar Auditorium" was, in fact, an old airplane hangar at Oakes Field airport. Nothing on the island was big enough, so they'd converted the hangar for the night, fitting it with rows all around like a circus. They'd fixed a makeshift dressing room for Mahalia, too—including bedroom furniture. They knew she'd want to rest.

Before she changed, Mahalia stretched out on the bed. She picked up the program left for her and burst out laughing as she read: "Entire proceeds go to the PLP Election Campaign Fund." They had signed on to a political event, and none other than Sidney Poitier was the emcee. Mahalia hadn't known the famous Hollywood actor was from The Bahamas.

The huge hangar was packed solid—no way of telling how many people were there. Sidney Poitier gave Mahalia a beautiful introduction, and she took it from there. Giving the audience more than they expected, singing one song after another. The islanders were enjoying every note.

After more than two hours—encore after encore—Mahalia exited to cheers and came into her dressing room reaching for dry clothes. "Baby," she panted, "with this night breeze sweeping in here, wet as I was, I didn't dare come off [the stage] in here and change."

Every minute she could, Mahalia wanted to soak up the sun. Except, she took time to find a church and thank God for all the beauty of the islands, the fine reception she had received; and to be able to sing to the glory of his name. Outside of that, she wanted just to relax. And then came Chauncey Eskridge, her lawyer, who had followed her from the states to talk about the chicken business.

One of Sidney Poitier's brothers was headwaiter at the hotel where Mahalia was staying. He, along with maids, waitresses, and porters eventually showed up at Mahalia's door to share information about their political problems. They were all eager for Miss Jackson to know the story of the past political uprising and how now they were trying to elect some people who could identify more with themselves, the native people of The Bahamas.

Mahalia listened to the words tumbling out, one topping the other. Jean sensed it was time to usher them out. When the two were alone she said, "Mahalia, you got to help these people!" Jean was surprised at herself; she hadn't known she was that committed. She knew what they wanted, but hadn't really made clear, was for Mahalia to come to their meeting in the park the next night. Mahalia nodded, thoughtful. "I'll come," she said.

The car made its way through the park to a roofed pavilion strung with lights. It was on a hill. Everybody would be able to see her. Mahalia got out, and as she walked toward the pavilion, the mass parted to let her through. Expectancy was in the air. The great Mahalia Jackson had sung for those with $5 or $10 at the hangar, but tonight she would sing for them, for free.

When she stopped singing, Mahalia spoke, her voice now barely above a whisper, her arms outstretched as a mother speaking to her children, shepherding the flock. She told them, while she had listened with interest to each of them as they shared with her about their political affairs, she hoped they would attend their own affairs as she was an outsider, and couldn't afford to get involved in their political conflicts.

It took several planes to get from Nassau to Mobile, Alabama. From Miami, a telephone call was made to the producer Joe Glaser, who said yes, the rest of the Mobile deposit was in. But at the auditorium, Mahalia had yet to see half the $2,500 still due. Mahalia was fully dressed, waiting as her aide hunted down the promoter.

At the front office, the aide received and counted the remaining payment, then hurried through the three dimly lit city blocks to get back to the stage entrance. Now what to do with the money? It was finally planted on Charles Clancy, Mahalia's organist who was deposited safely on stage.

The next day, they waited to receive the $1,500 deposit from Tampa. If they didn't receive it, the event would be forfeited. Then, Mahalia would have time to meet Judge Hooks in Nashville, Tennessee, and finalize plans for the chicken business.

Sarah Ophelia Colley Cannon was Minnie Pearl to Mahalia and most of the world. The two women had never met before but were mutual admirers, and about to be partners-in-stock. Mahalia had flown into Nashville on Monday night. On Tuesday, Governor Buford Ellington made her an honorary citizen of Tennessee. And they'd all eaten Minnie Pearl's Chicken and gone back to the office for business.

John Jay Hooker Jr. of Nashville—president and board chairman of the Minnie Pearl's Chicken System, Inc.—was sitting down with Judge Ben Hooks and his primary partner A.W. Willis of Memphis, plus various aides on each side. The group gathered to talk about the Minnie Pearl corporation taking 50 percent of Mahalia Jackson's Chicken System, Inc., by matching their cash investment. Starting a national franchise would take capital until the company's stock could go public.

Mahalia was visible evidence of the value and integrity of the plan, and its essential difference—all Mahalia franchises would be Black-owned and managed, just as the national management would remain Black. Mahalia listened as the figures and plans rolled on. Gulf Oil was interested in a station tie-in. The talk branched to a future donut shop chair and to Mahalia Jackson's budget-priced parlors.

"You could make them like New Orleans," Mahalia injected eagerly. "Put in some creole food." She heard it all out. Afterward, she called Bob Miller and made Chauncey Eskridge tell him. Bob Miller didn't think it was enough front money. Chauncey was furious. "You're not a lawyer," he grated. "You have no business interfering." Bob Miller didn't care. He was only interested in Mahalia.

Part 14

THE DEATH
OF A DREAMER

MAHALIA SITS ALONE, REFLECTING ON HER LOSSES:
HER DIVORCE AND MARTIN'S DEATH, APRIL 1968 (GETTY CREDIT).

Why God? Why Martin?

On Thursday, April 4, 1968, Mahalia woke up brooding. She looked out of her hotel window and declared to no one in particular, "I ain't flying today." Mahalia had told Dr. King she'd be in Memphis for the meeting on April 4, and Judge Hooks had arranged for them to fly to Memphis in his personal plane. Her aide told her the weather wasn't so bad, plus, the plane had two engines.

"That's not enough engines for me. I'm not flying today," Mahalia said, flatly. Chauncey Eskridge came by and talked more about the chicken business. Mahalia was restless. In the afternoon, they went to see J. Robert Bradley at the National Baptist Convention offices, and then went by his apartment. Mahalia watched television along with the others. The first thing they saw on the screen was the report that Martin Luther King had been shot in Memphis.

Mahalia was sure she hadn't heard right, then minimized it when she heard he'd only been shot in the butt. The news continued and sounded worse and worse. It was too much for her to take in. She couldn't even cry or be sad. Not yet.

Martin had become so much a part of her life in the last 10 years—her younger brother, her confidante, her spiritual leader, her reason for being more than just a singer, but a singer who used her stature and connections for a righteous cause. It was Martin who pushed her to live with a purpose. He had called her a sojourner for justice. She had never felt prouder.

Why God? Why Martin? And, in the midst of the cries and the moaning throughout the room, Mahalia collapsed.

Already, radio and television stations reported rioting in Chicago and cities across the country—rioting everywhere. Mahalia wrang her hands in confusion and indecision. Martin would've known how to calm the rioters, what to do next.

"What shall I do? What shall I do?" Mahalia's aide, Jean Childers, became fearful as Mahalia became overwhelmed. They needed to get her away from the center of rioting and danger. Chicago wouldn't be the place to be. And, now there were reports that Nashville was experiencing violence. Mahalia was distraught.

Early Sunday morning, three days after Dr. King's assassination, Russell Goode drove Mahalia and her aide directly to Ebenezer Baptist Church, Dr. King's church in Atlanta. They were led directly up to the front. Martin's brother A.D. King was delivering the sermon. Martin's father "Daddy King" followed him. Then Mahalia stood and sang her sermon—a song out of the gospel. God was on the side of the angels. *Hallelujah.*

When Mahalia later walked up to the front desk of the Regency Hyatt House in Atlanta, two double bedrooms magically appeared and were waiting. After she'd settled in, a boy brought up an entire meal—turnip greens, sweet tomatoes, ham, corn sticks, everything. On top of the meal was a big box of roses. The card said Coretta Scott King. Mahalia knew Coretta wasn't one who took to everybody, but Mahalia was someone who'd stolen her heart.

Bob Miller, Mahalia's longtime friend and business manager, was waiting in Atlanta when she arrived. He knew there'd be things Mahalia would want him to do, such as provide transportation for the musicians playing in the relays while Dr. King was lying in state. Miller leased a car as Mahalia needed it to meet Mrs. King who was coming from a memorial service in Memphis.

A Day of Mourning and Saying Goodbye

Mahalia was up at 5 a.m. for a day she had never allowed herself to imagine would ever come. That day she was saying goodbye to a man she considered her dearest friend, who had changed her life and her purpose for living. With all the danger that surrounded Martin's life, Mahalia had always believed God would protect him. She dared not ask, how it was that God had let this happen?

Mahalia's secretary Jean Childers helped her into the navy-and-white knit suit she'd bought in Chattanooga, Tennessee, for Martin's funeral. By 6 a.m., they were leaving for the church. There was a large crowd surrounding the church when they arrived. Mahalia had already been told that only a limited number would be allowed inside the church. She was met at the door by church ushers and escorted up to the pulpit with the ministers.

Mahalia sent Jean to the balcony where she'd keep note of who came through the door, and who was already seated. There'd come a time when Mahalia would want to know. Not now, she was in suspended disbelief and wouldn't remember anything that happened the day of Martin's funeral. It was all too much grief for her.

Jean spotted such Hollywood stars as Eartha Kitt, Harry Belafonte, Sidney Poitier, and New York Governor Nelson Rockefeller—*that must be his wife.* He was giving the woman his seat and moving to the wall to stand. Then, there were Mayor John Lindsay from New York City and Michigan Governor George Romney.

There was Bobby Kennedy—*that must be his wife Ethel sitting next to him.* Jean looked down into the pulpit, and it saddened her to see that Mahalia's face was strained, nothing like the warm face full of life she was most used to seeing. Thank God Mahalia didn't have to sing just yet.

Mahalia's spirits had lifted some as they left that service to go to the next one at Dr. King's alma mater, Morehouse College. Her friend Bob Miller walked up to tell her he was parked two blocks down the road. There was no way to get closer. They would walk the rest of the way to Morehouse. Mahalia made a not-so-silent groan. She was already feeling the expected results of the walk—her feet were killing her.

Reverend Abernathy was concerned when he saw Mahalia standing downstairs in the foyer of the Morehouse library. He was certain she was ill. Almost out of breath, she could hardly respond when Mrs. Abernathy spoke. Mahalia offered a weak smile, sweat now moving down the side of her face.

Morehouse President Dr. Benjamin Mays greeted Mahalia warmly but didn't tally as he was still working on his speech. Mahalia walked out onto the balcony to get some air. While there, she spotted Bobby Kennedy, who hurriedly rushed to greet her. "Mahalia!" They spoke quietly for a long moment.

Somehow Mahalia found the strength to walk up to the front and stand to sing her final goodbye song, an emotional performance of "Take My Hand, Precious Lord," for her friend. It was Martin's favorite song. She sang out her sorrow, sang a plea for forgiveness of mankind, sang for the soul she knew was sitting at Jesus' side. *Save me a place, Martin. Save me a place,* she whispered, when she finished.

The plane leaving Atlanta held a Who's Who of greats, including the acclaimed writer James Baldwin, noted gospel singer Clara Ward and her mother, and actors Brock Peters, Tony Franciosa, Marlon Brando, and others.

Minters Again

This was one of Mahalia's happiest moments in a long while. She and Minters were talking about remarrying. They just had to work out a pre-nuptial agreement. He was playing coy but serious about not wanting to be left out in the cold the way he was after their divorce.

The other big thing that put a smile on Mahalia's face was finally finding her new home. This time, she was moving from the bungalow in Chatham to Cornell Village, a high-rise condo building located in Chicago's affluent Hyde Park community. Her home would be the penthouse on the 26th floor of the building, which sat right across from Lake Michigan.

Mahalia called Chicago architect Ken Childers to look at the penthouse and draw up a plan. He would put together two apartments on the 26th floor and give her everything she wanted, including a den for Minters, a suite for his daughter Sigma, and a big living room.

Mahalia was then off again for performances in Milwaukee and Beloit, Wisconsin; Rochester, New York; then to California to produce another record.

In September 1968, Mahalia was happy and excited by the sketch that Ken Childers showed her of her new home. He spread the rough sketch before her with a flourish: an extra-large master bedroom. Everyone who knew Mahalia knew that was where she received most of her company anyway. It had a walk-in closet that was a room in itself, for all the singer's stage gowns and furs; a large formal living room, for Minters; and a spacious music room for Mahalia, with a view of Lake Michigan. Her new home also had a soundproofed den with a built-in stereo system so Minters could play his saxophone. A suite on the west side of the foyer was set up for Sigma. It included a bedroom, play space, a bathroom, a room for a governess or whoever would be taking care of the girl, and a guest bedroom.

A closed-circuit TV would be linked to the downstairs entrance to the building so Mahalia could see her visitors before they came up, as well as an intercom system that would allow her to hear conversations from the other rooms in the condominium.

After thanking Ken for seeing her vision, she hurried off to the dedication of the Mahalia Jackson Room at Greater Salem Baptist Church, and to participate in a "This is Your Life" kickoff benefit that would go toward building a $200,000 Mahalia Jackson wing on the new South Side YWCA.

At Christmastime, Sigmond was wary. Mahalia was silent, watching. Her breath was shallow. It hadn't been an easy two weeks. As soon as she got back from Hawaii, she'd been X-rayed in Los Angeles and advised to stay there to recover. She was in no shape for Chicago's freezing, snowy weather. She spent a strange Christmas in a furnished apartment at the Fountainview West, a high-rise on La Cienega.

Mahalia called her family in New Orleans. They said Ike had had a stroke and was trying to reach her. She called and told him to get a nurse, get two, whatever he needed. She'd pay for it. She called her friend Dinah

Shore…reached out to other friends. Mahalia sat down to a crowded table with Minters' godmother Mother Parks. And still there was a lonesome place inside her. Russell Goode came for two days before New Year's to help Dick Yancey drive Mahalia's car and her furs from Chicago.

On New Year's Day, Minters came. He'd spent Christmas with Sigma. He was frustrated, saying it was hard waiting around for Mahalia's attorney to figure out an agreement to guarantee he wouldn't come out worse off than he was now, once he went back into their marriage.

Minters didn't want to deal with the lawyer about their marriage. Still, he needed to know where Mahalia stood. The lawyer, Gene Shapiro, again spelled out the nature and terms of the prenuptial agreement which would stipulate that in the event of their marriage, Sigmond Galloway relinquished all claims to Mahalia's existing property—all assets of any nature—and she relinquished all claim to his. It was a quit-claim contract.

Sigmond relented and told the lawyer to draw up the agreement. As Shapiro left, Mahalia murmured quietly, "Now don't forget about that other…."

Mahalia was in such good spirits! Visitors joked it was the Japanese plum wine she drank for her heart, like Dr. Barclay had told her. Everyone knew Black Baptists had their own liquor code. Aunt Bessie always said there was "nothing wrong with taking a drink at home, just don't go sneaking into barrooms and mixing with the sinners."

The city of Long Beach, California, declared March 23, 1969, as Mahalia Jackson Day. Mahalia was giving her first concert in the city of a million people. For the first time in her life, she bought a $500 gown from Lane Bryant, a store for plus-size women. Mahalia never spent any real money on her clothes. But she liked the yellow gown so well she asked if the store had the gown in other colors, maybe in pink? She even bought an $80 hat—Halie, who never paid more than $6.50 for a hat in her life!

In March 1969, Mahalia was back in Chicago meeting with Ben Hooks and his Florida investors on the chicken franchise business. They now wanted her to sign on to starting a frozen soul food and canned vegetables side to the business. Judge Hooks needed her to come up with some recipes for a premium.

She then flew to Oakland, California, to open their Major League Baseball game with "The Star-Spangled Banner." To her surprise, they actually created something as close to "bombs bursting in air" as they could, when she sang that part. It was dark by then, and the bombing sound in the dark caused all kinds of havoc—something near a riot that night.

Mahalia returned to Chicago to see Dr. Barclay, then she would travel on to D.C. But before leaving, she had to make a formal denial that she was the mother of some girl who got herself free shoes in Norfolk, Virginia, claiming she was Mahalia Jackson's daughter. She even told the story to the people at *Jet* magazine. Mahalia didn't know whether to laugh or cry. The world didn't know, but those close to her knew that Mahalia was a barren woman—God had ordained it to be. She had long questioned why God did that, but she knew he had his reasons.

Still, she was outdone and angry…yes, angry, that people would put their children up to claiming they were hers, like the girl in Nashville some years ago. What she wouldn't have given to have children of her own. There was a time, she would have given just about anything.

In April 1969, Mahalia went to D.C. to participate in jazz great Duke Ellington's 70th birthday party at the White House. She had to hand it to President Richard Nixon. With all his darkness, he'd had the goodness to give Duke the night in style with everybody in the country trying to get invitations. Minters, as always, was in his element when he was around the rich and famous people. And, in all this time, all these days, he still had not signed the prenuptial marriage agreement and wouldn't say why.

Here she was in the White House worrying about her vaccinations for her upcoming international tour. Mahalia's agent Lou Mindling had told her not to bother about not having her shots yet, she could get that in Los Angeles right before she flew out.

Something was telling her something, and she wasn't getting it clear. She called her attorney Gene Shapiro and told him she was going to Los Angeles before she left for Europe to make a film. Then, she asked him about Minters, and Shapiro said he'd think about how to handle that situation.

Mahalia tried to just meditate after the plane got up in the air, but there was too much going around in her head. She was going to make some changes when they got back from Europe because Dr. Barclay warned her again to slow down.

A Spiritual Magician—Encore in Europe

In May 1969, the plane touched down at London's Heathrow Airport on Thursday at 10:30 a.m. Thankfully, Mahalia and her entourage were able to get through Customs without a hitch. They headed to the hotel, with no time for even a cup of hot tea. Mahalia held a press conference at 2 p.m. The London press seemed to love her.

Mahalia was hoping everything would go smoothly during this European tour. Two concerts a week. *Leave here with everybody feeling like a lily done bloomed.* After the press conference, Mahalia was escorted over for a radio interview, then another press conference.

Mahalia saw something from the corner of her eye. The tour sponsor and Minters having it out about the press conference. She hated to ask Minters what the commotion was about. She'd never get the straight of it.

Max Jones of *Melody Maker,* a weekly British music magazine, produced the first London concert and was ecstatic to learn there wasn't a vacant seat in Albert Hall concert venue. Mahalia promptly turned the usually proper English gathering to a spiritual event that was successful and enjoyable for the audience. She won the producer over, with him calling her a spiritual magician; a stupendous gift—and with such simplicity.

Max Jones made his way to Mahalia's dressing room after the last rousing encore and found her exhausted, resting in a chair. She rummaged through what seemed to be a miniature medicine chest and swallowed something.

"I wish I was as young as I was when you first met me, Maxie," she sighed. "There's so much to be done, and it's always me—if they want someone to ring the bell at church, they call on Mahalia."

While in bed that night, Mahalia's cramps and pains returned. She was frightened, traveling all the way over here and getting sick. She now felt her heart contracting. This wasn't good. She called Gwen Lightner, one of her pianists, who got ahold of Minters. Minters got a doctor who he heard was a top heart surgeon.

The London doctor found Mahalia in dire stress and pain. She had foreseen Europe crashing down on her. The doctor said Mahalia had had a heart attack, and she would have to go home. Mahalia asked if her doctors could come here. They would know what to do.

Dr. William Barclay was stowing his skis away and entering the British Columbia lodge when he received a call from London. He recognized the doctor's name—an eminent cardiologist who said he was calling at Miss Mahalia Jackson's insistence, but clearly she had had a coronary occlusion.

Dr. Barclay disagreed, saying he'd diagnosed Mahalia some years back with sarcoidosis of the heart. He suggested the British doctor boost her cortisone—her prednisone—up to very, very large doses.

While the cardiologist was astounded at such a high dosage, he said he would follow Dr. Barclay's prescription. He called back later to confirm that he'd increased Mahalia's cortisone and that her cardiogram had come back normal.

When Mahalia herself called Dr. Barclay, crying about her broken trip, he told her to go on—just rest a few days over this episode. He didn't think she would experience another such episode during her trip.

He had been right. She didn't suffer with further heart trouble during the trip. Not even when she almost blew a gasket after learning that CBS in Paris had canceled her concert in the French capital instead of waiting to see if she really did have to go home. To prove she'd done her part, she had Gwen take her picture in front of the Salle Pleyel concert hall to show that Mahalia Jackson was there the day she was supposed to be.

Mahalia and her group picked up the tour in Sweden. They went from the capital Stockholm to the Swedish cities of Malmo and Lund, where they visited a historical church. There, Mahalia came up with the idea to order specially made red choir robes to be flown in from California for her and Gwen's performance.

An outdoor crowd in Stockholm sat through a downpour, and Mahalia sang on, protected by a shell. She was amazed that, with her singing through all the rain, she didn't catch a cold.

After Sweden, Mahalia returned to Paris to perform to a standing-room-only crowd. French monks were so carried away, they came the next morning to quiz her about gospel music—they wanted to try it in their mass so people would get involved. Mahalia later laughed that they'd given her the 33rd degree and she loved it. As much as Mahalia wanted to, they didn't have time to sightsee or shop in the world's most romantic city.

Instead, Mahalia headed straight to Berlin, Germany, where, again, Minters bumped heads with the production people who told him he'd need a contract to film Mahalia's concert, in spite of what the U.S. government said. Yet, maybe to show there were no hard feelings, the producer presented Mahalia and Minters each with a beautiful watch to show the country's appreciation for Mahalia's presence.

After concerts in Frankfurt, Germany, and Basel, Switzerland, and the Swiss capital Zurich, Mahalia suddenly felt as if the concerts were closing in on her. She asked the promoters to book the events further apart, give her some breathing room. Especially now that she was having to ride trains between the Swiss cities. The Swiss refused to let her leave the stage. One reporter kept a tally, saying she sang 35 songs.

Mahalia said she wouldn't be able to make the concert in Vienna, Austria's capital, so they'd need to cancel it.

She would later tell the story of a young German girl who hitch-hiked her way around Europe to see Mahalia, then sneaked backstage at Zurich. Though she was caught once, she somehow found a way back a second time, and this time, she secured an audience with Mahalia herself, dropping to her knees in tears and saying that since she was a little girl, her dream had been to meet the gospel singer.

Mahalia had given the girl the gift of one of her warmest Mahalia hugs and ensured her that she could watch the performance unbothered. As she was leaving, the child told Mahalia it was the greatest moment of her life.

For the first time in a while, Mahalia was happy and content to have Minters with her. She loved him despite all their troubles and their differences, including the drinking that started early in the day and continued into the night and the ugly divorce that took a lot out of both of them. And now that they had returned home from her European tour, she and Minters could now focus on their plans to get remarried.

Mahalia had said she was ready to sign the prenuptial papers, knowing she would be handing over a large amount of money to Minters, enough to hold him over for some years for sure. Her lawyer Gene Shapiro had second thoughts. Mahalia should be present when the document was consummated. Besides, Shapiro had to incorporate the extended terms. They agreed on a date to sign the paperwork before Minters departed for Gary.

Mahalia was off to meet with Judge Hooks about the chicken shacks franchise and the new food business. From there, she wanted to catch up with Aunt Hannah and Alice, who she was happy to know were both all right.

Her next piece of business was getting the Hyde Park condominium ready to move in. She needed to find out how long it would take. She and Minters could be remarried right there in her new place. Minters had told her he wanted a large wedding this time "to show he was more than a piece of a man."

Mahalia longed for things to be the way she'd always dreamed they would be between her and Minters. She was happy when he came back from Gary and brought Sigma up to New York when she performed at a music festival in Harlem, and when she performed for Governor Rockefeller at Tanglewood in Lenox, Massachusetts.

Afterward, singer Stephanie Barber, owner of the Music Inn near Tanglewood, had them all over for dinner at her beautiful resort estate on the water in Lenox. Mahalia couldn't do much walking—her feet had begun to swell so bad—but Minters was such an attentive husband that she hardly noticed the pain in her feet.

Mahalia was happy as they began to make plans for their remarriage. She had questioned the fact that Minters rarely flew with her. But he had explained that his concern was if anything happened to him or Mahalia, Sigma would still have someone to look after her. Mahalia thought that was a good reason. She was excited to tell him the condominium would be ready to move into in September. He smiled and asked how a September wedding sounded to her?

Reverend Ralph Abernathy asked Mahalia to serve on the SCLC board, and he wanted her to be there for their meeting in Charleston, South Carolina. It was an important meeting. Since Martin's death, Mahalia had learned that a lot of the late-comers to the SCLC were strategizing to take positions in the organization. Some had it in their mind to replace Reverend Abernathy.

Mahalia was committed to being an ally for Reverend Abernathy. He was her friend, but even more important, he had been Martin's righthand man. No, he wasn't Martin, but he was the closest thing to him…and she didn't see another Martin in sight. The meeting lasted three days, and Mahalia didn't miss a meeting. She'd promised Ralph Abernathy, and she knew Martin was looking down and expecting her to keep her word.

Enough Is Enough

More than likely, it was a combination of things that caused Mahalia's collapse in July 1969. Earlier that week, she had performed concerts for ABC television network in Newark, New Jersey; in Kansas City; and in Dayton, Ohio. She was scheduled for a New York performance but canceled. Her body couldn't take the strain; enough was enough.

Mahalia's doctors kept her in the hospital until they could run tests. She was unhappy about the hospital stay but felt good about spending more time with Minters. Just a day after the doctor allowed her to go home, she was off to Philadelphia, where she performed without a hitch. But once she arrived at the apartment there, she was again experiencing shortness of breath, chest pains, and stomach cramps.

As Mahalia gasped for breath, her dear friends Albertina Walker and Dolly Dickens panicked and began trying to chase down the doctor who lived in the apartment complex. Finally, someone decided to call the paramedics. An ambulance arrived in five minutes. But Mahalia refused to ride in the ambulance. She was convinced that if she did, she would be dead before they arrived at the hospital. To everyone's surprise, the doctor's verdict was gastritis. Five doctors asked for her autograph.

Mahalia was almost too tired to be happy when her assistant Allen Clark finally finished moving her into her new home in Hyde Park. That first night in her new condo on the 26th floor of Cornell Village, she found herself wrestling with old and new emotions. She loved everything about this new place, but she didn't fall in love with it like she did her first home on Indiana Avenue. New beginnings weren't always good for Mahalia. What was she having to leave behind to make room for this new beginning?

Her memories went back to her childhood in New Orleans. "Nigger Town." She had recollections of so much, but not her mother Charity. Everyone told her she had the very same spirit and love for life as Charity. Mahalia believed she'd lost those things along the way. Now, she was more like her second mother, Duke.

But Duke, who they say was nothing like her younger sister, had taken Charity's place. And now Halie was remembering the old Duke, the hard Duke who loved with an iron fist. So different from the new Duke who had looked at her as an equal; who had smiled and hugged and said sweet things to her. Things Duke never found the need to say or do for the little girl Charity left in her care; the little girl who walked around in her own world, with a big black hole in her heart. It's funny how people gave the best of themselves to people who didn't need it and kept it from the ones who did.

Speaking of the past. Mahalia's first husband, Ike, would find her if she moved to a tunnel under the ground. Ike was certainly part of her past, but he refused to accept it. It was her first day in her new home, and he'd made his way all the way up to the 26th floor to ask her to loan him $500 for horses he had down in Virginia. *Lord, Ike. Still?* She told him she would be happy to help him if he wanted to start a business, but not with horses. He stayed a while before leaving, saying he'd let her know if he came up with any business ideas.

And, what of Minters who was part of her past and her present? She had made him president of her foundation and instructed her friend Ben Hooks to give Minters a good job with the chicken business because they were getting married again. Was she buying her husband? Paying him to come back to her? She never wanted to think that was what their marriage was built on. It worried her.

Dr. Barclay had slipped off from his new job at the American Medical Association to check out Mahalia's ailments. He admitted he was a bit worried about her seeming depression. The doctor had known and cared for Mahalia Jackson almost half of his life. The old Mahalia was full of joy and spirit. Where had that Mahalia gone? The woman he was looking at now seemed frightened of life, and maybe of death. And, of course, she understood that the sarcoid was progressing, and that exacerbated her other ailments…the cramps, the eye lesions, the heart palpitations, the chest pains. The other part of her ailments was in her head, and in her heart.

Mahalia was paranoid about her health, her financial security, her family, and more. With all the people in her life, she was still a lonely woman. Maybe she'd always been lonely, just moved so fast with so many people in her circle that she didn't notice it. Now that she'd slowed down, it was there staring her in the face.

On Thanksgiving, Mahalia sang at a barbecue in Mississippi at the bequest of Mayor Charles Evers. She was always happiest when she sang down home. It was there that she sang with her whole body and soul, felt free to release herself, to praise God to the very highest. On that day, she would say later, her songs were her prayer of thanks to God with every note. "Even for the burdens, for they make us strong."

Now, here it was Christmas in 1969, and Mahalia didn't know whether she was opening a door or shutting it, but what was inside was grand. The Christmas dinner table was loaded, and sitting around it were Minters and his daughter Sigma. The dinner guests also included Mahalia's godson John "Brother John" Sellers; her aunt Alice, who would take a Christmas plate to Aunt Hannah; the Reverend Branham and his wife; her friends Russell Goode, Robert Anderson, Josephine Davis, and Bertha; and more guests were on their way. It was like old times in Mahalia's house in the days before Minters.

And there was not a cross word or look. Maybe it was the food. Robert Anderson could surely cook a turkey. But Mahalia believed, from the way they dove in, that it was the chitlins that got everybody to eating with such a good face. Even Minters partook of the Southern delicacy. He caught her look and winked. Christmas was beautiful.

Mahalia had thought Bermuda would be warm. It was cold, and she wasn't feeling much better. She was thinking she might have caught the flu. Plus, she had been suffering chest problems since she left Memphis.

Promoter Eddie De Mello had his fingers crossed. But there she was—she had sung the one-hour matinee in marvelous form, and now tonight His Excellency the Governor of Bermuda, Lord Martonmere, and his wife Lady Martonmere were lending patronage and homage—yes, homage—to this amazing Queen of Gospel. One-hour provision forgotten, Mahalia was responding to "Encore!" again and again. Oh, indeed, she was fantastic!

Mahalia had landed back in New York when she learned there was no hotel availability…even for the famous Queen of Gospel. She and her entourage were at the airport, hunting a hotel reservation, and both the Hilton and The Waldorf-Astoria were full. They settled on the Wellington Hotel, with Mahalia mumbling that it wasn't "what it used to be."

By morning, Minters checked Mahalia into a hospital. She let the doctors know she couldn't stay more than overnight. She had a plane to catch to New Orleans the next day. She had to be there for her friend John H. Johnson, publisher of *Ebony* and *Jet* magazines, who was receiving his honorary Doctor of Journalism (PhD) degree.

A Family Reunion

Mahalia's New Orleans trip turned out to be a Clark-Jackson family reunion—the biggest one she'd had since she became famous. She was performing at Loyola University and was pretty proud of that, too. New Orleans had just recently began rolling out the carpet for "Little Halie from Nigger Town."

Both sides of her family—the Jacksons and the Clarks—were there in full force. Her Jackson siblings Yvonne, Pearl, Wilmon, and Johnny Jr. came with their children, and there were too many Clarks to count. Mahalia's ex-husband, Minters Galloway, was performing with her, his first time visiting Mahalia's hometown with her. Some of Mahalia's kinfolk were taking a wait-and-see position with this man they'd heard had been giving their Halie the blues.

Not only was the handsome Minters Galloway the program emcee, but he was accompanying his famous former wife on his beloved flute. Mahalia made her family proud, in spite of the fact that she was sweating so much her clothes were drenched by the time she walked off the stage.

Sunday morning, Mahalia was inside a family member's home, moving around in the kitchen. No need to dawdle, Duke often told her. She checked the pots and pans cooking on the stove in preparation for the day's dinner.

When she was satisfied everything was as it should be, Halie turned to cleaning up the kitchen, washing down the sink and counters, putting away anything that didn't have a right to be sitting around. She washed her dishcloth and smoothed it on the sink to dry.

When her aunts and cousins complained that she was working like a housemaid, Mahalia laughed. She'd done enough of that to keep her a lifetime. She shook her head, remembering. It had started in Aunt Duke's home. "That's the way Aunt Duke taught me, baby, that the Lord likes a clean kitchen."

She sat for a minute, breathing hard. Before it was time to head out to church, Mahalia's face was etched in pain, though restrained. She asked Gwen Lightner, her new organist, if she would represent her at the church. The mood in the house shifted as Mahalia admitted she just wasn't up to visiting the church that Sunday morning. If Mahalia was skipping the opportunity to visit her beloved childhood church, she wasn't well.

After her Sunday night performance, Mahalia traveled two hours to Baton Rouge, where she'd promised her friend Ida Beal that she'd perform at her church. From Baton Rouge, Mahalia flew back to Chicago. She stayed there for only two days before she flew out west, to Salt Lake City, in search of some relief. She was told that Utah was the place to go to get well. They swore the hot, dry climate would have her feeling like new. It was cold and raining when she arrived.

Mahalia was in a fretting mood. She hadn't been able to meet with her lawyer about plans for her temple. She somehow felt there was a time clock ticking on this temple business, and she was running from behind.

Back in Chicago, she pulled herself together in time to sing at a $100-a-plate fundraising dinner for Adlai Stevenson II, one of her political friends and one of Chicago's longest-serving political figures. He'd served as congressman and governor and had run for president of the United States three times.

The next day, her body punished her for putting on the only kind of performance Mahalia knew how to give—150%—no matter how she felt. She summoned Dr. Barclay to meet her at Billings Hospital.

After 20-plus years, it was hard for him to say no. He prescribed her medicine but took the opportunity to also remind her that he wouldn't be available to her again. His role as vice president of the American Medical Association precluded him from serving as her personal doctor. Surprised at her tears, he finally convinced Mahalia he'd find a way to check on her no matter what.

Mahalia Takes a Caribbean Islands Tour (1970)

In April 1970, Mahalia performed at the Brooklyn Academy of Music in New York, followed by a week of traveling and performances across the East Coast, from "The Dick Cavett Show" in New York to "The Mike Douglas Show" in Philadelphia, then on to Portland, Maine, and finally to Bowdoin College in Brunswick, Maine.

Mahalia's astounding whirlwind of performances after months of inactivity confirmed for Minters Galloway that his former wife's ailments were as much in her head as in reality. He was for certain, in the minority. No one else believed that. Neither her doctors nor her family thought Mahalia was "putting on." The woman was sick, sicker than most of her fans realized. Sicker than she'd ever been in her life.

It was miraculous to see her bounce back as if she'd never experienced a sick day in her life. She wouldn't have it any other way, even when she knew she'd pay for it the next day—sometimes that very night. It was because she was always representing God when she stood up in front of an audience, she said. She'd made a promise to him years ago that she'd never let him down, never embarrass him. Mahalia Jackson would have to be deathly ill to give her audience less than all of her. She gave everything she had, and then borrowed some more from God.

Mahalia had a full day of rest before she was off again, this time to the Caribbean islands of St. Croix, St. Thomas, St. Vincent, Guyana, Barbados, Jamaica, and Trinidad, where she was scheduled to perform six concerts and two one-hour shows.

Mahalia's first stop would be St. Croix, and before she boarded her plane, she wanted to meet with the promoter to make sure they were on the same page. Mahalia had learned over the years that "when you're working with promoters, you get all your money up front, before you take one step up on that stage." She also wanted to make sure she would have some rest days in between all those performances.

In spite of the fact that Mahalia had traveled halfway around the world over the last decade, this was her longest stay in any of the Caribbean islands. She was enchanted by the people, the history, the food, and the beauty of the islands. She was surprised and delighted that she had fans in the West Indies; the people on the streets recognized her immediately. She was treated like royalty at each of her stops; welcomed with pomp and circumstance by the governors of each island—including special per-formances in her honor. Residents crowded in to request blessings from Mahalia, referring to her as "Sis-tah! Sistah!"

After her first performance in Trinidad, however, she learned there were political troubles brewing in the country. Mahalia was the guest of Prime Minister Eric Williams and was escorted to her guest room in his palatial mansion. She was resting there when she heard shouting outside the prime minister's residence.

A crowd outside were obviously angry and making demands. More shocking was that her name—Mahalia Jackson—was included in the crowd's shouts. Perplexed, and a little frightened, she couldn't understand how she figured into the locals' problems. Before long, a knock came at her door. One of the prime minister's assistants brought a message from him. Would Mahalia speak to the crowd? Mahalia reluctantly agreed. She understood there were poor people all over the world, and who else would they complain to, but their leaders?

Mahalia stood at the window and listened to some of the words the crowd was chanting. She specifically heard the word "Black Power" loud and clear. She shook her head, walked with the prime minister's aide downstairs and out the door. As she stood on the steps of the mansion, there was an immediate silence.

Mahalia started out by telling the crowd, "I know I'm just a visitor in your land, but the governor asked me to come out and speak to you, and I said I would." She shared that she understood their complaints, but she personally was not a big fan of putting strong titles on movements. She believed people either did what was right or they didn't. Case in point, she said, was the "Black Power" rhetoric so many people were throwing around for their own purposes.

"What I believe in, and have said this everywhere I've gone, is civil rights and equal justice are for everybody. And I really think this can be achieved if we found a way to get good jobs, and if everyone used their right to vote. If we have those, then we can achieve Black Power, not just words that people use to manipulate other people."

She waited to see what their response would be. There were shouts of "Yes!" "Mahalia!" and "Our Sistah!" There were even some nods and smiles. Mahalia was relieved, but wary when she saw that the crowd were not disbursing, and there were still some rumblings.

The prime minister was by her side by then and whispered to her that the crowd's immediate grievance was that her concert had been too expensive for the common people to attend. Mahalia frowned and nodded. She agreed to return and deliver a free concert for underprivileged residents. She was happy she could calm the troubles on the beautiful island.

On to St. Vincent, Guyana, Barbados …the islands began to run together. There were three more, but nobody could remember where since they had been added after the original contract was signed. Now they added her return trip for the "poor people's concert" to her expanding schedule.

Since she had a few hours to herself, Mahalia, Sigmond, and Gwen drove up into the quiet of the mountains. Finally, she felt rested, calm, and at peace. She had no idea that she would be faced with another stressful situation when she returned. She sent for the promoter, and found herself embroiled in yet another messy confrontation—this time about payment for her performances. She hadn't been paid for the extra performances that were added at the last minute.

The sponsor was adamant that he'd already paid. The payment had been made to Mr. Galloway. Mahalia, incensed, reminded the sponsor that Minters Galloway was not her manager, and that his contract was with her, not Minters.

Mahalia stared over at Minters, who simply shrugged and said he'd given her everything the promoter gave him. Fuming, as all in her circle knew Mahalia could, she told them both that she expected full payment or she wouldn't go on to Jamaica. Everyone in the promotions circle should know how serious Mahalia was about getting her money. This wasn't her first rodeo. Surely, he'd heard the stories. Minters tried to dissuade her from pulling out of the Jamaica trip, but she was adamant.

Mahalia fumed. She could have been in New Orleans for Duke Ellington's surprise premier of his critically acclaimed *New Orleans Suite* studio album, which included a masterpiece he'd devoted to her—"Portrait of Mahalia."

Mahalia told close friends she was growing more and more disenchanted with other folk—mostly white men—who decided what was right for her and her career. One of the big decisions she had made was to end her recording contract with Columbia and return to her own sound, without all the bells and whistles of Hollywood. She needed time to sit and meet with her lawyer to get all that straightened out. Good or bad, she'd agreed to sign a two-year extension with Columbia since it would take some time to get her own recording company off the ground. Now she wanted to talk to her friend, the brilliant music producer and musician John Jay Hooker. She had been dodging Minters' ongoing request that she include him in her recording business.

June 1970 marked the debut of "Mahalia Jackson's Fried Chicken" shacks opening throughout the Midwest. Mahalia complained to her friend and business partner Judge Ben Hooks that it seemed a store was opening every week, and she was having to juggle her schedule to fly in and eat chicken for the cameras. Hooks was president of the franchise corporation.

"Mahalia Jackson tries some 'Glori-Fried' chicken prepared at the Mahalia Jackson Fried Chicken shack in Chicago this weekend," read the June 6, 1970, Sun-Times newspaper article. The restaurant opened that weekend at 83rd and South Evans streets, and was just the first of five store openings in Chicago.

Mahalia was the main attraction at Detroit Mayor Roman Gribbs' promotional event for his upcoming foundation benefit. Mahalia was sweating profusely, as she was worried whether she would get to her store in time for its opening.

As more and more people lined up to meet her at the governor's mansion, Mahalia grew more and more nervous that she would miss the announcement of the Chicago chicken shack. Finally, an escort with a screaming siren took her to the airport, and officers from the local sheriff's department escorted her aboard a plane in time to arrive at the Chicago restaurant and eat fried chicken for the press.

In spite of her overwhelming schedule, Mahalia's return checkup with Dr. Vondrasek was encouraging. Her blood sugar was more balanced, and she'd lost 10 pounds. Though he suggested it would be good if she'd spend a few days at the hospital for them to monitor her, Mahalia bolted, saying she had too much on her plate for the next week. Like always, she'd let the doctors know when she could come in.

Mahalia had chicken business the next day. And before she got back on the road with concerts and performances, she really needed to spend some time looking for her temple, especially now that she had the extra money from the sale of the house on Indiana Avenue.

On July 4, 1970, Mahalia would sing at the Omaha baseball stadium for 20-30 minutes at the beginning and close. Officials there wanted her to sing "God Bless America," but she didn't know the song by memory, so she would substitute it for "The Lord's Prayer."

It was a night game, but she wouldn't spend the night in the city. The next day was Aunt Hannah's birthday, and Mahalia had planned a dinner for her that evening. It wasn't often she got the chance to celebrate with her family. Three days later, Mahalia was in New York, and the next day she was in Philadelphia.

On July 10, Mahalia joined a long list of celebrities in Newport, Rhode Island, where she gave a show-stopping performance at the Newport Jazz Festival. The festival drew some of America's most notable Black performers representing gospel, blues, rhythm and blues, and jazz. She was excited to see so many old friends. Gospel down to the bone, Mahalia always said she could appreciate all kinds of music. Hugh Masekela and Nina Simone were two of her favorite performers at the festival.

How long had it been since she'd seen her old New Orleans brother Louis Armstrong? She had missed that big smile of his and that "way down in the throat" gravelly voice. They fell into each other's arms, and she laughed as he talked about "red beans and ricely! Nicely!" Their friend and music historian Bill Russell was up from New Orleans as well and happy to reconnect with Mahalia and Louis. Not even the rain could dampen the warmth of these reconnections.

Halie offered to cook Louis his favorite rice and beans when he visited her in Chicago. But she quickly told him it wouldn't be soon because she was on her way to Detroit, where she'd be raising money for her Mahalia Jackson Foundation.

Four days later, Mahalia was back in New York for a performance, and right after that she would be heading to the Berkshire Music Barn in Massachusetts for another performance.

Mahalia's next visit to Dr. Vondrasek wasn't a good one. Her hypertension had crept way up, and she was complaining of recurring chest pains and intermittent diarrhea. Her weight had also jumped up to 219 pounds. The doctor, worried, directed her to rest. No traveling or performing for the next two weeks.

Bob Phillips, her agent, grimaced when she told him what her doctor said. Just because Mahalia didn't feel well today, how could she tell she wouldn't feel well a week or 10 days from now? he complained. Finally, he relented, saying that if the doctor would send him a report, he'd get her events canceled.

By the end of July, Mahalia's doctor had approved her travel to California. She loved traveling to California in the summer to get away from Chicago's dangerously hot weather. Unfortunately, her ailments traveled with her.

On the day she arrived, she visited the doctor's office for a prescription for a decongestant. Mahalia was in one of her moods. No one called it depression, but she was again down in the dumps. She was scheduled to record with Columbia Records while she was in California, but complained she just couldn't. She called Toledo, Ohio, to cancel her next performance, as well.

By early August, Mahalia was back in Chicago, and back in Billings emergency room. She complained that the pains in her chest felt like a ton of bricks. For the first time, Mahalia was seeing a Black doctor, young Dr. Lloyd Ferguson, at Billings. Her beloved Dr. Barclay had stopped by to introduce her to the new doctor and for a precursory check of her vitals. He told her that the chest pain was caused by hypertension and suggested that Dr. Ferguson prescribe Valium to help with her pressure.

Mahalia touted this new Valium that her new doctor prescribed as something of a wonder drug. The very next day she felt up to flying to Toronto, Canada, to keep her engagement with "The Barbara McNair show," which she'd canceled two weeks earlier. The next night, she was in Detroit performing for a benefit in honor of one of her favorite people, Joe Louis, who was struggling after his son put him in the Veterans Hospital. She loved seeing Joe, and all of his old friends, many of whom were her friends as well—like comedian Red Foxx and jazz singer Billy Eckstein.

Mahalia's heart lifted with joy as she sang a tribute to the great boxer. Though Minters made sure he was there for most of the glamourous events such as this one, he was still whispering that most of Mahalia's complaints were in her head, or overblown. He didn't get it, how she jumped from being on the brink of death to belting out songs the way she had that night. Mahalia, used to his skepticisms, simply gave him one of her famous stares and half-joked that if she knew the answer to that, she'd never have to set foot in a hospital again.

Finally, Mahalia had a couple of weeks to devote to her own business. She spent those weeks working on her campaign to find herself a temple. She looked at the Swedish Club, just off Stony Island. It had a beautiful dining room, ballroom, kitchen, offices, and parking space. But she learned it would only hold but 500 people at most. She needed a place that would hold up to 1,500. What Halie wanted more than anything was to have her church sitting smack dab on Martin Luther King Jr. Drive on Chicago's South Side. That would really mean something to her. She asked her attorney to look for something on King Drive.

Mahalia had made a quick trip down home to New Orleans and was scheduled to fly out to join the National Baptist Convention. For the first time since they'd finally opened their doors to her, she told them she couldn't be there, that she wasn't in the best of health and wouldn't be able to travel there this year. Instead, when her pains let up, she traveled to Monroe, Louisiana, for a performance in her neck of the woods. She worked herself into a frenzy and had to be led off the stage.

Mahalia Takes her Gospel to Africa

One of Chicago's most admired politicians, U.S. Congressman William Dawson, had been the first person to teach Mahalia that politics wasn't just about power, but also about helping the community and making it better. In time, he'd become a good friend and someone Mahalia looked forward to helping get reelected each year.

Dawson had repaid her support many times over as she made her way in Chicago. When she told him she didn't know anything about politics, he took it on himself to guide her in how to vote, how to campaign, and sometimes who to vote for. Her friends were sorry to see Mahalia grieve so deeply when the congressman passed away on November 9, 1970. Of course, she agreed to sing at his funeral.

On that same day, Mahalia's new assistant Allen Clark, her cousin, was packing up for her trip to Africa. Her first trip to Africa. Mahalia was both excited and concerned to be going to the continent that she'd heard nothing but negative news about. She couldn't worry too much about her fears though, she had a concert to do in Virginia the next night.

Mahalia had to talk herself into this Africa trip. She argued against it in the beginning, even to perform at Liberian President William Tubman's 75th birthday party. It had nothing to do with the president. It was the big black snakes she saw on television. She wouldn't want to have to be carried through the jungles by natives, either.

Trying hard not to laugh at Mahalia's fear, her manager had told her that Liberia was a beautiful, modern country on the west coast of Africa. She wouldn't have to go into a jungle, and she'd be treated like royalty. Everyone revered Mahalia Jackson in Africa. In time, she settled down and agreed to the trip.

America's Queen of Gospel was greeted at the airport in Monrovia, Liberia's capital and largest city, by a welcome motorcade led by U.S. Ambassador Samuel Westerfield and Liberian Vice President William Tolbert. For the next two weeks, Mahalia was indeed treated like an African queen.

Mahalia and her organist Gwen Lightner were given the full second-floor suite in the ambassador's residence. They ate breakfast on the sunporch in the mornings while watching the passing ships on the Atlantic Ocean. Nowhere in the capital city was there not something to watch, even the way the women moved on the street.

They were amazed at the colors, the smells, the beauty of the people. They were guests at a Calendar Tea—a hospital benefit—and discovered an astonishing array of cookies and cakes, intricately decorated and soaked in rum.

The wives of the vice president and the president of the Bank of Liberia had made a beautiful, floor length Liberian garment—a grand bubu—for both Mahalia and Gwen. Mahalia's was a silken white lace threaded with gold which cascaded from its flowing headpiece.

Liberian politician and businessman Stephen Tolbert and his wife, who had arranged Mahalia's trip, hosted a dinner for Mahalia and her party, where they presented them with intricately worked 24-karat gold jewelry. Gwen received gold earrings and a nugget to match. Later, a group of admiring ladies presented Mahalia with ivory jewelry because she had responded so to the elephant symbol.

Ambassador Westerfield escorted Mahalia to the executive mansion for a private visit with President Tubman, who said her singing "thrilled his soul."

Later, at the presidential dinner and ball, Mahalia met dignitaries from a number of neighboring countries, including the global diplomatic corps. Everyone stood for the president's entrance. Mahalia was surprised to learn that guests could not remain seated any single time President Tubman rose for any purpose thereafter. The 75-year-old president led the grand march and started the ball with a little dance around the room by himself, to horns, sticks, and hand drums. *He could pass for 40,"* Mahalia whispered.

Thanksgiving at the U.S. Embassy included a candlelight dinner with turkey and trimmings flown in from the United States. The president's aides took Mahalia shopping, where she fell madly in love with the rich, colorful African fabrics. She ordered 12 dresses to be made before she left the country. The women looked puzzled, then shared with Mahalia that they could create a gown fit for a queen in less than an hour.

The aides took Mahalia sightseeing in the countryside, and she felt as if she was just a few steps from heaven…until she saw dead black snakes down in the valley. When the car stopped for them to walk around and view the countryside closer up, Mahalia refused to leave the car unless it was at the top of a hill. She still had the vision of the mamba snake that only needed to bite once to kill a person.

The next week, a U.S. Navy plane flew Mahalia and her entourage to Liberia's Maryland County, the capital of Cape Palmas, the region where President Tubman was born. By now, Mahalia felt that if she had to stand for one more toast to anything, she was going to disgrace her country. When they were taken to a children's presentation of the president's life, Mahalia sat in the president's box.

Without thinking, she slipped off her shoes. Luckily, an aide witnessed this and hurriedly urged Miss Jackson to put her shoes back on before the president noticed. Unbeknownst to Mahalia, this was a serious breach of protocol! Mahalia frowned, and fixed the aide with a stare. She had taken her shoes off in the White House, why couldn't she take off her shoes here in Africa? Her feet were hurting in the White House, just as they were killing her here.

Cape Palmas was Mahalia's final concert—so heart-felt, so soulful that, first, President Tubman, then his wife, flung their arms around her as she stood drenched and disheveled. They thanked her profusely for bringing such joy to their county and such personal joy to them.

The final event was a dinner in honor of visiting heads of state. Mahalia was not feeling well and was not feeling up to entertaining or being entertained. She forced herself to attend and was happy she did once she realized President Tubman was presenting her with Liberia's award of high distinction: the Grand Banner of the Order of the Star of Africa.

"We are all one, from America," said a beaming Mrs. William Tolbert, the vice president's wife.

Two weeks after her departure from Africa, Mahalia was back in New York, then back to California. The warm California climate agreed with her, even waking on Christmas Eve to snow falling.

Mahalia spent Christmas Day with Mother Parker, Minters' god-mother. They called all Mahalia's gospel buddies in the area to spend the holiday with her. The old house was rocking, and outside a crowd stood listening to Mahalia's voice, clear down the block.

A young boy who lived in the neighborhood told Mother Parker the next day, he would've paid $100 to just shake Mahalia Jackson's hand. Little did he know that if he'd knocked on the door, she would have invited him in and likely would have given him a big holiday hug.

Part 15

MAHALIA WOWS THE WORLD
(1971)

MAHALIA DURING EUROPEAN TOUR (GETTY CREDIT).

A New Year for Halie and Another World Tour

Mahalia returned to New York in time to bring in the new year, 1971. She couldn't believe she was into a whole new year. She felt it was even more imminent that she get her business organized—begin producing her own records, and get her temple in place.

She had made a decision during her time in California with her gospel friends. Her label would be called "Hallelujah!" She had lots to think about and plan for the new record business, like where she'd put her studio. Would she need to purchase her own equipment, or lease it? Would they run mail order, or lease the distribution? What about promotion and cost of distributing here and internationally?

Money wasn't Mahalia's problem, she admitted. It was getting a quality studio and a good manager of the studio. She needed some partners and investors she could trust. She talked with both Benjamin Hooks and John Lee Hooker who both said they'd be honored to be part of the business.

She wasn't worried about the records selling. She'd prayed on it, and she knew that returning to her old sound was going to reach young and old alike. Her voice was an instrument from Jesus. And it wouldn't just be her voice, there were some mighty good voices out there she'd help groom and bring into the recording business.

In the middle of her planning, Mahalia remembered one of her closest friends suggesting in confidence that she do something about her teeth. Over the years she'd lost some, and the remaining ones had been ground down to stubs. With her traveling all over the world, meeting with kings and queens and presidents, she really needed a presentable mouth. She might as well do something about her "ole raggedy teeth," she decided.

When Mahalia went to the dentist to get implants, she passed out in the dentist chair. But once it was over, her teeth were perfect—as even as a picket fence, her friends told her. She was sure Johnny Cash would pay her a compliment when she showed up in Nashville the next day.

Mahalia sang "Amazing Grace" on "The Johnny Cash Show," and the audience gave her a standing ovation. She left immediately afterward, to attend her niece's funeral. She found out once she arrived that she needed a white hat. She called her old trusty standby Ida Beal to bring her one. Even if it wasn't finished.

On February 10, at 6:01 a.m., a powerful earthquake struck the northern end of the San Fernando Valley. The Associated Press reported 64 dead, over 2,400 injured. Some 850 homes and 640 buildings were severely damaged. Another 4,800 homes, 265 apartments, and 1,125 commercial buildings had appreciable damage.

Mahalia's own building had been damaged, but not irreparably. She was still shaken the next week, reading her Bible most of the day. She was roused from her reading when someone yelled her name. She went to the door to find a man lying half-naked and half-dead in front of her door. She called the rescue squad, told them to put him in the hospital, she'd pay. All the time she was wondering why the man had come to her door, all the way up the steps to die on her doorstep?

March 1971 wasn't promising to be a great month, the way it was going already. Mahalia was spending as much time in the hospital or in a doctor's office as she was in her own home. Besides that, she had to prepare for another international trip. Another strange land is how she saw it, that she had to prepare her heart and mind for.

On March 24, Mahalia was in Dr. Peck's office in Los Angeles. He gave her gamma globulin to prevent infectious hepatitis and a new prescription to control her diabetes.

Five days later, on March 29, she was at Billings in Chicago. Dr. Siegler gave her a new stronger prednisone prescription and an extra supply. Later that same day, Dr. Vondrasek and Dr. Rosi kept their habitual late hours, and Dr. Rosi saw her. She had some epigastric distress—gas pains—which apparently had developed in the morning. He gave her something to relieve the condition. Mahalia was a walking pharmacy, hoarding medicine like she wouldn't be returning.

Aunt Bessie was at the house waiting for Halie to finish her meeting with Judge Benjamin Hooks. She couldn't put a finger on it, but Bessie was worried about her niece. Was it the trip? Was it this new business venture she was so high on? Was it how she'd come back from her sicknesses last year running a hundred miles a minute, knowing she was just making herself sick all over again? Bessie shook her head and frowned. She just didn't know what, but it was keeping her awake at night.

April 2 was Mahalia's departure day for a monthlong international tour. When she should have been on her way to the airport, she was sitting in Dr. Vondrasek's office. He prescribed an antibiotic as a general travel precaution.

Delta Air Lines' VIP agent kept a lookout for their most important traveler. Mahalia was nowhere to be found. It was past time to enter the restricted area for outbound passengers. But Mahalia was on the streets, waving at taxis, cars, anything moving to pick her up and take her to the airport. No one seemed to recognize the Queen of Gospel. The departure time was fast approaching, and Mahalia was praying.

She had, in fact, arrived at the airport early. But when she looked for her vaccination record, it wasn't there. Nobody had it—not Gwen, not Celeste—and there wasn't time to go all the way back to South Norton, miles and miles away, to get it. They had no option. Mahalia and her aide

Celeste rushed to find a doctor as close to the airport as they could. She would have to take her shots all over again and have a new record.

They eventually located a doctor who agreed to give her the necessary vaccinations. It wasn't until they were walking out of the doctor's office that they looked at each other, realizing they had no way back to the airport. Finally, a cab driver recognized Mahalia and made an illegal U-turn to pick her up.

Mahalia told the cab driver that God had his name and that he'd be blessed. She thanked him all the way to the airport and gave him a hefty tip. She was so grateful to find they were holding the plane door open, the stewardess beckoning. Gwen, her organist, did not board until they arrived. There Mahalia was, panting, sweating, looking distressed, but she'd made it back, and the plane was waiting. The VIP attendant's smile was a mile wide as she escorted her most important passenger aboard the plane.

Mahalia was in an upbeat mood, quipping about the stewardesses looking like porcelain dolls, and how they tried to feed you every 20 minutes. She slept, then woke with one of her God-inspired moments. "It struck me just before I left, as I was reading my Bible, and I had never noticed it before. Solomon was Black! The wisest man! And he didn't go to a university!"

Mahalia stayed cheerful through the hour layover in Honolulu, Hawaii, and took some time to walk outside to get rid of a leg cramp. A reporter immediately recognized her and dashed out to interview her. When she climbed aboard again, she asked for some brandy and a teaspoon.

Japan—Mahalia's Historic Performance

Mahalia arrived in Japan on April 7, 1971, exhausted with nothing but a bed on her mind. She learned immediately after settling in that she had an evening event. It was near midnight when the weary party arrived back from the official reception, just as a welcoming party stopped her before she entered the hotel. Cheering fans with flowers, flashing lights, and a giant welcome banner hoisted high. Mahalia was a "national honor guest," they told her.

The next morning, she was picked up at 7 a.m. by the CBS/Sony Records promotion director in Japan. She chuckled that she had thought Japan didn't know who she was.

Mahalia had learned from a public library inquiry that Emperor Hirohito's 70th birthday was coming up. She had been told that U.S.-Japan relations were scratchy—some drawn-out squabble over textile regulations. Mahalia thought it wouldn't hurt to give the Emperor a birthday gift from America: a gospel concert. She called Washington to Hale Boggs— the House majority leader and an old friend, plus a New Orleanian. The message got to Congressman Boggs, and he was all for it.

Mahalia was having brunch in her room when a call came in from the American Embassy: Mahalia might be invited to the Imperial Palace. Betsy Fitzgerald, the young U.S. Embassy Third Secretary cautioned Mahalia, however, that it was still up in the air.

She also cautioned Mahalia that there were certain niceties she must remember if the visit took place: *You don't make a direct overture of any kind. It's done by a Mrs. Matsudara. The invitation would come from the Empress.* If it happened, Miss Jackson would be the first Western entertainer ever to be invited to the Imperial Palace.

Mahalia had been reading the Buddhist bible she'd found in the night table. A reporter and interpreter entered her hotel room, asking for just a few words for the radio station. Mahalia thought it was supposed to be a rest day, and the press conference was the next day. Finally, saying yes, she decided she would be interviewed without leaving her bed.

Dekko, the Japanese liaison, came with exciting news. Princess Takako Shimazu—Princess Suga, the youngest daughter of the Emperor—would be present at Mahalia's first concert on Sunday. Though the Princess didn't attend after all, after her son's accident, she sent flowers and a warm greeting.

Mahalia was amazed by the report that 20 million viewers had seen her as she was welcomed as a national honor guest. A smiling magazine editor and his photographer appeared and trooped out with Mahalia to see the cherry blossoms. She stopped at a breathtaking tree with a smile and gestured to the translator that she would like an audience with their priest.

At the New Otani ballroom, Mahalia's delight changed to depression as she learned that Aunt Hannah was sick, and that her favorite Uncle Porter had had a stroke at his home in Cincinnati. Her depression only lifted after she returned to her hotel and received the news that she was invited to the Imperial Palace.

Miss Fitzgerald from the embassy called to go over the royal protocols and proscription for the historical visit: *Don't wear white, because it is the color for mourning. Don't wear yellow, that's the imperial color.* Her Majesty the Empress would wear a short silk suit. The palace needed to know what Mahalia was wearing, for approval. Finally, they required that Mahalia give them a list of 15 songs she was willing to sing so the Imperial Household may request eight.

The palace visit was set for April 23rd. Mahalia had days before then to continue her tour. The next day she crossed the city to the CBS/Sony building and rehearsed. The room was filled with photographers snapping her photo. Father Joseph Love came by—he would interpret her songs on Sunday. Japanese Baptists called. By the end of the day, Mahalia was having cramps in both her legs and her hands. But she wasn't feeling poorly.

On Saturday, she walked into the New Otani ballroom for her programmed press conference—and was confronted with some 200 writers and cameramen from all media. Microphones were set at the front of the room, and a banquet-length table was neatly covered with cloth; chairs there for interpreters; sponsors' representatives. Mahalia imagined there were more press here than the presidential press conferences back home.

Mahalia was itching to tell the media of her historic visit to the palace, but they'd sworn her to secrecy. Just then, a voice came from the back of the room: "Miss Jackson, do you have any plans to sing before the emperor?" Hirohito was the 124th in his line, and to gain the Presence would be, indeed, historic.

Another question, and another, and on and on. Mahalia smiled and politely answered their questions for over two hours. She was talked out. She rested after the press conference. It had worn her out. Then she learned she still didn't have a visa for India, and now the palace was asking for an explanation for each of the songs Mahalia chose to sing. An explanation? She rolled her eyes. Her song was the explanation.

When she awoke from her nap, Mahalia was sick. She searched everywhere for her medicine but couldn't find it. In pain and crying, she finally fell back asleep. She woke again with a hoarse voice, and her hands were cramped. Her feet were swollen, too, hardly fitting into her sharp-toed shoes. Her corns hurt.

Mahalia knew the only remedy was prayer. As she stared into the mirror, she asked for God's intervention and his mercy on his suffering child. As she prayed, she flexed her fingers, and tested her hoarse voice.

When she walked out on the stage, God had worked his magic, as he always did when Mahalia called. The next day's reviews confirmed it. Hisamitsu Noguchi, the dean of Japan's music critics, wrote: *"Her first concert gave so deep impression as I have never felt in any concert of classic, popular, and jazz singers. Her gospel songs have not only the perfect musical beauty, but also the very persuasive power by her belief…Though I am not a Christian, I could not stop running tears; tears of joy."*

So entranced was the critic, he returned for the night performance at Koseinenkin Hall. Backstage, greeted by her elated troupe, Mahalia shook her head, telling the enthralled crowd: "*What I tell you…that's God. He gives it to me or he don't. Sometimes I'm good, sometimes I'm bad.*"

When the tour agent's representative brought Mahalia's payment, she soon realized she was being paid in the Japanese Yen, not U.S. dollars. The poor woman had no idea what it meant when Mahalia narrowed her eyes and breathed through her nose. If she'd told these people once, she'd told them a thousand times, she didn't get paid in nothing but American dollars.

I told you, and I trusted you, and I sang—and I don't have my money. Cash. American dollars.

"Mahalia," she said, "you don't need $10,000 American dollars over here. We are working on it. We can't get all the dollars yet—they're scarce here. You can change the yen easily at home. Why don't you—"

Mahalia grew quiet. She was reliving all the times she'd been tried by men who promised her one thing and tried to give her something a lot less. She'd learned her lesson, and good. She'd not be caught up in that trick all the way over here in Asia. She stood ramrod-straight, eyes flashing. Mahalia calmly told the woman that she would catch the next train out of the country, if she didn't get her $10,000 cash in U.S. dollars.

The representative pleaded for Mahalia to give her until 6 p.m. Mahalia ignored her, reading her Bible. In the afternoon, she thawed out enough to say yes to touring the Meiji Shrine and Gardens in Tokyo. In spite of herself, she enjoyed the gardens. Gardens were God's handiwork, after all. They were manifestations of God's goodness. She smiled as she stared into the beautiful, pristine water, and the colorful fish and exotic trees. So filled with joy, Mahalia began to sing. She drank from the dipper at the sacred Shinto spring, which was said to have magical powers of health. "*Drink from the fountain of life…drink of the living water.*"

On the long ride back to the hotel, Mahalia continued to sing, now *"Who Made the Great Plan."* She abruptly stopped and declared to no one in particular that she now understood that God, in fact, was science. She decided she wanted to buy a kimono and obi to wear during her upcoming Carnegie Hall performance. *I want to look just like a Black Japanese.*

At 8 p.m., the night train for Nagoya pulled away. At that very moment, Mahalia was standing at the end of her bed staring down at stacks and stacks of dollars strewn across her bed. *This is business. We'll all count again.* The money was counted. Tallied. Proved. $10,000. The cash went into her traveling companion's purse. It was nobody's business that Japan actually forbade more than $200 in yen to be taken out of the country.

Nagoya's Prefectural Hall was already surrounded by thousands of fans more than an hour before the doors opened. In Osaka's Sankei Hall, they shouted Japanese phrases for the Amens and hallelujahs. Men listened and wept as Mahalia sang.

The next day, Mahalia was uplifted and talkative. Her childlike curiosity made her drink in every new thing she experienced or saw—the ancient palaces, the well-preserved gardens and Buddhist temples. She was especially moved by the cleanliness of Japan's streets. She bought film for her 8-mm movie camera and purchased delicate tea sets for all her aunts and pearls for herself, although she proudly shared that the huge, faceted ring she wore had cost her only $1.

Mahalia lingered after dinner with Father Love and some 60 of his fellow Jesuits at Japan's Sophia University, where one priest cheerfully hand-pumped an ancient organ so Clancy could play for them all to sing, and Gwen's recipe for "destroyers" had the Jesuits reeling. She kept Gwen busy with writing letters back to the States about the tour and about the possible

TV shows she'd like to do upon her return. Pearl Bailey and Flip Wilson shows were at the top of her list.

There was a string of calls from the U.S. Embassy in Tokyo, imploring Mahalia that details must be precisely worked out for the historic performance at the Imperial Palace. The ambassador was drawn in—Armin Meyer and his wife would be the only guests outside the royal circle. There was a correction extended by the embassy: Mahalia's wasn't the first Western performance. A European harpist had performed there shortly after World War II.

Mahalia thought for a minute. *That's all right. I'm the first singer.* Finally, she was finalizing her list of songs, 15 total. They were pushing her to sing "Deep River." She hadn't sung it since President Kennedy's death.

The palace selected eight of the 15 songs, including "Who Made the Great Plan." The U.S. Embassy would create a memento of the night for the Emperor, a scroll with the words from the song printed onto it. The Emperor was a scientific man, and this song was about science and religion. Mahalia wanted to give the scroll to His Imperial Highness herself but was told that no one could physically give the Emperor gifts. They were sent in advance and screened for suitability.

Never before had an Imperial Palace guest arrived in a taxi. The taxi driver was so flustered by the address that he wouldn't go all the way up to the gate where soldiers guarded the high forbidden stone walls. He let her out at the wrong gate, forcing her to tiptoe over millions of small black stones to the correct East Gate—about a football field away. A limousine picked her up at the East Gate, driving past various buildings which jointly were "the palace"—all tucked discreetly among serene grounds and gardens.

They were joined by Master of Music Abe, a lean elder with wise eyes peering from a face out of an ancient print. He spoke no English, but through Honda-san. With dawning horror, it was learned that Mahalia Jackson must not only abide by a set of songs for the first time in her life—but also she must move minute by set minute.

Mahalia had asked for small American flags to wear on her dress. They didn't have any. Mahalia pressed down on the pink silk dress and jacket outfit that was approved just a few days ago. They'd said short or long, but this seemed more right, with the Empress in a suit. *Do I need to curtsy? Just bow? Do I wear the pearls?*

It was the "rehearsal moments." The auditorium was like a jewel box! Microphone, piano, organ. Exactly at 2:20 p.m., the curtain opened to a packed court. Seating, like everything else, had been prescribed. Mahalia stood, still, as the musical introduction ran its course. The head bowed, her signal, and she began softly singing "The Lord's Prayer." The house was totally silent.

The applause was loud. Genuine. Mahalia prayed her thankfulness.

"He's so Wonderful"—*and isn't it wonderful, Lord, that these people would pick this song?* Heads began to nod, feet to tap—the Empress herself was smiling. By the time she began "Didn't It Rain," Mahalia had to force herself not to do a holy dance. As she walked off stage, the applause was just as loud and seemed not to be near its ending. *Thank you, Jesus, no encores.*

Exhausted, Mahalia fell heavily into the one seat in the room, a straight-backed chair in the crowded little space. She pushed off her spike heels and pulled on slippers—panting. She was startled by the man who hurried into the room. "Her Majesty the Empress wishes to know, will Miss Jackson sing one more song?"

The Empress later received Mahalia, escorted by the U.S. ambassador, Armin Meyer, in a private audience. The room was filled with the Empress' family. Quiet and beautifully attired in her silk suit, she reminded Mahalia of the rich white women in New Orleans. "Miss Jackson, your music was very moving of the spirit. I thank you so much from my heart," she smiled.

"I thank you so much, Your Highness. It's a great honor to be singing for Your Majesty and for the Emperor—even if he isn't able to be here—and for such a great and old and spiritually minded country as Japan."

Over and over Mahalia heard how much they had loved the American gospel music—Crown Prince Akihito, Crown Princess Michiko, Prince Mikasa, Princess Mikasa, Princess Chichibu…the names ran together, and all so enthusiastic. After the royal reception, Mahalia went to the resting room, where she admired more closely the gifts her hosts had bestowed upon her: a lapis lazuli blue porcelain vase with the Imperial crest and a box of Japanese tea-ceremony candies in a brocaded box.

Her party was served fragrant hot tea in Imperial porcelain cups. Mahalia, too excited to sit still, rounded up groups for her movie camera. The jubilant American ambassador Armin Meyer shared with Mahalia what a great honor this had been for his wife and him, who had been there for two years and had "never been invited to the palace before." Meanwhile, the wires of the international new agencies—The AP, UPI, Reuters, the World—were humming.

Mahalia was tired, and her voice was hoarse during her last performance at the Shibuya Kokaido in Tokyo. She started off slow, worried that she would disappoint the polite audience. She closed her eyes and prayed. Suddenly, slowly, her voice gained strength until it was Mahalia singing like Mahalia always did. The applause let her know it was true.

Mahalia said later that she had surprised herself. Panicking, she'd begun an acapella song she hadn't sung in 20 years, "I Woke Up This Morning with My Mind Stayed on Jesus." Before it was over, she declared, the Japanese audience was talking in tongues! Some people were praising, some were screaming—in every language except Japanese. Mahalia was astounded.

The American Embassy was stunned by the world's interest in Mahalia Jackson, as was evidenced by the deluge of priority cables sent between Delhi and Tokyo during the two weeks she had been in Japan. The whispered secret was that Prime Minister Indira Gandhi wanted to attend Mahalia's concert in India, and in fact, she wanted to meet with Miss Jackson privately!

Armin Meyer, America's veteran Asian/Eastern envoy, ruffled through the cables. In the diplomat's eyes, this Negro woman Mahalia might be the world's most powerful woman. Who else was so beloved by the Soviets, the Japanese, the Americans, and now the Indians?

India at the time was teetering on the brink of war with Pakistan. Cholera raged through the country. Poverty and hunger were everywhere. Indira Gandhi had won the election by a landslide and was said to be working from dawn to midnight to bring change for her people. Yet, the prime minister would make time to meet and talk with Mahalia Jackson. And, like a teenage fan, visit her backstage during intermission!

Mahalia was pleased that the prime minister wanted to meet her. But more pressing were the cramps in her hands, along her arms. They weren't going away, and despite taking pills, they were returning faster than usual. And her breathing was scaring her. It was shallow, leaving her wrung out after every song.

This trip gone be my last. It's getting too much for my body. I'm sick, been sick. I'm writing [Chicago Mayor] Daley to be on the lookout for something for me to do; I'm getting tired of being on this road.

Mahalia's Gospel Takes India by Storm

Mahalia was told that she was just 40 miles from the Bangladesh border as they traveled through endless parks filled with thousands of men and women. The driver said they were war refugees, Hajongs, who traveled to India seeking respite and safety to worship as they pleased. Mahalia wondered if they'd found it here. They looked hungry, tired, full of despair. She knew the look.

As they arrived at the American Consulate in Calcutta (Kolkata), there were uniformed men standing guard at the entrance—armed soldiers who were posted there after a bomb was thrown over the wall during the election. Mahalia's eyes found something that made her smile, giant frangipani trees covered with white flowers like the ones that were hung around her neck when she landed. They also reminded her of the giant trees she grew up around in New Orleans—the crab apple and cherry blossom trees.

She noted with alarm how men squatted beside their trays heaped with fruits and vegetables, while other men bicycled around like a Chinese rickshaw with great bales of hemp passing by on carts. It was almost a place of make-believe.

But there was Mrs. Herbert Gordon, the wife of the consul general, whom Mahalia didn't find much to not like about. The woman was wonderful, and Mahalia found it a joy to watch her move around the house at work.

Mahalia learned that tickets to her concert were selling like gold. One hour after the tickets went on sale, they were sold out. Interested buyers were offering twice the price of the tickets. The consul general was ecstatic as if somehow it was a feather in his cap.

Mahalia was astounded—how did these people on the other side of the world learn about her or her singing? She'd received a personal note from the Chogyal (king) of the Kingdom of Sikkim, a monarchy in the Eastern Himalayas, and his American queen, Hope Cooke, who'd attended Sarah Lawrence College. At his coronation, Cooke became the Gyalmo (queen consort) of Sikkim. Mahalia shook her head. This was getting curiouser and curiouser. It reminded her of the fairytale books in the white people's houses with all the strange people dressed in strange costumes.

The Chogyal wasn't well that evening, but the Gyalmo came, a vision of pampered perfection, and beautiful cloths thrown across her body. Saris—all the Indian women wore them, and they were all so beautiful and so colorful. Mahalia would ask Mrs. Gordon to help her buy some before leaving India.

337

The Gyalmo walked over to where Mahalia sat half-reclining on a chaise lounge. Her tiny voice forced Mahalia to bend to hear her. Mahalia found herself drawn to the young woman, and to many of the interesting people in the room. She learned that each of them was important in one way or another. Heads of government, business, even a swami.

Swami Nityaswarupananda was quite interested in American spiritual gospel. Mahalia was entranced and was sorry when someone tugged at her from the other side. It was a Mr. Ashok Mehta, owner of the only company in the country licensed to press foreign records. Her ears quickly perked up. *I make my own. We might can talk business, Mr. Mehta.*

Mahalia smiled over at the man's wife, who she learned was from a part of India where the women ruled and the children took the mother's last name; where everyone was musically inclined, and everyone was Christian. Mahalia's smile widened as the woman shared that in her part of India, they had their own brand of Indian gospel.

Before her concert at St. Paul's Cathedral, Mahalia's legs began cramping and her heart began its on-again, off-again fast beats. But, like always, when she arrived onstage at the Cathedral all the day's pains disappeared. She was ready to sing for God. She sang like Mahalia sang. The critic Amrita Bazar Patrika wrote in The Statesman, an English-language newspaper in India: *"The near-legendary singer…almost hypnotized her audience…inspired. Between a high-pitched vocal cyclone and the softest, almost inaudible cadence…matchless."*

New Delhi. Just minutes after Mahalia dragged herself aboard Air India for New Delhi, the next leg of her tour, the stewardess whispered to her, the departure was slightly delayed. "What's the matter?" Mahalia asked, frowning up at the young, brown woman. "I'm sure all will be fine," the young woman promised. Minutes later, the whispers reached Mahalia—security was searching the plane for a bomb. *"Lord,"* Mahalia muttered under her breath, shaking her head. She closed her eyes and prayed silently. She changed her mind yet again about the safety of riding on planes.

After about 10 minutes, Mahalia looked up to catch the smile and nod from the young stewardess that everything was okay. The young woman lightly patted Mahalia's shoulder. "We're about to leave, Ms. Jackson." Mahalia looked askance at the girl, though she was no longer surprised when strangers knew her name.

The welcome committee met Mahalia in Delhi with a bouquet of flowers. The tall and lanky Daniel Oleksiw, director of the United States Information Service, was joined by American Ambassador Kenneth Keating. A decision was hastily made to have Mahalia Jackson reside at the ambassador's residence, rather than the Roosevelt House in the U.S. Embassy with the steep circular staircase.

The Oleksiw home reminded her of New Orleans' mansions on St. Charles Avenue. The lady of the house smiled and said their home was actually designed by an Indian architect. Lunch was a beautiful and color-ful spread of meats and vegetables. Mahalia was fascinated by the hot and spicy herbs. She asked a million questions.

I'd love to take some of these spices home with me. You know, Japan had some really tasty spices too, and I'd meant to get some there…but, I just love the food here. The only other place you can find food this spicy is in my old hometown, New Orleans.

Mahalia wasn't looking forward to the interview scheduled after dinner. She was feeling poorly again. *My fault, I stayed up too long talking last night.* Mrs. Oleksiw, though, was worried and called the embassy doctor to come in and look at Mahalia.

The American doctor Thomas Wiegert, aware of Mahalia's health history, decided it was her hypertension bothered by the travel and fatigue. He prescribed a relaxant and suggested the singer rest. "Maybe a massage would do you good," he smiled. Mrs. Oleksiw hastily called in her own personal masseuse, Ram Lal. Mahalia fell asleep shortly afterward. She thanked her host profusely, saying it was exactly what she needed.

The evening's dinner was a garden party in Mahalia's honor. Mahalia loved it. She was reminded of how much she missed having a garden she could plant and watch grow outside her kitchen window. By the end of dinner, Mahalia's energy was lagging again, and her breathing labored.

Her hosts were worried the next morning when Mahalia was slow to come down for breakfast. Jim Ascher, the deputy information chief, sent word to cancel the day's tours of the Roosevelt House, the Voice of America offices, and the New Delhi press interviews.

As Mahalia relaxed in the Oleksiw home, she had no idea the kind of stir her presence was causing in the country. The first newspaper announcement that she would appear in four cities resulted in a call to the ambassador's office, asking to purchase tickets for Mrs. Gandhi. Of course, they would love for her to come as their personal guest. Falling over themselves apologizing, the Americans explained that no one thought she would attend, so no one had invited her.

The Gospel Queen Meets the Prime Minister

Another surprise. The prime minister of India requested a private meeting with Mahalia during her performance intermission. Here was the leader of the country, whose time was parceled out sparingly and who rarely took time for social niceties. It was unbelievable that she took such an interest in the American gospel singer.

The prime minister's office called twice more to confirm that the concert would begin at the announced time, to inquire how long the first half of the program would last, and what time Miss Jackson would leave the stage. When Oleksiw shared the prime minister's inquiry with Mahalia, she smiled and shook her head.

"Now that's one thing I can't tell you. I sing what the Lord wills me to sing. I don't know if it's going to be a two-minute or a three-minute or a five-minute song. And I don't know about encores. Just as the spirit moves me. But I'll start on time, they can tell you that. But you got to get the doctor back. I'm not well," she said.

The doctor returned. After examining her, he told Mahalia to rest as much as she could and take her medication. Mahalia sighed and decided she'd forego checking the auditorium this morning like she always did.

Director Daniel Oleksiw learned that evening that the prime minister had fired a good part of her cabinet and was meeting that night with the rest. He was doubtful she would attend the performance. Mahalia smiled and said she understood. *A woman like that, with so much power, must have a lot of important business to deal with.*

The prime minister had come after all and was waiting outside to meet Mahalia Jackson. Mahalia was inside the plush Vigyan Bhavan, where a conference room had been especially fitted as a dressing room for her, including a chaise lounge for resting. Director Oleksiw waited impatiently with the prime minister. He was nervous. Mahalia Jackson was keeping the prime minister waiting. A woman who had a hair-trigger temper and waited for no one.

Mahalia had insisted that she change from the sweat-soaked dress she'd performed in before meeting the prime minister. She needed to freshen up, smooth her disheveled hair. It would have been disrespectful to meet the powerful Indian leader looking like she just finished wrestling a Louisiana alligator!

Mahalia quickly wiped sweat from her face and forehead, swiping her face with a powder sponge, combing her glistening curls. She was in pain, but she wouldn't complain. Not now. The white chiffon dress was becoming—perfect for the occasion. Mahalia didn't look her 58 years.

There was applause as America's Queen of Gospel entered the room. It was a room half-full, but Mahalia's tiny black eyes focused only on the woman she knew immediately was Prime Minister Indira Gandhi, who stood with Ambassador Keating. Mahalia noticed that Indira Gandhi was a small, fragile-looking woman dressed in a sari. Her skin was a beautiful olive tone, and there was just a sprout of gray, highlighting her dark wavy hair. Her eyes were black, lustrous, intense. The two women stared at each other, smiling as they greeted each other, then sat and talked in low voices.

"When you coming to America?" Mahalia asked, eyes never leaving Mrs. Gandhi's.

"I don't know just yet," smiled Mrs. Gandhi.

"Well, when you do, you come stay with me in Chicago," said Mahalia. Mrs. Gandhi smiled. Such a simple, innocent offer. Mrs. Gandhi would later tell the American ambassador, *"I will never hear a greater voice; I will never know a greater person."*

The prime minister said she was not able to stay for the second half of the concert, though Mahalia's performance was surely partially inspired by Mrs. Gandhi's visit. The mostly Indian crowd was swept away by Mahalia's voice, her songs, her spirit. She left the stage to the deafening sound of "Encore!" Again, she was soaked with sweat. Even after an encore, the cheers wouldn't stop. They couldn't know the performer was again feeling poorly.

Dr. Wiegert, the American doctor, watched, worried. He saw familiar signs. After the encore must come the flowers—the traditional Indian salute which signals the real end. Over the footlights poured a stream of young Indian beauties in saris, arms filled with baskets of blossoms.

Puffing, triumphant, Mahalia was finally heading to her dressing room, but the eerie silence from the crowd, the entire audience standing in tribute, changed her mind. Back on stage she went for yet a final encore. One more song, *for the young people,* which turned into another and another, a full performance.

It turned out that the prime minister had not only stayed until the end, she left and came back for the encores. She stood in the fire exit to listen. The message was delivered to Mahalia onstage. She smiled, glowed as she grasped the lectern.

"I have been gospel singing for 42 years. Maybe I have got 42, 52, or 62 more years to do it. But today, I have so much to be grateful to God for, and when Madam Prime Minister stayed—is still here—that is a blessing from God. That's why she's the prime minister. When people learn to serve their fellow man and be part of them and don't worry about titles, that's what makes you great. For a fine, fine lady to stay here after the program.

"You know, they can say what they want about us women—and I say this all over—but really, it takes a woman to really do something. Now ladies, and all the good men, too—men are proud of great women; they are, you know. They don't always show it, but behind their back, child, you ought to hear them brag! So, I think everyone ought to stand up and give her a great big ovation, giver her a great big hand—men and women and children and all."

There was thunderous applause, led by Mahalia. Wave after wave as Mrs. Gandhi stood, smiling, delighted. Somewhere along the way, a slight Indian man in nondescript cotton homespun clothing, sitting in one of the end seats in the cheaper row by the exit, realized with a start just who was standing nearby. He scrambled to his feet and offered Mrs. Gandhi his seat. Her security cordon hurriedly regrouped. But nothing bad could happen this night in the Vigyan Bhavan in New Delhi. Revolt and plague and the cabinet could wait for the one enchanted evening.

Mrs. Gandhi had left reluctantly when the flowers came over the stage and was almost at the main entrance with Ambassador Keating at her elbow when she heard the ringing applause of Mahalia's re-entrance and the music. She hurried back down the long side corridor to the entrance-way nearest the stage to stand and listen.

The last note of the last encore was the song most shouted for throughout the auditorium when Mahalia asked them to decide upon one final choice: In the lilting English of India, they joined her for "We Shall Overcome." Mahalia made clear that it held a broad meaning, that "with God's help, we shall overcome the evil raging throughout the world."

The electricity could be felt through the reception rooms of the Oleksiws' post-concert reception. "My God, what a diplomatic coup!" gasped the Yugoslav envoy. "I said the same thing," trumpeted a West German diplomat.

"And, did you notice," said a smiling Indian woman, "the prime minister had her head uncovered the whole evening? That is most unusual; she usually has her sari draped over her head, even indoors."

Across the hallway, in her small wing, Mahalia lay writhing in pain. Her heart. It was almost like England—but was it like England? She'd gotten up and continued on from there. Dr. Wiegert hurried in and said he thought she'd better give up tomorrow.

At 4:30 a.m., the Reverend Hendrix Townsley—district superintendent of the Methodist Church in Southern Asia—began typing a letter to the president in Washington, D.C. In his *"more than 28 years in India,"* he wrote that he *"had never before experienced anything like the goodwill engendered by this one lady last night. Send her back!"* he implored the president.

Mahalia was groggy the next morning. Whatever the doctor had given her to make her rest and rid her of the pain she had made it impossible for her to become fully awake, and she felt the pain returning. Director Dan Oleksiw, still worried, canceled the film crew for the Taj Mahal. Mahalia, though, wanted to visit the Taj Mahal and decided, against the doctor's orders, she would still do the filming.

She was enthralled to see a real, live circus along the road to the Taj Mahal. There were camels, a black dancing bear, an elephant, and a snake charmer! As afraid as she was of snakes, Mahalia braved the hot, searing Indian sun to complete the filming at the Taj Mahal.

Madras. It was back to the airport the next morning for Mahalia's next stop in Madras, located on the Bay of Bengal in eastern India. Om Prakash, a silent young Indian who was Mahalia's constant security guard during her time there, knelt and asked that she touch his head for blessings. To Mahalia's surprise, as he rose, others knelt and asked that she do the same for them. Mahalia laughed softly, half surprise, half amazed. She raised her hands to the skies and told the cheering crowd: "Just remember, it's not me, or anybody on Earth who can bless you. It's God who delivers the blessings."

Mahalia stayed at the home of an American couple, Mr. and Mrs. George Henry, in Madras, rather than with the new Consul General Stephen Palmer, who hadn't settled in yet. The next day, however, Mr. Palmer hosted her in his garden. Mahalia was entranced by the beauty of the garden, lit up with colored bulbs that highlighted the temple flowers, the flame trees, and bougainvillea. Her eyes teared up as she remembered the bougainvillea in New Orleans. That evening, she was even more amazed when she visited one of the seven sacred temples in Mylapore.

In spite of the excitement of the day, Mahalia was faced again with the problem of foreign currency exchange. This time, however, when her hosts sought to pay her with the local rupees, not dollars, the American Embassy immediately came to the rescue and resolved the problem.

There were back-to-back press and radio interviews. The Indian people and the Indian press were fascinated with the statuesque Negro singer from America. At the end of the last interview, Mahalia went directly into a 30-minute Air India Radio concert. Later that night, she performed to another sold-out concert.

Bombay. Mahalia's next stop was the sprawling, beautiful city of Bombay (Mumbai). She was put up in a royal palace, once owned by a prince. The residence, all marble, overwhelmed the New Orleans native. Mahalia couldn't help but be reminded of how far she'd come from the three-room shotgun house in New Orleans' "Nigger Town." That was almost 60 years ago. See how God had blessed her!

It wasn't long before Mahalia was ailing again. She asked that the doctor be called, wanting to make certain she was healthy enough for the upcoming Whitney Young Memorial Concert. The doctors prescribed calming medicine and implored Mahalia to take her medicine and rest when she could.

Mahalia was pleased when she learned the concert would be held in a cathedral—built before America was even a country. She was even more pleased to learn that a women's group, the Time and Talents Club, who couldn't get tickets to the sold-out concert, had set up 500 seats on the grounds to hear the concert by loudspeaker. Mahalia was disappointed to learn that thousands had been turned away.

Mahalia's jaw dropped when she learned the Cathedral of St. Thomas forbade applause. Not even a clap! *Lord, what have I got myself into?* She was a bit amused, wondering how the audience would manage that. Her fans back home were known to clap, sing, holler, stand, and even dance in the aisles. The women's group was just as disappointed. Mahalia assured them it was a new experience for all of them, but it would be fine.

The concert was a huge success, in spite of the silence which Mahalia admitted she could never get used to. The hospitality in Bombay was wonderful. Dinners and parties galore.

On her second day, Mahalia visited the cathedral again, but for some unexplained reason she announced that she needed to leave a day early. No one was brave enough to argue with the Queen of Gospel.

Bangkok. Mahalia's next stop was the bustling city of Bangkok, the capital of Thailand, and one of the most visited cities in the world. She was thinking of Bea Thompson from her childhood days in New Orleans. She had told the journalists in Bombay that it was hard to find real friends like Bea, the longer she lived.

Back in Los Angeles, Mahalia was ducking out of as many friends' gatherings as she could. *Lord it's good to be back home*, she sighed. She hadn't been home a week before she got the letter about August concert dates in Sweden, Norway, Italy, and Israel. Her agent promised there would no more flights to Europe for now since she was experiencing so many health problems.

Mahalia could hardly believe the India tour was finally over. It seemed as if it would never end. Her time with Prime Minister Indira Gandhi was something she'd never forget. But it was good to be home, piddling around her Los Angeles apartment, overseeing some of the work her half-brother Johnny had workers doing.

She was preparing to get back to her real home, Chicago. Finally, her own temple was about to become a reality. And she needed to see Dr. Vondrasek as soon as she set foot back in Chicago. This thing been going on long enough; it's embarrassing. And it sure got to be fixed before her performance at Marymount College.

Dr. Vondrasek saw Mahalia around mid-May. Her diarrhea had started in Bombay, India, and had continued for three weeks. Nothing showed up in the tests to account for it, but the doctor said they would give her some treatment for it. Yes, she was still taking her diabetes medicine and prednisone.

Dr. Mahalia Jackson

An honorary degree of Doctor of Humane Letters from DePaul University! When they presented Mahalia with the St. Vincent DePaul medal "for serving God through the needs of man," the tears began to flow. Mahalia Jackson, Charity Clark's baby girl, Aunt Duke's orphan girl. She was overwhelmed with gratitude that the Lord had let her travel so far in life.

The June 1971 ceremonies took place downtown Chicago at the Auditorium Theater. The highpoint for many in attendance was the presentation of an honorary degree and the St. Vincent DePaul Award to gospel singer Mahalia Jackson, who sang for graduates in what would be one of her last public appearances.

Of all the things she'd been involved in during her singing career, receiving the honorary doctorate touched Mahalia most deeply. As much as she tried, she couldn't hold back the tears as she remembered how far she'd come, how not too far from DePaul University she had been the washerwoman for a white family just 30 years before.

Mahalia had been a good student who loved learning; and when she allowed herself to think back, she still felt robbed of a childhood and an early education. Walking the corridors of the school with Illinois Governor Otto Kerner, Mahalia felt self-conscious as she watched all the young men and women receiving their degrees. Governor Kerner had praised her as a humanitarian before conferring upon her the honorary doctorate.

Mahalia was scheduled to travel to Little Rock, Arkansas, in a few days, performing for the Sunday School Congress with minister and singer Reverend Jodie D. Strawther. She'd have to find a way to gather up her strength.

Mahalia was thinking more and more about getting things settled for her Mahalia Jackson Foundation benefit. Her famous jazz friends Duke

Ellington and Dizzy Gillespie had already committed. But she was still ailing. Nothing had changed with her diarrhea. It was a problem for her to go out and sing. She was swelling, now. The doctor could give her something for that. Her family were getting concerned. Seemed like Halie was running a drugstore in her house. She was tired, too. Too tired to even go see her doctor.

Judge Ben Hooks was helping Mahalia with the proposal Mayor Daley had offered her to head up a project for at-risk youth. He'd outline a program for her to combat the drug menace. He told her that with her appeal, she could be a tremendous force. She let him know that even with this, she hadn't lost sight of the temple.

Mahalia imagined her temple on Martin Luther King Drive. The place she had her eye on fell through. The woman wouldn't sell it to her for any price. *The Lord works in mysterious ways.* But first she needed to get to Billings Hospital to see the doctor. Her heart was racing again. She lay awake last night thinking about her will. They'd gone back and forth on it. Her and her attorney Gene Shapiro. She felt the Lord was pressing her to get it done.

Now, she had Oral Roberts to rehearse for on Monday, tape on Tuesday. The next two days she had rehearsals for "The Flip Wilson Show," and taping the next day.

Mahalia arrived back in Chicago on May 31, 1971, just in time for the Miracle Tent Revival. Dan Stewart's "Compassion Explosion" revival and faith-healing crusade was the first revival tent permitted in Chicago since 1958. *Praying for my own miracle, that the Lord will save me from having to travel to Europe.* Hadn't her agent already got the lady in Sweden to change the dates so that now she didn't have to travel there until September?

Mahalia was back on her mission. Her longtime friend and counsel Bob Miller stopped the car. Mahalia drank in the vision. She was remembering that Sunday morning so long ago when she walked onto the floor of Mt. Moriah Church, not even 5 years old yet—remembered how she'd stepped in front of the congregation and sang. "Hand Me Down My Silver Trumpet, Gabriel!" She had that same feeling as she scanned the majestic building on Drexel Boulevard and 51st Street. God had sent her.

God had led her to this place, on this day. A building of marble and stone, like a temple in Rome. It was over two stories high, and had a building in back! She wouldn't get out; didn't want people to know it's Mahalia Jackson because then the price would go up.

K.A.M. Temple was right smack on Drexel—in Hyde Park, near the University of Chicago, and no more than 15 blocks from Mahalia's condominium. There was talk that the temple was moving outside the city and willing to sell. *How Great Thou Art!*

Gene Shapiro heard the eagerness in Mahalia's question, *How much will they sell for?* The contract he'd drawn up was neutral, but the synagogue officials said they hadn't fully decided to sell. It hadn't been listed yet. Shapiro had called the realtor again, but wouldn't divulge who his client was. The listing was $450,000. He'd checked the appraisal value—$350,000. He urged Mahalia to name an offer, and suddenly she was hesitant.

What they take?

"I don't know. What will you offer?"

How much it takes?

She called and asked Judge Hooks to come. She had told him time and again she didn't blame him for the failure of the chicken shacks. She accepted his explanation that the market fell through, there was faulty financing and over-extended production requirements. After all that high-falutin reasoning, for Mahalia it came down to trying to do too much with too little.

The judge hadn't taken a dime from her and had put money in her hand—though mostly it ended up as stock. At any rate, she was the winner…she had Benjamin Hooks at her disposal when she called on him. She met him, Gene Shapiro, and Bob Miller at Bob's funeral parlor since Bob could hardly get away with his partner being so sick.

After the meeting, they'd driven to the temple. Mahalia sat in the car. Bob Miller came back. "Mahalia," he whispered, "I've sworn the caretaker to secrecy. You've got to come take a look at this thing inside with Judge Hooks and me—we can't advise you until you see inside."

Mahalia had to sit. The building seated over 1,200 people. Stained glass windows, balcony, pipe organ, sound system, choir room. Toilets for men and women…and look at this in back! Community hall with a stage and a grand piano, chapel, big kitchen, six schoolrooms with desks, chairs, all equipped. A library, and a nice big office with its own rest room.

A basement, too? Oh, Lord! You do provide. Look at this: four-room apartment and a mailroom down in all this quiet. Make the records in the basement, charge off the rent, and help support the interdenominational Temple of God. Hallelujah!

In early August 1971, Mahalia woke up with a racing heart and pain. She was scared as she walked into Billings Hospital. Would they send her back home again with another round of pills to take? The doctor said she checked out alright—her EKG was all clear—and he gave her a prescription for Valium with directions to take them three times a day, to calm her. She should be fine traveling to Connecticut the next day.

Mahalia appeared on actress June Havoc's "Youth Bridge" television show, with a gaggle of children all pushing to be the one next to Mahalia Jackson. Mahalia was there to help June get support for her theater project for disadvantaged children. She used the opportunity to push the fact that programs for children worked best when Blacks and whites were together, not apart.

After the show, Mahalia stayed on with her friend. For whatever reason she shared with her, her unexplainable dread in traveling to Europe later that year. She couldn't get out of it, the promoter had told her that unless there was a doctor's report that said it was dangerous for her to travel, she'd have to go.

Mahalia's concert in Montreal, Canada, was canceled due to inclement weather. *A gulley washer*, Mahalia laughed. She called Ben Hooks to talk about her temple plans. He was less enthusiastic about the plans than she'd hoped he'd be. It was easier face to face, Ben Hooks agreed. He didn't want to rain on Mahalia's enthusiasm, but as her friend, a lawyer, and a businessman, he advised her strongly against moving ahead. Mahalia heard him out, but when she answered at length, he knew the truth. Her real love was evangelistic work, revival work. This temple would be the sum, the culmination of her life—to concentrate her time on bringing sinners to the alter for conversion.

Judge Hooks wasn't the only one trying to change Mahalia's mind. She said, "Everybody trying to tell me. I've got enough money to do it on my own; and if I want to do it, I'm going to do it. The Lord told me to do it."

"IF the Lord wants you to do it, Mahalia," said Judge Hooks gently. "You do it."

"It won't cost me nothing. It's *his* money. I just want to live to see the day," Mahalia said, almost in tears. "If I go to Germany, I'll die." She really believes it, Ben Hooks decided. At first, he'd thought this business of not wanting to go was some sort of talk-up. But, no, she was convinced.

Part 16

THE GERMANY TOUR:
MAHALIA'S FINAL BOW

"Didn't It Rain"—The Last Encore

In September 1971, Mahalia was set to fly to Germany, with concert dates in Hanover, Frankfurt, Berlin, and Munich. But before she left, she wanted closure on her temple. She wanted the church for $250,000.

"$450,000 is the asking price," Shapiro told her. "Do you offer them $235,000?"

Yes, but I wants it!

"We'll see."

By Sunday morning, Mahalia was worrying less about the temple and more about the trip to Europe. She was told she had no option. She was prepared to travel. No smiles, no excitement. She asked Gwen, her organist, to bring her mother to pray over her.

I have to go, and only the Lord knows if I'll come back alive.

Dr. Quentin Young came that evening with yet more pills for Mahalia. Pills to ease the pain in her back, which seemed worse than ever. She had slept, but it hadn't lightened the load she was carrying inside. Her friend Harry Dale was driving her to the airport. He'd always been able to get a smile out of Halie. Not today. She was in a deep slump.

It was during her flight to Germany that Mahalia's spirit lifted some—as she and Gwen were laughing at the movie they watched on the plane. "This is all I'm going to fly, from now on," Mahalia said.

Hanover. Gwen called the hotel doctor. Mahalia's spirit darkened as soon as they landed in Hanover, Germany, changing from depressed to frightened.

"These pains—like terrible knots in my chest—an oppression," she whimpered. *I don't mind dying, Gwen. God knows I'm a Christian. I just don't want to die alone."*

She was scaring Gwen, who moved into Mahalia's room and slept in the spare bed. The doctor checked Mahalia's pulse, her heart, her breathing, and told her he didn't hear any irregularities in her heartbeat or breathing. Before leaving, he gave her something to relax her, to let her sleep.

The next morning, the sponsor's road manager, Eugene Schaeffer, came for her. Mahalia dressed and held a press conference. The next night, she sang, giving them all they sought from her…"Mah-HAHL-ya!" Schaeffer sighed with relief.

Mahalia didn't respond the next morning when she was asked how she was feeling. She boarded the plane for her travel on to Dusseldorf, then Nuremberg. She'd made up her mind. Her complaints were lost on deaf ears. She would finish the tour, get home, and curl up in her bed. The pattern repeated itself: travel—pains, weakness—doctor, pills—dress, press conference—sing.

Mahalia openly resisted at every stop, protested—insisting she was too sick to go on. The tour sponsors ordered EKGs and declared her health was "fine." They were determined this trip would not end like the one in 1967 when a too-hasty, too-cautious hospitalization had collapsed their tour.

Then, there were moments when Mahalia was Mahalia, roused, even cheerful. Gwen wrote to the family, to Ike Hockenhull, to Mayor Daley. She wrote a desperate letter to Gene Shapiro, Mahalia's attorney, asking about the progress with the temple.

What Mahalia didn't know about the wrangling over the sale of the temple, wouldn't upset her. The sell was not going as simple as real estate sells should go. Was it because the buyer was Mahalia Jackson, or was it yet another case of redlining, *even in the Lord's business?*

By mid-September, her assistant Allen Clark and her friend Bob Miller handed the broker Mahalia Jackson's $15,000 check, ending all speculations the property owners might have had. The buyer was, indeed, "the" Mahalia Jackson.

That night in Gütersloh, Germany, Eugene Schaeffer, the road manager, was in awe. Mahalia, who was so despondent and obviously in pain during most of the trip, put on an amazing performance for the excited,

stomping, clapping, chanting auditorium jammed with college students…
and came back for six encores.

"Mah-HAHL-ya!" they called. Hundreds of students swarmed on
stage and swept her into a second round of "When the Saints Go Marching
In." Mahalia was in her holy dance. Schaeffer was confident that the fräu-
lein was in good shape.

Frankfurt. Mahalia and her entourage arrived in Frankfurt the next day.
She was still mildly rejuvenated, likely a carry-on from the exciting night
before. She ate a good dinner in the hotel restaurant and carried on a lively
conversation. She was most excited by a message she'd received from Mayor
Daley. He was planning a big welcome home program for her. Her friend
Harry Belafonte had agreed to be the emcee. Mahalia had even walked outside to get some fresh air. She felt like her old self for the first time during
the tour.

The next morning, she woke with a low pain, and pressure. A doctor
was called. He found nothing out of the ordinary. Her heart is fine, he said.
He prescribed more pain medication. That night, again, she performed just
as the old Mahalia would, infused with the spirit. The packed audience
received four encores. "Mah-HAHL-ya!" they screamed to the auditorium's ceiling.

Finally, Mahalia arrived back in the dressing room where she gave
out and slumped in her chair. "I'm sick," she declared. There was something darker in this declaration. She roused herself enough to change to
her street clothes, before being escorted to her hotel room.

Berlin. On to Berlin, Germany's capital and largest city. Had Mahalia been the old Mahalia, she would have loved this place and its people. How she was feted like the royalty that she was…the blond child named Mahalia bearing flowers and the 24-karat gold medallion struck by German retailer Heinz Wipperfeld to commemorate Mahalia's first concert at the new home of the Berlin Philharmonic Orchestra, the Berliner Philharmonie concert hall. There was also the commitment offer from German lawyer Reiner Schroeter to underwrite a Hallelujah Records office in Germany.

On September 23, Mahalia was transported to the hospital with her road manager Eugene Schaeffer with tearful complaints of persistent chest pain. Two doctors examined her, and both declared there was nothing unusual in her electrocardiograms. Mahalia, sobbing and anxious, was fearful of the strange doctors who refused to believe she was sick and continued to ply her with drugs to ease her pain, but not address her larger health issues.

"We going home tomorrow. Be ready," she whispered.

Mahalia returned to the dressing room, forced to go on with her performance. Heaving and exhausted, she dressed, then walked onto the stage. What started out slow, gradually transformed into a Mahalia performance. The vessel pouring out God's message in song. An encore.

The audience was transfixed as Mahalia returned and sang one of her staples—"Didn't It Rain?"—and danced, and her hair swirled, and the sweat fell down her chin and onto her bosom. Moving offstage, she was still dancing, sweating, singing; her eyes tightly closed. And it was over. She couldn't return to the stage to take the final bow. *Tell the people I'm sick and thank you.*

Mahalia Falls Ill in Munich

Munich. On Friday, September 24, Mahalia was in Munich. By night, she was swathed in pain. She held the small yellow pill, the newest prescription for pain and exhaustion, in her hand. *"I want an American doctor!"* she wailed.

Finally, Gene Shapiro was on the other end of the phone all the way in Chicago. He was straining to hear Mahalia. It seemed the contract was breached—by the tour sponsors' failure to deposit second funds in New York before Berlin. His lawyer's mind was already mapping the moves; they couldn't push Mahalia around. *We can't find an American doctor, and we need one now!*

Shapiro reached out to the 24-hour duty man he'd called on once before at the U.S. Consulate General in Munich. Shapiro was told there was no one available, not one doctor, and to try calling the U.S. Army Hospital at McGraw Kaserne…but they weren't supposed to treat civilians, not even civilians like the world-famous Mahalia Jackson.

At 3 a.m., the ambulance backed into position, and Captain James Schlie admitted Mahalia to the emergency room. There were 24-hour EKG tests. No visitors were allowed. Washington called. The EKG came back clear on Saturday, as did the one on Sunday. More tests were taken. The doctors chided Mahalia; she may be simply exhausted. The sponsors asked if she could sing on Wednesday. More EKGs.

Again, the EKG was clear on Monday. By Tuesday, the EKG showed irregularity. Mahalia was in severe pain. Major Santos, the chief cardiologist from Frankfort, was flown in. A public information desk was set up. Major Foster from Heidelberg was flown in.

Tuesday's readings: electrocardiographic changes which supported a diagnosis of coronary artery disease with angina. The press release was fed to hungry media around the world. In his AMA office in Chicago, her old doctor, Dr. Barclay, shook his head. "Sarcoid," he said. If Mahalia didn't stay on the prednisone, the sarcoid would get completely out of control.

"Can't I just go home, to my hospital?" the anxious patient asked. The official response: "The possibility of early medical evacuation was discussed with Miss Jackson, but in the interest of Miss Jackson's health, it has been decided best for her to receive more conservative care."

The flood gates flew open once the world knew that Mahalia Jackson was hospitalized in Munich, Germany. There was an endless barrage of flowers, phone calls, cables, letters, and cards. A reporter from the Netherlands was barred from entrance. Singer/actress Pearl Bailey cabled; Mayor Daley called (and deputized Colonel Reilly to follow Mahalia's care). She received letters from General Davison, commander of the U.S. Army in Europe, and from President Johnson and Vice President Humphrey. The Gordons cabled from Calcutta; as did Dan Oleksiw from the U.S. Embassy in New Delhi, and Reverend Abernathy from the SCLC.

Prayer cloths came in from troops and schoolchildren written in English, French, German, and Dutch; and from 500 missionaries from Austria, New Zealand, India, Belgium, and Japan. The messages were read to Mahalia, who was forbidden to talk.

Alone in the intensive care unit, Mahalia fingered the one cable she'd kept nearby. *"I'LL COME IF YOU WANT ME TO. LOVE SIGMOND."* She'd need to cable him money to travel. She coaxed the orderly into rolling her bed close to a telephone. No answer. Mahalia lay back thinking. Call Shapiro in Chicago. *I can't find Minters, Doc; he's not home. Call his sister Ruth—get her to find him; but you find him and buy him a ticket to come.*

Gene Shapiro, her attorney, reached out to Ruth and asked her to tell Minters he wanted to talk to him. He refused to say why. The question was, what did Mahalia want them to do? The Grand Hotel Continental was elegant, expensive—the tour sponsor's choice. But now the cost for her and her traveling aides was all on her.

Finally. *I guess you all better go on and get back home.* Mahalia sighed. She didn't know how the contract business would end, with the promoters insisting she was obligated to continue the tour when she was well or she owed them money, and her attorney Shapiro saying she wouldn't.

Doc, why Minters not here yet? she asked in desperation and sadness. Shapiro hadn't found him. *Then you come,* Mahalia sighed. *They don't believe I'm really sick; they think I can go on. So, you come. And bring my coat. It's getting cold over here; I need it to go home.*

He couldn't come, but he'd ask Mahalia's assistant Allen Clark. Allen could bring Mahalia her coat. Mahalia didn't answer yes or no. Shapiro called Allen to see if Galloway had contacted him and to tell Allen about the coat.

"I'll take the coat," said Allen.

Shapiro called the McGraw Kaserne Adjutant General's office and asked that the tour management be barred from disturbing Mahalia; that only such persons as she named be admitted to see her at all.

Mahalia's voice was lighter this time. *I asked the doctor, and they going to let you all stay out here at the Bachelor Officers' Quarters. I told them I needed you for my business. You all can come now.*

Mahalia had been in the hospital for almost four weeks. Peculiar weeks. Right from the first day, but in a different room, when the bird came to the window messaging the death of an old friend from Mahalia's early gospel days. She had two doctors, Major Thompson and Major Hansen. Both were nice, but neither allowed her to eat foods she liked. *Thank God the Black dietitian allowed her a little seasoning.*

Mahalia was ready to return home. She didn't understand why they wouldn't allow it. She'd rest better in her own bed. Besides, she had to finish the business with her temple.

Finally, they agreed Mahalia would return home, but not by commercial flight without medical attendance. They didn't want to release her from Army medical care until she was in the United States. She would be flown home by Air Evacuation military transport plane.

What does that mean? Mahalia asked cautiously.

Colonel Howard shared that Mahalia would be taken by helicopter to Rhein-Main Air Base near Frankfurt, where she'd stay overnight and be checked at their hospital. The next day, they'd fly her into Andrews Air

Force Base near Washington, D.C., where she'd stay at their hospital overnight. The following day, she would be flown to Great Lakes Naval Hospital near Chicago. An ambulance would then drive Mahalia from there to Billings Hospital in Chicago, to be signed over to her preferred doctor. They'd contacted him in advance.

Dear Jesus, all that instead of flying straight to O'Hare? Great Lakes must be 30 miles away. "It's regulations. They have to land at a military field, and that's the closest."

Home at Last

Mahalia landed in Chicago on October 23, 1971, in time to celebrate her 60° birthday at home. The press covered her arrival, a historic moment— the great gospel singer Mahalia Jackson being lifted down on a canvas stretcher by Army medical corpsmen, flanked by her assistant Allen Clark and her attorney Gene Shapiro. Also present were Mahalia's aunt Alice and her longtime friends Tina Choate and Harry Dale.

Two days later, on October 25, Mahalia was escorted from Billings Hospital to her home in Hyde Park. She had planned to go to Alice's where she knew her aunt would not allow people to bother her. But, as the trip stretched out, she needed to be home, in her own bed. Alice could come up there and not let them in.

All the tests at Billings Hospital showed that nothing was wrong. Still, they gave Mahalia three more prescriptions, including more Valium. Billings had secured Mahalia Jackson's medical records with its newest diagnostic notation, "sarcoidosis." Dr. Thompson, the American doctor in Munich, said even if Mahalia's heart had been weakened, all she needed now was "rest and light exercise, and she could sing in six months if she started easy."

Mahalia's family and friends were scurrying around planning a birthday party, but the doctor's order was rest and no party. Mahalia was complaining again of pain in her back and chest; no matter that the EKG registered as clear.

There was her friend Russell Goode with the yellow legal pad to work on Mahalia's new will. She was happy to see him, but before they could get started her stomach was turning over yet again. She'd have to wait and work on the will another time.

Mahalia had gained enough strength to start planning for her temple. Mayor Daley would provide her with a nursery school or kindergarten, then she'd get her teacher friends to teach the arts and her music friends to come in and give lectures. *Now we getting somewhere.* And, she'd need to line up preachers for daily prayer meetings.

Call Josephine Davis, ask her and George to paint inside the church auditorium—that's all the place actually needs. And send out a choir call. CBS already wanted a Mahalia Jackson Christmas Special from her temple! Of course, the money question was still up in the air.

Mahalia wrote a wire and had it sent to Mrs. Gandhi in care of President Richard Nixon: "*Welcome to our country. With the world on the brink of war, God has given you the power to lead men. He is leading you through a divine plan. All things work together for the good of those who trust in God.*"

With all her heart set on that temple, there was some nervousness. Mahalia had gotten wind of trouble; rumblings about the temple. Some said the price was high for the property. Shapiro wanted her to put the temple in the church's name, not hers, so she could raise money.

There was a setback now with the temple. The owner had stripped it clean, beyond the agreement, which only allowed for the removal of the organ and the Judaic objects. But Gene Shapiro had stood his ground, and it was all going back. All except the grand piano, which was someone else's property. This hadn't been shared with Mahalia. She was upset that they'd taken it. Shapiro was still wishing he could talk Mahalia out of the purchase before the deadline. He knew he couldn't. It would have to be her decision.

Shapiro made two points abundantly clear to Mahalia: She must have control of the temple by herself. She could appoint a board, if she wished, but she must always keep control. He had structured it that way. Then he'd done quite a bit of shopping to come up with a loan at 6% when they were paying her 5% on certificates of deposit, so her money was costing her only 1%.

The men sitting around Mahalia's breakfast table raised their voices when Mahalia told them she couldn't hear them. Bob Miller, Gene Shapiro, Judge Hooks, Reverend Parnell, Reverend Lewis, and the key visitor, Roland Burris of Continental Illinois National Bank.

"Talk up! I still can't hear what you saying!" Mahalia was in her bed, attending the temple finance session two rooms away. Judge Hooks single-handedly picked her up, brought her in, and deposited her in a comfortable chair. She looked gratified, but not unduly.

"I'm the one going to have to pay this thing, you know," she said to Mr. Burris. "Go ahead and talk." When all her questions were answered—first mortgage, second mortgage—she signed the waiting papers. The remaining $185,000 of the $225,000 purchase was secured. Mr. Miller was glad Mahalia would have revenue right off from leasing the school, with the mayor's help.

"*…The Mahalia Jackson Group is to take possession of the K.A.M. Temple, Dec. 15,*" the newspaper read. "*Reported purchase price is $2,225,000, personally guaranteed by Miss Jackson.*"

"Great God in the morning!" Mahalia wailed. "They off $2 million."

The doctor noted continued chest pain when Mahalia woke, increasing when she spoke and aggravated by walking. Mahalia didn't want to remain in bed. She felt her body weakening. Yet, when she tried to walk, it was painful. Doctors noted that her hypertension was in check, and there was no evidence of cellular damage. Her blood sugar level was normal. Yet, she was on a coronary dilator, diabetes medication, a tranquilizer, and the prednisone she'd been on for decades, now.

On November 18, Dr. Vondrasek wrote that Mahalia's heart was pounding irregularly, her appetite had improved, and she'd gained six pounds. Her tolerance for sugar had also improved. He reduced the diabetes dosage and gave her sleeping medication.

Mahalia's only excitement was the temple. She was still planning when she wasn't in pain.

On Thanksgiving 1971, a neighbor offered to cook Thanksgiving dinner for Mahalia, but Allen was already prepping to cook. Mahalia was in a tizzy, angry and suspicious. She changed the locks on the condominium the next day.

Again, she called Allen to come with the yellow legal pad. She needed to make some changes to her will. But not before he took her to the emergency room. She needed some help. Again, the doctors examined her and told her there was nothing they could find. They even said they were just taking her money and not finding anything wrong.

The Christmas Special for CBS was still on Mahalia's schedule. But, how in the world would she be in a position to do anybody's special in the shape she was in?

Shapiro called to tell her the house on Indiana Avenue had finally sold. Something to make her smile. She told Shapiro she couldn't find the key to her safety deposit box, that she hadn't had it in years.

Mahalia went back to Billings emergency room, again. She was so weak she could hardly stand. Nothing was keeping her going now except her dream of the temple.

No Temple for Mahalia

In early December, Shapiro was there with Judge Ben Hooks, telling Mahalia they would be closing on the temple on December 15.

December 15, we'll close. Mahalia rolled the words around with her thin lips. What happened to that gleam in her eyes every time she thought of the temple? All weekend she prayed. She couldn't sleep. Her finger traced Psalm 83:1. *Keep not thou silence, O God; hold not thy peace, and be not still, O God.*

Four days later, just two days before closing on the temple, Mahalia called Shapiro and told him she wouldn't be buying the temple, after all. There was enough shock to go around. No one had an inkling this was the direction she was going. She hadn't breathed a word.

"You'll forfeit the $40,000," Shapiro told her. He knew there was no need in arguing with her once she made her mind up. He relayed her decision to the realtors, brokers. "Ms. Jackson decided she did not want to buy," said Gene Shapiro, "due to the state of her health—which is obviously not good—and that she does not have her own source of funds."

Ben Hooks who had encouraged her against the purchase all this time could hardly believe she'd talked herself out of it.

Now, Mahalia was worrying about losing her $40,000. Judge Hooks was glad he was there to calm her down as she questioned Shapiro. After Shapiro left, she showed Ben her will. She was still worried.

Albertina Walker and Mahalia Jackson had been friends for as long as Mahalia had been in Chicago. They'd cut their teeth on gospel music. Albertina, younger by a few years, had looked up to Mahalia even though she was singing the gospel for almost as long. The joke was that Mahalia was the Queen and Albertina and the others were just part of her court.

Albertina fussed that she'd been trying to get ahold of Mahalia, but Mahalia's circle of busy bees blocked her at every turn.

Mahalia's aunts Bessie, Alice, and Hannah and cousins Missie Wilkerson and Allen Clark—all the family—were there praying for the tide to turn for Halie like it always did. That Halie would wake up the next morning and bound out of that bed and say she's ready to sing. It had always been that way. Her ailments didn't ever keep her down for long.

This time was different, though. Tears were rolling from Mahala, as she was complaining that nobody believed she was as sick as she was, not even her own doctors. She wanted Minters. She needed him to come.

Missie was the go-between. She'd get him there if it was the last thing she did. And she did just that.

On Christmas Eve, Mahalia was walking back in her door from Michael Reese Hospital. For the first time in her adult life, Mahalia didn't celebrate Christmas—do it up big with a houseful of people eating and drinking and making merry. There were no decorations, and no Christmas dinner to speak of. When has Halie had this in her grown life? No Christmas dinner to feed all these people. She was ashamed.

There was a tableful of Christmas cards—from President Nixon and from former President Lyndon Johnson and his wife Lady Bird. And, there at the door was the best Christmas gift she could imagine, Minters, with his sister Ruth.

Mahalia worried that God was punishing her with this illness that wouldn't go away. *What could it be I done wrong that he's punishing me?*

Minters had visited Mahalia at Michael Reese every day after work. Mahalia had asked him to bring Sigma. She'd given him a key to her home. And what's more—and she hadn't even broached this with Minters—they would be remarried.

Minters had just consulted lawyer Bob Tucker about the marriage quit-claim. The lawyer said it would hold; it was valid. What if he signed and married Mahalia, and she threw him out again for some reason? It wasn't easy to get a job. But still—Mahalia sure had perked up at the idea.

Russell Goode wondered if Mahalia would ever be able to sing again.

Oh, I'm going to sing again!

Mahalia opened her mouth, and it was as if nothing had changed in these hard, ugly months of illness. Her voice was just as strong as ever. Russell leaped to the piano, and she sang something else—kept it up about five minutes.

Mahalia said she wouldn't make Martin's birthday memorial service in Atlanta on January 15, his birthday, but she could be there April 19 for Dr. King's Memorial Center board meeting.

On December 28, Mahalia was back at Billings Hospital.

By New Year's Day, Mahalia couldn't decide whether she needed her friends to protect her, or whether she needed them to leave her alone so she could spend time with Minters.

If Minters and me can get together one more time, I'm going to move away from here and go to Jamaica or Hawaii or somewhere these folks can't afford to follow.

Albertina, I got news for you—Minters and me going to get together again! I'm ready now, but Minters says wait "cause they'll say I tricked you while you were sick and your mind's not all there." But I got all my sense—I know what I want to do.

Mahalia and Minters called Russell Goode, asking where he'd hid the will.

"It's in that big straw pocketbook you got in the islands, remember? In your big closet?"

Bessie's Dream—A Bad Omen

On January 4, 1972, Mahalia called Gene Shapiro. She wanted to cash in all her savings certificates. *I want my money, and I want it now, and I want it in cash.*

The lawyer met Allen at the bank in Melrose Park, got a cashier's check for the $100,000 certificate, drove to Mahalia's condo on Cornell, took the elevator up to the 26th floor, and gave her the $100,000 check and every certificate of deposit. Shapiro insisted that Mahalia note that everything was in her name, not his. He then went to his office and resigned as her lawyer, by letter, effective January 6, 1972.

The day after Shapiro resigned, Mahalia was in tears. Aunt Alice and Aunt Hannah were there, looking from Halie to each other and shaking their heads. She'd begged Shapiro to come back as her attorney. He'd refused.

Mahalia called Dr. Rosi, since Dr. Vondrasek wasn't due in until the afternoon, complaining of abdominal pain, nausea, and vomiting. Dr. Rosi told her to come in for some tests. Minters took her to Billings instead, to a woman doctor who suggested Mahalia see a psychiatrist, that there must be something on her mind she won't talk about, making her feel like this.

Bessie Kimble woke up frightened. It was the second message on her niece within a week. The first time, look like Bessie could see Mahalia off in a place—sad looking. Bessie had called Doodutz, then Isabell. *"Isabell, you all say Mahalia ain't sick, but Mahalia is sicker than what you think. I know. I had a dream."*

Bessie had said that in the second dream she had lost a piece of jewelry. *That means that somebody you love, you're going to miss them. They're going to die.* It was the same before her niece Little Alice passed. But they'd laugh at her now, if she told them. It's not like she used to be—used to could just sit down and vision, almost as bad as her sister Bell.

On January 5, Mahalia had been ill all night, nauseated and vomiting. "I feel like I'm dying, doctor." She told Dr. Rosi that the prescription Dr. Vondrasek had phoned in hadn't helped. Dr. Rosi studied his X-ray.

There was gas within the small bowel, and he considered the possibility of an early, incomplete bowel obstruction. He gave her three prescriptions and stressed to her cousin Allen the time factor in taking them. If Mahalia wasn't appreciably better tomorrow, he'd put her in Little Company of Mary Hospital for observation.

Zephaniah 3:14-20: Mahalia's Bible lay open there, left behind. There'd be one at Little Company of Mary.

On January 19, Mahalia was admitted to the hospital. Her admitting diagnosis was intestinal obstruction and coronary heart disease. Her abdomen was somewhat distended. She was installed on the second floor south. The medical staff began intravenous feeding, they gave her medication for sleep.

The next day, Mahalia was in good spirits. She asked Allen to bring her checkbook, joking that all he wanted was to help her spend her money.

Mahalia was waiting for Minters, who was now working for the City of Gary. He said he'd talked to Dr. Vondrasek—knew him from back when they were married—and the doctor wanted him to talk to her about running a suction tube down her throat to help clear out the intestine and the gas and so on. The doctor had told them, "This is the conservative approach to incomplete intestinal obstruction, or to paralysis of the bowel."

"*Unh-unh. Not down my throat! Ruin my vocal cords? That would be the last thing—I told that doctor.*" Mahalia fretted, smoothing her hand over her swollen stomach. She whispered to Minters that they could get married right then. Right there. He shook his head. He wouldn't have anyone accusing him of undue influence on a sick woman.

Mahalia called Shapiro on Sunday. *Get my money from the church, sell all my property, get the money for Indiana Avenue, and sell the condominium—I'm moving to Arizona.*

Worried, Shapiro asked if someone was pressuring her into this. She surprised him when she told him she was going to be operated on the next morning. He tried to pin her down on exactly what was to be done, but she really didn't seem to know.

Just unlocking my bowels.

Before hanging up, Mahalia calmly told Shapiro she was going to marry Minters.

There visiting was Aunt Alice, who had been sick with her diabetes, and Aunt Hannah, with her high blood pressure. This was their first visit in a while. Mahalia hurried them out before it began to snow or something. As they gathered themselves, Mahalia said quietly, *"I want you all to kiss me before you leave."* She didn't mention the operation.

When Missie arrived, Mahalia asked her to comb her hair. "Look at it. Look just like it has not been done for months. Time to get the braids loose." Mahalia's spirits were lifting.

She asked Minters if he'd stay all night, being that she was to be operated on in the morning. But he had a band job at the Holiday Inn in Gary that night. He promised he'd be back the next day as soon as he could—before she was out of surgery.

There was no option, Dr. Vondrasek agreed with Dr. Nester Martinez, the surgeon. He was deeply concerned. The X-ray did not show anything causing the obstruction, but it existed. One other problem was that for some reason, her pulse was getting very fast.

Ever since she'd been admitted, Dr. Vondrasek had found Mahalia morose, just lying there. He hadn't been able to cheer her up—or get permission to insert the tube. With this cardiac problem, she just wasn't in good condition. They couldn't wait, he agreed.

On Monday, January 24, Dr. Martinez performed abdominal surgery and cut adhesive bands for release of partial intestinal obstruction. Mahalia was taken to the Intensive Care Unit. The problem was not post-surgical, in that sense, but severe tachycardia, or rapid heartbeat.

On Tuesday, the doctors were hopeful. Mahalia seemed to be in better spirits. Her high blood pressure began to drop. Minters Galloway, taking his customary route, found himself barred. Family only.

On Wednesday, Mahalia's circulation was failing. Her kidneys were malfunctioning, and her heart rate was going far too fast.

It was early morning, on Thursday, January 27, when doctors noted a sudden increase in Mahalia's blood pressure, followed by a sharp drop to zero. They could not save her. Mahalia Jackson, the world-famous Queen of Gospel, died. Alone.

AFTERWORD

The news of Mahalia Jackson's death spread quickly through the City of Chicago and then the nation and the world. Many of her followers refused to believe the great gospel performer was gone. When her pastor said her remains could be seen at Greater Salem Baptist Church, Mahalia's church home, fans came to see her for the last time. Some 50,000 people, Blacks and whites, filed past her coffin. In subzero weather, they stood outside the church in a slow-moving line, waiting to view Mahalia's body, which was clad in a long, blue satin gown with silver and gold sequins and resting in a mahogany casket. Mean and shifty gales swept off frozen Lake Michigan, battering the mourners. But the cold could not discourage those who came to say goodbye to one of the greatest voices of the 20th century.

The next day, 6,000 people came to Mahalia's funeral service at McCormick Place. Aretha Franklin sang gospel songs that Mahalia had taught her, including "Take My Hand, Precious Lord," the same song Mahalia sang at the funeral of her friend Martin Luther King Jr.

Three days later, the people of New Orleans, Mahalia's birthplace, were given a chance to pay their respects to the Queen of Gospel. The funeral was like none the city had witnessed before. The governor of Louisiana and the mayor of New Orleans led some 50,000 people in a final tribute past her open glass-enclosed casket.

For her memorial service, 4,000 people filled every seat and yet another 4,000 stood outside silently pressing forward. A choir of 550 voices from all over the city sang. There were also a U.S. military color guard, a mixed honor guard (black/white/women) of city police officers, as well as the mayor, the governor, and many other dignitaries.

The next morning, gleaming black limousines rolled past Mt. Moriah Church where once there were no shoes for Sunday school for Mahalia and where her singing talent had first sprouted. Then Mahalia was driven the eight miles to her final resting place, the grassy greens of Providence Memorial Park in Metairie, Louisiana—beside the Mississippi River and not far from Water Street.

There were headlines around the world—even in Brazil, where Mahalia never set foot but was revered. In Jamaica and in Nassau in The Bahamas, her music was poured into the streets by loudspeakers for 24 hours of mourning. In Calcutta, India, Duke Ellington sat for hours with Mrs. Herbert Gordon reminiscing their own eulogy for Mahalia.

In New Delhi, Prime Minister Indira Gandhi—visibly moved—spoke her tribute. At the White House, President Nixon issued a statement of mourning for the nation.

In Hollywood, California, the famous but quiet jazz singer Ella Fitzgerald startled her publicist by declaring she was flying, on her own, to the funeral of "a great lady," even though she must fly back the same night.

Three Mahalia records were chosen for the White House library. A posthumous Grammy award was designated.

In Paris, the French music critic and record producer Hugues Panassié, who co-founded the acclaimed *Jazz Hot* magazine, asked jazz historian Madeleine Gautier to prepare the publication's tribute to Mahalia Jackson.

British jazz author Max Jones shared his memories in London, and in Chicago, Pulitzer Prize-winning historian Studs Terkel shared his memories of the great gospel queen.

Mahalia would have been proud. *Pretty good for a little bare-foot girl from Nigger Town.* She had done good, by herself, and by so many others. She received hundreds of requests on any given week. And she'd tried her best to oblige, until her body finally said "no." Then, in 1964, when she must have known that her health had reached the "danger" point, Mahalia paused for a time, then doubled down on life. *How could she stop singing God's words? She'd promised she would.*

No one knew the troubles she'd seen, or had to carry. While some knew the physical ailments, only a few knew the emotional toll of her long journey.

In 1971, when she was 60, the government asked her to fly to an American outpost in Japan to sing for the soldiers. Mahalia's doctors had warned her against such trips.

"I have hopes that my singing will break down some of the hate and fear that divide the white and Black people," she'd said.

When she got back from Japan, they had another chore for her. It was to be in Germany, this time. There was trouble between Black and white American troops stationed there. Maybe Mahalia's golden voice and majestic presence would bring peace between them. That Thanksgiving 1971 found her at a U.S. Army post in Germany. She sang the old gospel songs with a special tenderness. But that was when she collapsed on the stage and was rushed to an Army hospital, gravely ill.

The doctors had wanted to keep her there until she was strong enough to return to America. Mahalia shook her head. She thought she'd have a better chance of recovery back home. She did not want to die away from family and friends. If the end was coming, she wanted it to come in her own land.

They brought Mahalia back to Little Company of Mary Hospital in Evergreen Park, a Chicago suburb. And the newspapers told the story. "Sister Halie in a hospital," people said. This had happened often before. Even so, the hospital's switchboard was kept busy night and day as people called to find out how Sister Halie was doing. The president of the United

States called. Letters poured in for the gospel queen. Flowers from friends and strangers flooded her room. All this fuss over a down-home girl. Mahalia had been poor so long she never got used to a lot of attention.

On May 18, 1972, four months after Mahalia's death, Sigmond Minsters Galloway, Mahalia's second husband, died of cancer (detected only shortly before his death). Isaac Hockenhull, Mahalia's first husband, died in July 1973, about a year after Mahalia's death. Mildred Falls died in 1974, two years after Mahalia, and Aunt Hannah Robinson died shortly thereafter.

All her life, Mahalia reshaped names to suit some inner sense, but she never knew the import of her own. Rabbi Julian B. Feibelman of New Orleans has provided an arresting translation from the Hebrew language: Mahala—meaning *melodius song*. And, in an extended form, Mahalaleel— meaning *the one who praises God*.

MAHALIA JACKSON

Timeline

1911 October 26—born in Uptown New Orleans

1927 November—departed New Orleans for Chicago

1934 Made her first recording "God Gonna Separate the Wheat from the Tares"

1936 Married Isaac Hockenhull, a chemist (divorced in1941)

1939 Met composer Thomas A. Dorsey and began touring around the country with him

1947 Recorded "Move on Up a Little Higher" for Apollo Records—her first hit song, which became the best-selling gospel record of all time

1950 Became the first gospel singer to perform at historic Carnegie Hall in New York City

1952 First tour of Europe, performing before sold-out crowds

1955 Named music director for the National Baptist Convention

1956	Purchased her dream home at 8358 S. Indiana Avenue on Chicago's South Side
1956	Met Martin Luther King Jr. and Ralph Abernathy for the first time
1956	Engaged to New Jersey minister Russell Roberts (He died not long afterward.)
1957	Became the first gospel singer to perform at the Newport Jazz Festival in Rhode Island
1959	Portrayed a funeral soloist in the film *Imitation of Life,* singing "Trouble of the World"
1961	Performed at the inauguration of President John F. Kennedy
1962	Recorded the Christmas album *Silent Night: Songs for Christmas*
1962	Won Grammy Award for Best Gospel for "Every Time I Feel the Spirit"
1963	Won Grammy Award for Best Gospel for "Great Songs of Love and Faith"
1963	August 28—Sang at the March on Washington, inspiring Martin Luther King's famous "I Have a Dream" speech
1964	Married Sigmond Minters Galloway, a jazz musician and salesman (divorced in 1967)
1968	April 9—Sang "Take My Hand, Precious Lord" at the funeral of her friend Dr. Martin Luther King Jr., who was assassinated five days earlier on April 4

1968-1971 Embarked on world tours that included Europe,
the Caribbean, Africa, Asia

1970   Moved to Cornell Village Condominiums in Chicago's affluent
Hyde Park community

1972   January 27—Died of heart failure and other complications at
Little Company of Mary Hospital in Evergreen Park, Illinois

1977   Won Grammy Award for Best Soul Gospel Performance for
"How I Got Over" (posthumous)

1978   Inducted into the Gospel Music Hall of Fame (posthumous)

1988   Received a star on the Hollywood Walk of Fame (posthumous)

1997   Inducted into the Rock and Roll Hall of Fame (posthumous)

ACKNOWLEDGMENTS

This book took several years to complete, and it could not have been completed without the libraries, museums, and archives I visited over the years—including Louisiana State University, Baton Rouge's Special Collections unit; Ancestry.com; the New Orleans Jazz & Heritage Festival and Foundation; The Historic New Orleans Collection; New Orleans Arts and Cultural Host Committee; the Chicago Defender newspaper; the Chicago Tribune; the National Archives and Records Administration and a special thank you to the Mahalia Jackson Residual Family Corporation, and to Senator and Mrs. Roland Burris, who started me on this journey.

RESOURCES /
REFERENCE MATERIALS

Research Documents

John McDonogh, namesake for Mahalia Jackson's elementary school—
    McDonogh 24 Elementary School

John McDonogh, Wikipedia, the free encyclopedia

Books and Other Document References

https://studsterkel.wfmt.com/programs/brother-john-sellers-discusses-
    his-career-blues-artist-and-how-church-music-inspired-his

wftm.com / Studs Terkel Archives / Brother John Sellers Interview / 1982

Movin' On Up, by Mahalia Jackson with Evan McLeod Wylie,
    Hawthorn Books, 1966

Just Mahalia, Baby: The Mahalia Jackson Story, by Laurraine Goreau,
    Word Books, 1975

Mahalia: A Life in Gospel Music, by Roxanne Orgill; Candlewick Press, 2002

Make a Joyful Noise unto the Lord, by Jesse Jackson, Thomas Y. Crowell
    Company, 1974

The Governors of Louisiana, by Miriam G. Reeves, Pelican, 2004

Rising Tide: The Great Mississippi Flood of 1927 and How it Changed America, by John M. Barry, Simon & Schuster, 1997

Sundown Towns: A Hidden Dimension of American Racism, James W. Loewen, Simon & Schuster, 2005

The Negro Motorist Green-Book, John C. Dillard, editor; Victor H. Green, Publisher; 1936

Louis Armstrong: An Extravagant Life, by Laurence Bergreen, Broadway Books, 1997

Coretta: My Life, My love, My legacy, by Coretta Scott King with the Rev. Dr. Barbara Reynolds; Picador, 2017

Mahalia Jackson: Born to Sing Gospel Music, by Evelyn Witter, Mott Media, 1985

Jabir, Johari, *On Conjuring Mahalia: Mahalia Jackson, New Orleans, and the Sanctified Swing,* American Quarterly, 61 (Sept. 2009), pp. 649–70.

Tony Heilbut, *The Gospel Sound: Good News and Bad Times,* Limelight Editions, 1997, ISBN 0-87910-034-6.

Horace Clarence Boyer, *How Sweet the Sound: The Golden Age of Gospel,* Elliott and Clark, 1995, ISBN 0-252-06877-7.

Hettie Jones, *Big Star Fallin' Mama: Five Women in Black Music,* Viking Press, 1974.

Jules Schwerin, *Got to Tell It: Mahalia Jackson, Queen of Gospel,* Oxford University Press, 1992, ISBN 0-19-507144-1.

Bob Darden, *People Get Ready: A New History of Black Gospel Music,* New York: Continuum, 2004. ISBN 0-8264-1436-2

Jean Gay Cornell, *Mahalia Jackson: Queen of Gospel Song,* Champaign, IL: Garrard Pub. Co., 1974. ISBN 0-8116-4581-9

Viale, Gene D. *I Remember Gospel and I Keep on Singing.* AuthorHouse. ISBN 978-1-4490-7681-8.

Caroline Merrick, *Old Times in Dixieland: A Southern Matron's Memories* (New York: Grafton Press, 1901);

The Merricks of Pointe Coupee Parish / Caroline Thompson Merrick

Caroline Merrick and Women's Rights in Louisiana, by Samantha LaDart

Notes from Caroline Merrick's Life

History.com/black history/Montgomery bus boycott / chapter 1

www.ebenezeratl.org/ chapter 1

https://kinginstitute.stanford.edu/encyclopedia/montgomery-improvement-association-mia / Chapter 1

2010 The New York Times Company; Obituary, Alden Whitman

A Knock at Midnight: Inspirations from the Great Sermons of Martin Luther King, Jr.; edited by Clayborne Carson and Peter Holloran; Warner Books, 1998

www.influenzaarchives.org

https://soulphoodie.com/2020/08/08/americas-first-black-owned-restaurant-franchise-mahalia-jacksons-glori-fried-chicken/

Earning her Place in The Sun: My Great Respect for Mahalia Jackson; Sherman Houston, Jr., www.assistnews.net

New York Times / Obituary /Jennifer Dunning, *Brother John Sellers, 74, Blues Singer, Dies,* April 11, 1999

Kendall's History of New Orleans, The Lewis Publishing Company, Chicago and New York, 1922

Mississippi River Flood History 1543-Present (weather.gov) – pg 65

https://en.wikipedia.org/wiki/Robert_Charles

https://prcno.org/louisiana-sugar-rice-exchange-1884-1963/ -

Hoovervilles of the Great Depression – Legends of America – page 139

http://www.slaverebellion.info/

https://knownolablog.wordpress.com/2020/07/27/the-hero-of-new-orleans-robert-charles